First World War
and Army of Occupation
War Diary
France, Belgium and Germany

20 DIVISION
Divisional Troops
96 Field Company Royal Engineers
2 August 1915 - 29 May 1919

WO95/2107/3

The Naval & Military Press Ltd
www.nmarchive.com
Published in association with The National Archives

Published by

The Naval & Military Press Ltd

Unit 10 Ridgewood Industrial Park,

Uckfield, East Sussex,

TN22 5QE England

Tel: +44 (0) 1825 749494

www.naval-military-press.com

www.nmarchive.com

This diary has been reprinted in facsimile from the original. Any imperfections are inevitably reproduced and the quality may fall short of modern type and cartographic standards.

© Crown Copyright
Images reproduced by permission of The National Archives, London, England, 2015.

Contents

Document type	Place/Title	Date From	Date To
Miscellaneous	2107/3		
Heading	20th Division Divl Engineers 96th Field Coy R.E. Aug 1915-Apl 1919		
Heading	20th Division 96th F.C.R.E. Vol I Aug To Oct 15		
Heading	War Diary of 96th (Field) Company R.E. From Aug 2nd 1915 To Oct 31st 1915 Volume I		
War Diary	Bac. St Maur	02/08/1915	09/08/1915
War Diary	Bac. St Maur Sailly	10/08/1915	10/08/1915
War Diary	Sailly	11/08/1915	27/08/1915
War Diary	Rue De Paradis Laventie	28/08/1915	31/10/1915
Miscellaneous	Trench Fortification Lecture To Officers And N.C.O.'s 96th Coy. R.E., 20th Division	07/08/1915	07/08/1915
Diagram etc	Organization of A Sector of Defence		
Diagram etc	Support & Reserve Trenches		
Diagram etc	Avenues		
Heading	20th Division 96th F.C.R.E. Vol. 2 Capture Strong Nov 15		
Heading	War Diary of 96th Field Coy R.E. Nov 1st 1915 To Nov 30th 1915 Volume No. II		
War Diary	Rue De Paradis Laventie	01/11/1915	20/11/1915
War Diary	Rue De Paradis Laventie Sailly	21/11/1915	21/11/1915
War Diary	Sailly	22/11/1915	30/11/1915
Heading	20th Div. 96th F.C.R.E. Vol 3		
Heading	War Diary of 96th Field Company R.E. From Dec 1st 1915 To Dec 31st 1915 (Volume 3)		
War Diary	Sailly	01/12/1915	31/12/1915
Heading	20th Div. 96th F.C.R.E. Vol 4 January 1916		
Heading	War Diary of 96th Field Coy. R.E. Volume IV		
War Diary	Sailly	01/01/1916	10/01/1916
War Diary	Grand Sec Bois	11/01/1916	11/01/1916
War Diary	Morbecque	12/01/1916	22/01/1916
War Diary	Oudezeele	23/01/1916	31/01/1916
Heading	96th F.C.R.E. Vol 5		
Heading	War Diary of 96th Field Coy. R.E. From 1st February To 29th February 1916 (Volume V)		
War Diary	Oudezeele	01/02/1916	03/02/1916
War Diary	Houtkerque	04/02/1916	12/02/1916
War Diary	A. 23.a 2.6 C. 25.a.5.9 Sheet 28	13/02/1916	29/02/1916
Heading	War Diary of 96th Field Coy. R.E. From March 1st To 31st 1916 (Volume VI)		
War Diary	A.23.a.2.6 C.25.a.5.9 Sheet 28	01/03/1916	31/03/1916
Heading	War Diary of 96th Field Coy. R.E. From April 1st To 30th 1916 (Volume VI)		
War Diary	A.23.a.2.6 C.25.a.5.9 Sheet 28	01/04/1916	17/04/1916
War Diary	Herzeele	18/04/1916	27/04/1916
War Diary	Winnizeele	28/04/1916	30/04/1916
Heading	War Diary of 96th Field Coy. R.E. From May 1st To 31st 1916 (Volume VII)		
War Diary	Winnizeele	01/05/1916	19/05/1916
War Diary	H.7.a. A.28.c Sheet 28	20/05/1916	22/05/1916

War Diary	H.7.a. A.28.c Sheet 28 Ypres	23/05/1916	31/05/1916
Heading	War Diary of 96th Field Coy. R.E. From June 1st To 30th 1916 (Volume VIII)		
War Diary	H.8.a.8.8 A.28.c. Sheet 28 Ypres	01/06/1916	30/06/1916
Heading	20th Divisional Engineers 96th Field Company R.E July 1916		
War Diary	H.8.a.8.8 A.28.c Sheet 28 Ypres	01/07/1916	07/07/1916
War Diary	H.7.a.5.9. A.28.c. Sheet 28 Ypres	08/07/1916	15/07/1916
War Diary	H.7.a.5.9. A.28.c. Sheet 28 Ypres Winnizeele	16/07/1916	16/07/1916
War Diary	Winnizeele	17/07/1916	18/07/1916
War Diary	Winnizeele Berthen	19/07/1916	19/07/1916
War Diary	Le Don by B 55 Sheet 36.c	20/07/1916	23/07/1916
War Diary	M.12.D.2.5 Sheet 28	24/07/1916	24/07/1916
War Diary	M.12.D.2.5 Sheet 28 Bouque Maisons	25/07/1916	25/07/1916
War Diary	Bouquemaison Authie	26/07/1916	26/07/1916
War Diary	Authie Rossignol Farm	27/07/1916	27/07/1916
War Diary	Rossignol Farm J.3.C. Sheet 57 N.E	28/07/1916	29/07/1916
Heading	20th Divisional Engineers. 96th Field Company R.E. August 1916		
War Diary	Rossignol Farm J.3.c. Sheet 57 D	30/07/1916	16/08/1916
War Diary	Rossignol Farm J.3.c. Sheet 57 D I 17.d Sheet 57 D	17/08/1916	22/08/1916
War Diary	A.14.a.5.3 F.21.d.4.6 Sheet-Albert	23/08/1916	27/08/1916
War Diary	A.14.a.5.3 L.9.c.9.3	28/08/1916	29/08/1916
Heading	20th Divisional Engineers. 96th Field Company R.E September 1916		
War Diary	A.14.a.5.3 L.9.c.9.3 Sheet-Albert	30/08/1916	28/09/1916
Heading	20th Divisional Engineers 96th Field Company R.E. October 1916		
Heading	96th Field Coy Vol 13		
War Diary		29/09/1916	28/10/1916
Heading	20th Divisional Engineers 96th Field Company R.E. November 1916		
War Diary	A.8.c.1.4 F.21.b.3.0 Sheet Albert	29/10/1916	10/11/1916
War Diary	A.8.c.1.4 F.21.b.3.0 Sheet Albert Ville	11/11/1916	11/11/1916
War Diary	Ville	12/11/1916	15/11/1916
War Diary	Treux	16/11/1916	26/11/1916
War Diary	Treux Vecquemont	27/11/1916	27/11/1916
War Diary	Vecquemont	28/11/1916	29/11/1916
Heading	20th Divisional Engineers 96th Field Company R.E. December 1916		
War Diary	Treux Vecquemont	29/11/1916	09/12/1916
War Diary	Treux	10/12/1916	11/12/1916
War Diary	Bernafay Wood And S.29.d	12/12/1916	22/12/1916
War Diary	Corbie	23/12/1916	30/12/1916
Heading	War Diary of The 96th Field Coy. R.E. January 1917 Vol 16		
War Diary	Corbie	31/12/1916	31/12/1916
War Diary	Corbie Citadel	01/01/1917	01/01/1917
War Diary	Citadel Combles Wedge Wood	02/01/1917	02/01/1917
War Diary	Combles Wedge Wood	03/01/1917	27/01/1917
War Diary	Franvillers	28/01/1917	03/02/1917
War Diary	Franvillers Meaulte	04/02/1917	04/02/1917
War Diary	Meaulte	05/02/1917	07/02/1917
War Diary	Meaulte S.30.a	08/02/1917	08/02/1917
War Diary	S.30.a	09/02/1917	11/02/1917
War Diary	S.30.a. T.16.a.	12/02/1917	18/02/1917

War Diary	S.30.a T.16.a. T.9.d	19/02/1917	19/02/1917
War Diary	S.30.a T.9.d	20/02/1917	01/03/1917
War Diary	S.30.a	02/03/1917	07/03/1917
War Diary	S.30.a T.9.d	08/03/1917	16/03/1917
War Diary	S.30.a Ginchy Bull Dump	17/03/1917	23/03/1917
War Diary	S.30.a T.16 Central	24/03/1917	28/03/1917
War Diary	S.30.a	29/03/1917	29/03/1917
War Diary	S.30.A N.34.a	30/03/1917	30/03/1917
War Diary	Q.34.a Sheet 57.c	31/03/1917	10/04/1917
War Diary	O.34.a. Ypres	11/04/1917	13/04/1917
War Diary	Ytres	14/04/1917	14/04/1917
War Diary	Ytres P.26.a.9.4 Sheet 57 C	15/04/1917	03/05/1917
War Diary	Metz Ytres Bertincourt	04/05/1917	04/05/1917
War Diary	Metz Ytres Bertincourt Ruyaulcourt	05/05/1917	07/05/1917
War Diary	Metz Ytres	08/05/1917	10/05/1917
War Diary	Sieve Wood	11/05/1917	14/05/1917
War Diary	Metz Ytres	15/05/1917	20/05/1917
War Diary	Ytres	21/05/1917	21/05/1917
War Diary	Le Transloy	22/05/1917	22/05/1917
War Diary	Favreuil	23/05/1917	23/05/1917
War Diary	Vaulx-Vraucourt & C 29 D 2.4	24/05/1917	27/05/1917
War Diary	Favreuil Vaulx-Vraucourt	28/05/1917	30/05/1917
War Diary	Favreuil Vaulx	31/05/1917	04/06/1917
War Diary	C.20.a 0.0 And Vaulx	05/06/1917	14/06/1917
War Diary	Noreuil Vaulx	15/06/1917	20/06/1917
War Diary	I 2.c.3.2	21/06/1917	21/06/1917
War Diary	I.2.C.3.2 Sheet 57. C	22/06/1917	25/06/1917
War Diary	Gomiecourt	26/06/1917	29/06/1917
War Diary	Gorges	30/06/1917	01/07/1917
War Diary	St Leger Les Domart	02/07/1917	09/07/1917
War Diary	La Chaussee	10/07/1917	13/07/1917
War Diary	St Leger-Les-Domart	14/07/1917	21/07/1917
War Diary	F 10 A. 5.2 Sheet 27	22/07/1917	30/07/1917
War Diary	Sheet 27 F 10.a.5.2. All C.7.7 Sheet 28	30/07/1917	30/07/1917
War Diary	A 11 C.7.7	31/07/1917	05/08/1917
War Diary	B.21.D.5.7	06/08/1917	16/08/1917
War Diary	B.21 D 5.7. F 10.A.5.2 Sheet 27	17/08/1917	17/08/1917
War Diary	F 10.A.5.2	18/08/1917	23/08/1917
War Diary	F 10.A.5.2 Sheet 27 B 10 D 7.3. B 9 D 4.8 (Sheet 28)	24/08/1917	24/08/1917
War Diary	B 10 D 7.3 B 9 D 4.8	25/08/1917	29/08/1917
War Diary	B 10 D 7.3. (Sheet 28)	30/08/1917	31/08/1917
War Diary	F 10 A 5.2 (Sheet 27)	01/09/1917	10/09/1917
War Diary	F 10 A 5.2 (Sheet 27) B 23 B 6.4 Sheet 28	11/09/1917	11/09/1917
War Diary	B 23 B 6.4	12/09/1917	27/09/1917
War Diary	B 23 B 6.4 Sheet 28	28/09/1917	28/09/1917
War Diary	F 10 A 5.2 Sheet 27	28/09/1917	01/10/1917
War Diary	N 18 C Sheet 57 C	02/10/1917	05/10/1917
War Diary	N.18.C.46 W 13 C	06/10/1917	07/10/1917
War Diary	W 9 B 9.4 Q.36 D 6.9	08/10/1917	05/11/1917
War Diary	W 15.b.1.2 W 19.c	06/11/1917	08/11/1917
War Diary	W 9 B 9.4 Q 36 A 6.9	08/11/1917	08/11/1917
War Diary	W 15.b 1.2 W 19.c	09/11/1917	11/11/1917
War Diary	W 9 B 9.4 Q 36 A 6.9	11/11/1917	11/11/1917
War Diary	W 15 B.1.2 W 19.c	12/11/1917	13/11/1917
War Diary	W 9 B 9.4 Q 36 D 6.9	14/11/1917	14/11/1917
War Diary	W 15 B.1.2 W 19.c	14/11/1917	16/11/1917

War Diary	W 9 B 9.4 Q 26 D 6.9 W 15 B.1.2 W 19.c	17/11/1917	20/11/1917
War Diary	R 13 B 6.1	21/11/1917	29/11/1917
War Diary	Villers Plouich Sheet 57.C.	30/11/1917	03/12/1917
War Diary	Fins Sorel	04/12/1917	30/12/1917
War Diary	Racquinghem	31/12/1917	05/01/1918
War Diary	Voormezeele	06/01/1918	20/02/1918
War Diary	Nesle	21/02/1918	21/02/1918
War Diary	Campagne	22/02/1918	27/02/1918
Heading	20th Divisional Engineers 96th Field Company R.E. March 1918		
War Diary	Campagne	28/02/1918	04/03/1918
War Diary	Chauny	04/03/1918	11/03/1918
War Diary	Ognolles	11/03/1918	15/03/1918
War Diary	Chauny	16/03/1918	31/03/1918
War Diary	Sheet Amiens 17 1/40000 Boves	01/04/1918	01/04/1918
War Diary	Fresnoy Au Val	01/04/1918	01/04/1918
War Diary	St Aubin Montenoy	03/04/1918	09/04/1918
War Diary	Brocourt	09/04/1918	09/04/1918
War Diary	Bouttencourt	10/04/1918	10/04/1918
War Diary	Beachamps	11/04/1918	17/04/1918
War Diary	EU	18/04/1918	20/04/1918
War Diary	Guestreville	20/04/1918	30/04/1918
War Diary	Lens 11 Guestreville	01/05/1918	29/05/1918
War Diary	Ablain-St Nazaire	31/05/1918	29/09/1918
War Diary	West of Avion	30/09/1918	10/11/1918
War Diary	Sheet Valenciennes 12	11/11/1918	30/12/1918
War Diary	Hurtebise Farm	30/12/1918	29/04/1919
War Diary	Hurtebise Farm Famechon	30/04/1919	29/05/1919

21/07/13

20TH DIVISION
DIVL ENGINEERS

96TH FIELD COY R.E.
AUG 1915 - APL 1919

12/7595.

30th Division

96th F.C. R.E.
Vol I
Aug to Oct 15
Api.9

CONFIDENTIAL

WAR DIARY

OF

96TH (FIELD) COMPANY. R.E.

FROM AUG 2nd 1915 TO OCT. 31st. 1915.

VOLUME. I

Army Form C. 2118

WAR DIARY
or
INTELLIGENCE SUMMARY.
(Erase heading not required.)

Place	Date	Hour	Summary of Events and Information	Remarks and references to Appendices
BAC. ST MAUR.	2/8/15	7.0 am	Marched to B'Illeth in BAC. ST MAUR. Adjutantine and No1 Section attached to 15th Field Coy., No2 Section to 2nd Field Coy. No 3 & 4 Sections to 1st Home Counties Coy. Half of each section working in trenches nightwork.	RE
"	3/8/15	7.15 p	Reported to C.R.E. S.I Division G.O.C. 24th Brigade + went round certain works with O.C. 15th Fd Coy.R.E.; also Billets & Workshops of 15th Coy R.E. Went round works in No 3 Section & Civis with O.C. 15th Coy R.E. to No 1 Section to No 2 Section out on work night of 2/3 August 1915. + Mudfet day work in R.E. workshop.	RE
"	4/8/15		Went round works on No 1 Section of line with O.C. 15th Coy Rl. 1/No 1 Section & 1/No 2 Section out on work night of 3 August 1915 other half on day work in R.E. workshop on 4/8/15 O.M. CHAPMAN. 1045642 wounded at 1.20 p.m. whilst working in the trenches. Lieut Ryrie L.Y.S. also 2nd Lieuts G.	RS
"	5/8/15		Went round works on No 3 Section of line with O.C. Ryrie L.Y.S. Butter Yeomanry. 1/No 2 Section out on work night of 4/8/15 other 1/2 on day work in R.E. Workshop on 5/8/15. No 45642 O.M. CHAPMAN.C died at 8.30 am in No 19 Field Ambulance.	RE
"	6/8/15		Went round works on No 4 Section of line with O.C. 15th Coy R.E. 1/No Section & 1/No2 Section out on work night of 5 August 1915 other half on day work in R.E. Workshop on 6/8/15.	RE

Army Form C. 2118

WAR DIARY
or
INTELLIGENCE SUMMARY.
(Erase heading not required.)

Instructions regarding War Diaries and Intelligence Summaries are contained in F. S. Regs., Part II. and the Staff Manual respectively. Title pages will be prepared in manuscript.

Place	Date	Hour	Summary of Events and Information	Remarks and references to Appendices
BAC. St. MAUR.	7/8/15		Went round works on No 3 & 4 Section of line & No 2 Section out on work night of 6/7 August 1915 a hot section on day. Work in R.E. Workshops on 7/8/15.	
do	8/8/15		Sunday	
do	9/8/15		Went round 2nd Inf. R.E. line with O.C. 2nd Lon R.E. Inspection working on 2nd & 15th Inf brigades + 3 + 4 Sections work with 1st Home Counties R.E.	
BAC ST MAUR {SAILLY}	10/8/15		Marched to new Billets at Sailly. Went over Section of line (Reserve trenches & entrenchments in rear) with 19th Brigade area taken over from 1st Home Counties R.S. and arranged for night work. (R.E. ng to commence on evening of 10th-11th. Two parties (R.E. only) went out for night work (10/11.8.15)	
SAILLY	11/8/15		Two parties (R.E. ng) proceeded to dry work on dry-pits behind Reserve trenches and revetting of Reserve trench. 2 parties to Regt of line (about 1/2 to right of line) relief of 19th Brigade after being out for 36". Coy on day work a night work with sand bag revetting of Parapet on own lantiers (Blaney) and on dummies support Reserve trenches to right - a traverse in reserve line and building Onston Bridge on east of Sailly Bridge. 1A. - 38 Wellsomen	

12-8-15

WAR DIARY or INTELLIGENCE SUMMARY

Army Form C. 2118.

Place	Date	Hour	Summary of Events and Information	Remarks and references to Appendices
SAILLY	13/8/15		(N.C. only) Party, working on reserve for Pontoon bridge; parties from Nos 1 & 2 Sections working on dug-outs F1 & F2 an ctong day-out. Frames for F3 & F5 ready. Host Section party. Sand-bag revetting, day work. Party on night work on outpost trenches.	RE
do	14/8/15		Party working on reserve for Pontoon bridge. Parties (RE only) working on reserve and communication trenches & revetting of Reserve trench parapet. (day & night work). Making dug-out frames (No 1 Section)	RE
do	15/8/15		Sunday.	RE
do	16/8/15		No 1 Section trimming up trenches in Reserve line. No 2 Section (party day & night work) Sand-bag revetting of Reserve trench, & making gangway bridge & drain tice. No 3 Section (party day & night work) on dug-outs on outpost trench. No 4 Section dismantling Pontoon bridge & removing to new site & erecting	RE
do	17/8/15		No 4 Section on Pontoon bridge. No 1 Section with 60 men from 10th KRR on excavation in Dyolo trench night. No 2 Section sand-bag revetting party 16 & Suffolk from No 2 Section on night work with 36 10th KRR making & deepening outpost trench. 12 NCO's & men of No 3 Section day work mending revetment on reserve trench No 3. No 3 Section day work with NCO's & men & day-outs on outpost trench. and 5 NCO's & men from 11th KRR excavating dug-outs. Engine — 37 men 5 brgs & 1 am-oft & making parapets Lavrentie front North. 26 " 3 " 1 do (on trench Lavrentie front East.	RE

Army Form C. 21

WAR DIARY
or
INTELLIGENCE SUMMARY.
(Erase heading not required.)

Instructions regarding War Diaries and Intelligence Summaries are contained in F.S. Regs., Part II. and the Staff Manual respectively. Title pages will be prepared in manuscript.

Place	Date	Hour	Summary of Events and Information	Remarks and references to Appendices
SAILLY	18/8/15		No 1 Section :- Rety Centrally. Supervising party 60 (10th KRR) deepening existing fire trench in 70 yd line F1 & F2. - 8 Sappers sandbagging revetting F1 & F2 reconnecting obsercvation post. Am-up trenches F1 & F2 taped out.	
			No 2 Section :- Supervising party 36 (10th KRR) undergrs 70 yd support trench to left of communication trench 13. Party N.G. making material in workshops. Party N.C. sand bag revetting 70 y support trench.	
			No 3 Section :- R.E. party revetting traverse in 1A communication trench - night work.	
			No 4 Section :- Building Pontoon Bridge.	
			Sappers :- Making parapet - LAVENTIE post north. Reconnoitring trenches LAVENTIE post south.	R.E.
do	19/8/15		No 1 Section :- Supervising party 10th Infantry digging run-up trenches in F1 & F2 from 70 yds line. 18 Sappers sandbagging in no 1 com trench @ F1 & F2. 70 yds trench.	
			No 2 Section :- Supervising party of Infantry widening no 14 com trench from RUE TILLELOY to support trenches & widening support trench to left. 18 no 14 com trench. Party of R.E. meeting drain in no 14 com trench & sandbag revetting support trench & bailing water.	
			No 3 Section :- Supervising party of Infantry revetting 1A avenue & traverse in 1A com trench making parapet of support trench.	
			No 4 Section :- Building Pontoon Bridge.	R.E.
do	20/8/15		Sappers :- Making parapet of road to LAVENTIE. Had a party in trenche LAVENTIE earth avenue. Supervising Infantry working on Brigade Subgrantère on Avenue behind FELON a cleaning main avenue behind FELON widening no 14 Comm. trench clearing trenches to left of 14 comm trench & widening support trench near 15 comm trench. Raising parapet of support trench on right of 1A Comm trench. Deepening trench left of 1A post RUE DU BOIS. R.E. & Infantry revetting on 1A Avenue 91A Comm trench north of 1A post. R.E. only:- In shops - an artillery observation post near TEA SHOP. Stone frame at M.12.a.9.7. widening & revetting recruit trench & clearing Comm trench south of 1A post.	R.E.

1577 Wt.W10791/1773 500,000 1/15 D.D. & L. A.D.S.S./Forms/C. 2118.

WAR DIARY or INTELLIGENCE SUMMARY

Army Form C. 2118.

Place	Date	Hour	Summary of Events and Information	Remarks and references to Appendices
SAILLY	21/8/15		Supervising infantry working on 59th Pole dugouts, excavating avenue behind FELON. "14" comm. trench on reserve trench (sand-bag revetments) left of 14 comm trench & widening 14 comm trench.	
			Supervising infantry revetting façade of support trench right of support. Trench right of 14 comm. trench & widening from 1X. R.E. laying't avenue behind FELON & widening & revetting reserve trench. R.E. laying't avenue behind FELON east side fort 1A. R.E. re-revetting loop hole east side fort 1A. R.E. in workshops making materials.	
do	22/8/15		Sunday.	
do	23/8/15		Supervising infantry working on 12 & 13 comm. trench — revetting 14 & 91 trench, a working on 59th Pole dugouts — excavating Winchester avenue & Pols between reserve line & RUE TILELOY — excavating reserve line in FELON & dug-outs behind same — and by revetting of reserve french between 14 & 15 comm. trenches — excavating reserve trench & widening support trench between 15 & 16 comm trenches & excavating new avenue in front of from post 17 — connecting run-up laying to drain trees & making parapet of support-trench on right of 1A comm. trench — excavating avenue from 1X. R.E. revetting 17 comm french south of RUE TILELOY, revetting 1A avenue. R.E. & working on dug-outs on reserve left of 1A. R.E. & 18 infantry working in shops making materials.	
do	24/8/15		Supervising Infantry excavating main avenue & working on 59th Pole dugouts, revetting sides of no 15 & 17 Comm. trenches, widening 14 comm trench & revetting of reserve trench between 15 & 16 comm french between 15 & 16 comm trenches and revetting of reserve trench between 15 & 16 comm trenches & evacuating trench through.	

WAR DIARY
or
INTELLIGENCE SUMMARY.

(Erase heading not required.)

Army Form C. 2118

Instructions regarding War Diaries and Intelligence Summaries are contained in F. S. Regs., Part II. and the Staff Manual respectively. Title pages will be prepared in manuscript.

Place	Date	Hour	Summary of Events and Information	Remarks and references to Appendices
SAILLY	24/8/15		Supervising Infantry working 11 comm. trench between reserve line and RUE TILLELOY, making 1A Avenue north of RUE TILLELOY excavating main avenue from 17 & deepening and widening reserve trench left of 1A. R.E. making dug-outs in reserve trench left of 1A. R.E. 91st Infantry in workshops.	
do	25/8/15		Supervising Infantry working on 59th Role Auger excavating main avenue behind FELON, excavating no 12 comm. trench from reserve line to no 11 comm. trench & reserve line, excavating change in reserve line & RUE TILLELOY & revetting in no 12 comm. trench from RUE TILLELOY. Widening no 14 & 15 comm. trenches working on support trenches connecting up two comm. trench on dug-out behind support out, widening support-trench between 15 & 16 comm. Trenches & reserve trench right of 16 comm. trench – revetting 17 comm. trench, revetting 1A avenue. north of RUE TILLELOY, revetting on PICANTIN Avenue, excavating day outs in 12 & support trenches right of 1A, & reserve 1P output trench, widening a deepening reserve trench left of 1A & building dug-outs in support line & excavating main avenue from 11 & strengthening down-stream parts of artillery & revetting infantry in workshops. R.B. constructing dug-outs R.B. 918 Infantry in workshops.	
do	26/8/15		Supervising Infantry working on Rue Auger excavating main avenue behind FELON, excavating no 12 comm. trench from reserve line also no 11, excavating change in reserve line at RUE TILLELOY a revetting comm. trench from RUE TILLELOY. Widening no 14 comm. trench also 15 working on comm. trench from support to "first line", and making support trench between 15 & 16 no. 0 dug-outs	

WAR DIARY
or
INTELLIGENCE SUMMARY.
(Erase heading not required.)

Army Form C. 2118.

Place	Date	Hour	Summary of Events and Information	Remarks and references to Appendices
SAILLY	26/8/15	(contd)	Supervising Infantry excavating reserve trench left of 16 comm trench. — revetting 17 comm. trench — revetting 1A avenue making cut PICANTIN avenue excavating dug-outs on 12 support trench — widening & deepening reserve trench left of 1A & building dug-outs in support line — excavating main avenue from 1 x. R.E. strengthening R.A. Obs post & instructing Infantry in construction of dug-outs. R.E. & 18 Infantry in workshops.	R.E.
do	27/8/15		Moved into fresh billets at RUE DE PARADIS, LAVENTIE – 9.8.m Instructing Infantry in construction of dug-outs, & strengthening Obs post of Artillery. Infantry working on main avenue behind FELON excavating reserve trench between 1A & 17 comm trench and widening & clearing out 16 & 17 comm. trench. Ups supple of trench left of 17 comm trench.	R.E.
RUE DE PARADIS, LAVENTIE	28/8/15		Supervising Infantry working on 59th Bde fatigue trimming up main avenue in FELON, excavating reserve line between 13+14, deepening No 13, widening No 11, chafing parapet between 11 & 12, and 12 & 13, widening & deepening 15 comm trench, and laying revetment of reserve trench & support trench & working on dug-outs, working on 1A comm trench making parapet for 1A comm trench, 17 comm trench making cut avenue from PICANTIN POST to 1A redoubt, excavating dug-outs behind support line to right of 1A comm trench, widening trench left of 1A post, putting in fire step, thickening dug-outs, excavating main avenue from 1 x. R.E. instructing Infantry in construction of dug-outs.	R.E.

Army Form C. 2118.

WAR DIARY
or
INTELLIGENCE SUMMARY.
(Erase heading not required.)

Instructions regarding War Diaries and Intelligence Summaries are contained in F.S. Regs., Part II. and the Staff Manual respectively. Title pages will be prepared in manuscript.

Place	Date	Hour	Summary of Events and Information	Remarks and references to Appendices
RUE DE PARADIS, LAVENTIE	28/8/15		R.E. and bag revetting of Support Line & parry wire revetment on main avenue. R.E. & 18 Infantry in workshops.	R E
do	29/8/15		Sunday	
do	30/8/15		Supervising Infantry trimming up reserve line between 13 & 14 – working on S9th Bde advanced Report Centre – cleaning up 11 from RUE TILELOY – cleaning up 670 yds line between 12 & 11 comm trench – widening & deepening 13 comm trench – sandbag revetment of Support Line parapets – thickening parapet of Support Line from left of 14 m.m. – excavating recesses & approaches to dug-outs – sandbag revetment of 6 IA comm trench 917 comm trench – on dug-outs for support trench right of IA comm trench – widening & revetting Support Line – excavating main avenue from IX. R.E. instructing Infantry in construction of dug-outs – erecting line steps in Support trenches – erecting dug-outs for Infantry at Post 17 & working at Avenue revetment. R.E. & 24 Infantry in workshops.	R E
do	31/8/15		Supervising Infantry trimming up reserve line between 13 & 14 – working on S9th Bde advanced Report Centre – cleaning up 11 comm trench – cleaning up 70 yds line between 12 & 11 comm trenches – widening & deepening 13 comm trench – sandbag revetment of Support Line parapets – thickening parapet of Support Line from left of 14 m.m. – excavating recesses & approaches to dug-outs – sandbag revetting IA comm trench – sandbag revetment of 17 comm trench – widening & making up parapet – on dug-outs for support trench right of IA comm trench – widening and revetting Support Line – excavating main avenue from IX – excavating PICANTIN Avenue – staff meeting dug-outs for Support at trench right of IA comm trench	R E

Army Form C. 2118.

WAR DIARY
or
INTELLIGENCE SUMMARY.
(Erase heading not required.)

Place	Date	Hour	Summary of Events and Information	Remarks and references to Appendices
ROE DE PARADIS.	31/8/15		Instructing Infantry in construction of dug-outs. Strengthening Artillery observation post at N.8.a.0.2. A & 24 Infantry in workshops.	
LAVENTIE				
do.	1/9/15		Supervising Infantry widening 12 a & 12 b comm. trenches — widening reserve line behind F1 — working on sap — Brigade Advanced Rep. at Centre — working on new trench of Queens behind F1 — widening 16 comm trench — deeping dug-outs — revetting Supt at trench — working on new berm pit thickening existing parapets — revetting 17 comm trench — excavating trench round traverse in 1A comm. trench — fixing firing step in Supt at trench — fixing dug-out frames behind Support trench — revetting 1A comm. trench making parapet for 1A comm. trench — working out run up trenches between 16&17 comm. trenches — clearing 17 comm. trench — widening & deepening Support trench & building parapet dug dyke — excavating main avenue from 1 & — A & B working on firing step & revetting — Q & a 24 Infantry in workshops.	R.E. R.E.
do	2/9/15		Supervising Infantry deepening 12 a & 12 b comm. trenches — widening reserve line in F1 & F2 — deepening avenue in F1 — revetting revetment of 70 yds line parapet — in dug-outs behind Supt pit — widening No.14 comm. trench — deepening reserve trench Left of 17 comm trench — fixing firing step in 70 yds line near 26 of 1A comm trench — revetting — digging up 17 comm. trench — clearing eye of parapet of 1A comm. trench excavating trench round traverse — revetting revetment of 1A comm. trench — fixing revetting frames — revetting run — also between 16&17 comm. trenches & wiring 70 yds line filling in redans under parapet. deepening & widening on Sth Brigade Advanced Report Centre. A & B working on Sqt	R.E. R.E.

WAR DIARY
or
INTELLIGENCE SUMMARY.
(Erase heading not required.)

Army Form C. 2118

Place	Date	Hour	Summary of Events and Information	Remarks and references to Appendices
RUE DE PARADIS, LAVENTIE	3/9/15		Supervising Infantry revetting 70 yds fire line parapet — excavating dug-outs to left of 15 comm. trench — from revetting (parados in main avenue — excavating from RUE BACQUEROT to 1A — widening & deepening 70 yds line & building parapet — from revetting (parados making up parapet fb 17 comm trench — excavating & clearing 1A comm. trench — dug-outs for 70 yds line — widening & deepening neave trench left of 17 comm trench — on D assembly trenches — working on 59th Brigade Advanced Report Centre — deepening 12 A comm trench.	RE
			1B a 24 Infantry in workshops	
do.	4/9/15 DAY		Supervising Infantry on assembly trenches — excavating 12a comm trench — working on 59th Brigade Advanced Report Centre — excavating avenue in F1 — excavating main avenue to right of DEAD END Post — excavating new avenue to right of RED HOUSE — revetting 1A & 17 comm trenches — filling in recess in 70 yds line parapet — excavating main avenue from RUE BACQUEROT — R.E. revetting main avenue.	
			1B a 24 Infantry in Workshops.	
		night	Supervising Infantry working on avenue in F1 — on trench of main avenue west of DEAD END Post near RUE TILLELOY — excavating run-up trenches between 16 & 17 comm trenches — making parapet in 17 comm trench — revetting 1A comm. trench — making out BURLINGTON ARCADE — excavating main avenue from RUE BACQUEROT to 1A.	RE
do.	5/9/15 DAY (Sunday)		R.E. revetting main avenue — building shelter at R.P. Stns in RUE BACQUEROT. Evil towlite REEDGE HUSH (erased). Supervising Infantry working on 59th Brigade G.H. Report Centre — on assembly trenches — on 12A comm trench — working on machine gun emplacement in front line — excavating main avenue west of DEAD END POST - west of RED HOUSE & from RUE BACQUEROT to 1A.	RE

Army Form C. 2118.

WAR DIARY
or
INTELLIGENCE SUMMARY.
(Erase heading not required.)

Instructions regarding War Diaries and Intelligence Summaries are contained in F.S. Regs., Part II. and the Staff Manual respectively. Title pages will be prepared in manuscript.

Place	Date	Hour	Summary of Events and Information	Remarks and references to Appendices
RUE DE PARADIS LAVENTIE	5/9/15	night	Supervising Infantry excavating Main Avenue west of DEAD END POST ? from RUE BACQUEROT to IA. R.E. working on machine gun emplacement in Front Line.	R.E.
ditto	6/9/15	DAY	Supervising Infantry working on 59th Bgde. Adv. Report Centre – on Assembly trenches – excavating Main Avenue, west of DEAD END POST, north of RUE TILLELOY west of RED HOUSE – from RUE BACQUEROT to IA – revetting IA + 17 comm. trenches – widening & deepening 70 yds Line – shelters for reserves in 70 yds Line. R.E. a machine gun emplacement in F2. R.E. a 24 Infantry in workshops making materials. R.E. working on machine gun emplacement in F2.	
ditto	7/9/15	night	Supervising Infantry on Assembly Trenches in F1 – working on 59th Bde. Adv. Report Centre – excavating new Main Avenue west of DEAD END POST – revetting Main Avenue near RUE TILLELOY – revetting IA Avenue – revetting 17 comm. trench – repairing new Main Avenue west of RED HOUSE – laying firing step in 70 yds Line right of IA comm. trench – rebuilding Parapet & reserves in 70 yds Line "E" of IA – excavating Main Avenue from RUE BACQUEROT to IA near RUE BACQUEROT and near RUE TILLELOY. R.E. machine gun emplacement in F2 – revetting Main Avenue near RUE TILLELOY. R.E. 24 Infantry in workshops making materials.	R.E.
		night	Supervising Infantry excavating Main Avenue in F1 west of DEAD END POST ? west of RED HOUSE – excavating Avenue from IX to 70 yds Line. R.E. revetting Avenue from EXE.	

Army Form C. 2118.

WAR DIARY
or
INTELLIGENCE SUMMARY.
(Erase heading not required.)

Instructions regarding War Diaries and Intelligence Summaries are contained in F.S. Regs., Part II. and the Staff Manual respectively. Title pages will be prepared in manuscript.

Place	Date	Hour	Summary of Events and Information	Remarks and references to Appendices
RUE DE PARADIS. LAVENTIE	3/9/15	Day	No 3 Section of 101st infantry Coy joined for course of instruction at 4.0 p.m. Supervising infantry on Piccadilly trenches — excavating main avenue west of DEAD END POST — west of PICANTIN POST. R.E. on machine gun emplacement in F2, revetting main avenue west of DEAD END POST — an Avg-arts in 70yds line — laying lining steps in 70 yds line right of IA comm. trench — R. Co 24 Infantry in workshops.	
		night	Supervising Infantry excavating main avenue in F1, west of DEAD END POST west of RED HOUSE & east of PICANTIN POST, and from EXE to 70yds line. R.E. on machine gun emplacement in F2 revetting main avenue west of DEAD END POST & revetting avenue from EXE.	R2
ditto	4/9/15	Day	Supervising Infantry — on Piccadilly trenches — working on Sgt Pete Adv. Report Centre — working on "Strand": excavating main avenue west of DEAD END POST— excavating "St North Road" — on parapets of 17 & IA comm. trenches — on dug-outs in 70 yds line right of IA comm. trench — Excavating "PICCADILLY". R.E. on m.g. emplacement in F2 — on Avy. arts in 70yds line — revetting main avenue & west of DEAD END POST — fire step in 70 yds line. Supervising Infantry excavating in workshops. "ST NORTH ROAD" & "PICCADILLY "STRAND" — on m.g. info from 14 comm. trench — excavating R.E. revetting 14 comm. trench — revetting "HAYMARKET".	R2

WAR DIARY
or
INTELLIGENCE SUMMARY.

(Erase heading not required.)

Army Form C. 2118.

Place	Date	Hour	Summary of Events and Information	Remarks and references to Appendices
RUE DE PARADIS. LAVENTIE	10/9/15	DAY.	Supervising Infantry working on "STRAND" — on 5q/th Bde. Adv. Report Centre — an Assembly trenches — excavating Main Avenue west of DEAD END POST — excavating "Gt NORTH ROAD" — widening 1A a 17 comm. trenches — on dug-outs in 70 yds line — on right of 1A comm. trench — excavating "PICADILLY". R.E. on M.G. emplacement in F2. — on Bns-auts in 70 yds line — revetting firing step in 70 yds line.	R2
		NIGHT	Supervising Infantry on No. 1 Battn. Adv. Report Centre — excavating Main Avenue west of DEAD END POST — excavating run-up to right of 17 comm. trench. R.E. on M.G. emplacement in F2. 1No4 Section left at 4.50 p.m. for School of Mortars. ST. VENANT.	
ditto	11/9/15	DAY	Supervising Infantry working on Assembly trenches — on 5q/th Bde. Adv. Report Centre — on No.1 Battn. Adv. Report Centre — on "STRAND" — on Bns-auts in 70 yds line in F2 & 3 — excavating "EDGWARE ROAD" — excavating "Gt NORTH ROAD" — on Bns-auts in 70 yds line — on No2 Battn. Adv. Report Centre — excavating "PICADILLY" — on Bns-auts if firing step in 70yds line. R.E. on underground gallery in front line in F3. — on Bns-auts in Workshops. 2nd Infantry in Workshops.	R2
		NIGHT	Supervising Infantry on "MASSELOT" Avenue — on No. 1 Battn. Adv. Report Centre — excavating "EDGWARE ROAD" — on 70 yds line Bns-auts a borrow pit between 14 & 15 comm. trenches — on run-up to right of 17 comm. trench — on chis-auts left of 17 comm. trench — excavating "PICADILLY" — on Bns-auts if firing step in 70 yds line. R.E. revetting 14 comm. trench.	R2

Army Form C. 2118

WAR DIARY
or
INTELLIGENCE SUMMARY.
(Erase heading not required.)

Instructions regarding War Diaries and Intelligence Summaries are contained in F. S. Regs., Part II. and the Staff Manual respectively. Title pages will be prepared in manuscript.

Place	Date	Hour	Summary of Events and Information	Remarks and references to Appendices
RUE DE PARADIS LAVENTIE	Sunday 12/9/15	DAY	Supervising Infantry on Ammunition trenches — on Sqth Bde Adv. Report Centre — on No1 Battn Adv. Report Centre — on dug-outs in 70 yds line — excavating "EDGEWARE ROAD", "G^t NORTH ROAD" & "PICCADILLY" — on No 2 Battn. Adv. Report Centre — widening 1A comm trench. N°6 on front line Galleries N°s a 24 Infantry in Workshops	
		NIGHT	Supervising Infantry excavating "PARK LANE" "EDGWARE ROAD" & "BURLINGTON ARCADE". On Dug-outs in 70 yds line N°6 on M.G.-line galleries	
do	13/9/15	DAY	A.G. only — On Sqth Bde. Adv. Report Centre — No1 Battn & No2 Battn. Adv. Report Centre — resetting & taking covers off "ROTTEN ROW" — on galleries in front line — clearing away outhouse near entrance to 15 comm. trench — on Dug-outs in 70 yds line — o on "BURLINGTON ARCADE." N°s a 24 Infantry in Workshops	K2
		NIGHT	A.G. only — On M.G. emplacement in F2 — Sandbag revetment of 70 yds line — deepening Sap in front line — on Dug-outs in 70 yds line.	K2
do	14/9/15		N°3 Section of 10½ Field Coy left at 10 a.m.	
		DAY	A.G. only — On Sqth Bde Adv Report Centre — No1 Battn Adv Report Centre — M.G. emplacement in F2 — on galleries in y-ont line — on No 2 Battn Adv. Report Centre. N°s a 24 Infantry in Workshops	
		NIGHT	A.G. only. — Connecting up 30 feet Gaps between F3 & F4 in front line (32 Infantry assisting). do making out Dug-outs in 70 yds line left of 17 comm trench.	K2
do	15/9/15	DAY	Supervising Infantry on "MASSELOT AVENUE" — on No1 Battn & 2 Battn. Adv. Report Centre — on Sqth Bde. Adv. Report Centre — on "PARK LANE" ("NORTH ROAD" & "EDGEWARE ROAD" — excavating "PICCADILLY" — a "BURLINGTON ARCADE" — excavating 1A comm trench — Dug-outs in 70 yds line. a mm — who night of 17 comm trench.	K2

WAR DIARY
or
INTELLIGENCE SUMMARY.
(Erase heading not required.)

Army Form C. 2118.

Instructions regarding War Diaries and Intelligence Summaries are contained in F. S. Regs., Part II. and the Staff Manual respectively. Title pages will be prepared in manuscript.

Place	Date	Hour	Summary of Events and Information	Remarks and references to Appendices
RUE DE PARADIS LAVENTIE	15/9/15	DAY	A Coy on galleries in front line – sandbag revetment of 70 yds line. B Coy 24 Infantry in workshops.	R.E.
		NIGHT	Supervising Infantry on run-ups in F.B – excavating "EDGWARE ROAD" and "BURLINGTON ARCADE" – on Brig-arks on run-ups in 70 yds line.	
do	16/9/15	DAY	Supervising Infantry on Assembly trenches – trimming off corner in "FLEET ST." – on sqm Rde Adv. Report Centre – on No1 Battn + No1 Battn Adv Report Centre – excavating "STRAND", "FLEET ST" "GT NORTH ROAD", "EDGWARE ROAD", "PICCADILLY" and "BURLINGTON ARCADE" – on Brig-arks in 70 yds line. A Coy on galleries in front line – on Brig-arks in FB – on M.G. emplacement in F.2. B Coy 24 Infantry in Workshops.	R.E.
		NIGHT	Supervising Infantry on run-ups in FB – excavating "EDGWARE ROAD" and "BURLINGTON ARCADE" – on galleries in front line. B Coy only on galleries in front line.	
do	17/9/15	DAY	Supervising Infantry on Assembly trenches – on sqm Rde. Adv. Report Centre – on No1 Battn 9/2 Battn Adv Report Centre – trimming off corner in "FLEET ST" – excavating "STRAND", "PARK LANE", "GT NORTH RD", "PICCADILLY", and "EDGWARE ROAD" and "BURLINGTON ARCADE". – on Brig-arks in 70 yds line. A Coy on galleries in front line + on Brig-arks on Brig-arks in workshops. B Coy 24 Infantry in Workshops.	R.E.
		NIGHT	Supervising Infantry on run-ups in FB, – excavating "EDGWARE ROAD" and on Brig-arks in 70 yds line. B Coy on galleries in front line & marking out run-up.	R.E.

Army Form C. 2118.

WAR DIARY
or
INTELLIGENCE SUMMARY.
(Erase heading not required.)

Place	Date	Hour	Summary of Events and Information	Remarks and references to Appendices
RUE DE PARADIS LAVENTIE	18/4/15	DAY	Supervising Infantry excavating "STRAND" — working on M.T. Battn. Adv. Report Centre — on Sgt. Bde. Adv. Report Centre — on Assembly Trenches — running o/b covers in FLEET ST — excavating "GT NORTH ROAD" — excavating "EDGWARE ROAD" — excavating "PICCADILLY" — preparing Road for Artillery — working on No. 1, Battn. Adv. Report Centre — on Eng. subs in 70 yds Line — excavating "BURLINGTON ARCADE". R.E. only on galleries in front line — on Eng. subs in 70 yds Line —. No. 8, 24 Infantry in Workshops.	R.E.
		NIGHT	Supervising Infantry on gun emplacement in F 2 & 3 — excavating "EDGWARE ROAD", and Eng. subs in 70 yds Line. R.E. only on M.G. emplacement in F 2, and on galleries in front line.	
do.	19/4/15 (Sunday)	DAY.	Supervising Infantry on Assembly Trenches — excavating "STRAND" — running o/b covers in "FLEET ST" — on No. 1 Battn. Adv. Rep. at Centre — on M.G. Stops in 70 yds Line — excavating "GT NORTH ROAD" — excavating "EDGWARE ROAD" — excavating "PICCADILLY" — excavating "BURLINGTON ARCADE". R.E. only on galleries in front line — on Eng. subs in 70 yds Line — on screening work along RUE TILLELOY. No. 8a 24 Infantry in Workshops	
		NIGHT	Supervising Infantry excavating gun emps in F 2 & 3 — excavating "EDGWARE RD" — on Eng. subs in 70 yds Line — excavating "BURLINGTON ARCADE" — preparing ground for Road for Artillery — on Parapets for Road for Artillery — on screening. R.E. only on galleries in front line — on Parados for Road for Artillery — on screening. Work along "RUE TILLELOY."	R.E.

WAR DIARY
or
INTELLIGENCE SUMMARY.

(Erase heading not required.)

Army Form C. 2118.

Instructions regarding War Diaries and Intelligence Summaries are contained in F. S. Regs., Part II. and the Staff Manual respectively. Title pages will be prepared in manuscript.

Place	Date	Hour	Summary of Events and Information	Remarks and references to Appendices
RUE DE PARADIS. LAVENTIE	20/9/15	DAY.	No. 24 Infantry working in shops (on mining gallery frames). Preparing barbed wire gooseneck pickets. Bangalore torpedoes for discharge of Bangalore torpedoes. Reconng. along RUE TILLELOY. – Preparing slaying out Indian Infantry Boards along avenue, Comm. trenches & mines.	The 2nd South Wales Borderers relieved
		NIGHT	NIL.	
ditto	21/9/15	DAY.	Supervising Infantry on Assembly trenches – excavating "STRAND" – excavating & mining off corners in "FLEET STREET" – excavating "Gt NORTH ROAD" – excavating "EDGWARE ROAD" – excavating "PICCADILLY" – of No. 2 Battn. Adv. Report Centre – on Dug-outs in 70 yds Line – preparing Road for Artillery – on admired stores. R.E. on Dug-outs in 70 yds line – on mining slope in 70 yds line – on galleries in front line.	
		NIGHT	No. 24 Infantry Carpenters in Workshops. Supervising Infantry excavating "MASSET" – on Dug-outs in 70 yds line – on Dug-outs in 10 yds Line – on "BURLINGTON ARCADE" – preparing Road for Artillery. Q.R. on advanced Stores in Front line.	
ditto	22/9/15	DAY	Supervising Infantry on Assembly trenches – deepening "STRAND" – excavating "EDGWARE ROAD" – excavating "Gt NORTH ROAD" – excavating "PICCADILLY" – on Dug-outs in 10 yds Line – working on No. 2 Battn. Adv. Report Centre – working on 3 advanced R.E. Stores. R.E. on galleries in front Line – on Screening Walk along RUE TILLELOY – preparing & laying out Indication Boards along avenues & Comm. trenches. No. 24 Infantry Carpenters in Workshops.	

Army Form C. 2118.

WAR DIARY
or
INTELLIGENCE SUMMARY.

(Erase heading not required.)

Instructions regarding War Diaries and Intelligence Summaries are contained in F. S. Regs., Part II. and the Staff Manual respectively. Title pages will be prepared in manuscript.

Place	Date	Hour	Summary of Events and Information	Remarks and references to Appendices
RUE DE PARADIS LAVENTIE.	22/9/15	NIGHT	Supervising Infantry on run-up in F2 & 3 – excavating "GT NORTH ROAD" – excavating "PICANTIN" – excavating "BURLINGTON ARCADE". R.E. only on Bng-arts in 70 yds Line. – on Advanced R.E. Store. –	RE
ditto	23/9/15	DAY	Supervising Infantry excavating "STRAND" – on Assembly trenches – excavating "GT NORTH ROAD" – excavating "PICANTIN". – on Bng-arts in 70 yds Line. – on No2 Battn. Adv. Report Centre – R.E. only on advanced R.E. Store. – on Galleries in front Line. – on Revesting along Rue TILLELOY, and laying out Indication Boards along Avenue Comm. Trenches. R.E. & 24 Infantry in Workshop.	RE
		NIGHT	Supervising Infantry excavating "PICANTIN" – Improving road for Artillery – on Bng-arts in 70 yds Line. – on parapet of "PICANTIN"	RE
ditto	24/9/15	DAY	Operations – nil. Company standing by.	
do	25/9/15 26/9/15 27/9/15		No 4 Section returned from Gt VENANT at 4-6 p.m.	RE
do	28/9/15	DAY	Laying trench boards in run-ups in F2 & 3. – Revetting parados for Bng-arts in 70 yds Line. – R.E. & 24 Infantry in Workshop.	RE
		NIGHT	NIL.	

WAR DIARY
or
INTELLIGENCE SUMMARY.

(Erase heading not required.)

Army Form C. 21

Place	Date	Hour	Summary of Events and Information	Remarks and references to Appendices
RUE DE PARADIS. LAVENTIE	29/9/15	DAY	R.E. only, revetting in "FLEET ST." – revetting firing step & laying trench boards in 70 yds Line in N.13/5 – Inspecting new Area. 98 Rfs. 2/4 Infantry in Workshops	
		NIGHT	R.E. only revetting in "FLEET ST." – removing R.E. Stores – marking out Borrow Pits for front Line	
do	30/9/15	DAY	R.E. only revetting in "FLEET ST." – working on new Adv. Report Centre – altering & fitting a revetting Stores to new Depot – on Aug. out into 70 yds Line – fitting firing step in 70 yds line – supervising work on Galleries in front Line	
		NIGHT	R.E. & 2/4 Infantry Carpenters in Workshops. R.E. revetting INDIAN AVENUE.	
do	1/10/15	DAY	Supervising Infantry excavating NORTHUMBERLAND AVENUE – banking up behind revetting frames in "FLEET ST." – on new Adv. Report Centre – widening & deepening "INDIAN AVENUE" Galleries & Bug out, constructing firing line – returning 70 yds to "RUE BAQUEROT" – on new Aug out for Stores at junction of MIDLAND RLY & "RUE BAQUEROT" – widening & deepening 70 yds line – widening & cleaning up "S. ELGIN ST."	
		NIGHT	R.E. & 2/4 Infantry Carpenters in Workshops R.E. only revetting "FLEET ST." and "INDIAN AVENUE" (No Infantry working)	
do	2/10/15	DAY	Supervising Infantry on new Adv. Report Centre – excavating "NORTHUMBERLAND AVENUE" – revetting parados of 70 yds line – widening & deepening 70 yds line – cleaning up "LONELY EARTH" & "S. ELGIN ST." – on Bug. out for new Line – working on retg "MIDLAND RAILWAY"	

Army Form C. 2118.

WAR DIARY
or
INTELLIGENCE SUMMARY.
(Erase heading not required.)

Instructions regarding War Diaries and Intelligence Summaries are contained in F.S. Regs., Part II. and the Staff Manual respectively. Title pages will be prepared in manuscript.

Place	Date	Hour	Summary of Events and Information	Remarks and references to Appendices
ROE DE PARADIS LAVENTIE	2/10/15	DAY	R.E. only laying French Boards in "ROTTEN ROW" – no fatigues of Inf. onto front line. N.G. & 2. Infantry Carpenters in Workshops.	
		NIGHT	R.E. & Infantry parades of front line in N.13/4. – on new advanced R.E. Store.	
do	3/10/15	DAY	(Sunday) 8 R.E. & 2 Infantry revetting "MIDLAND RAILWAY."	
		NIGHT	NIL.	
do.	4/10/15	DAY	Supervising Infantry widening deepening & revetting 70 yds line – titting widening & deepening "LONELY ERITH" – widening & deepening "S. EGLISE ST" – working on new R.E. Store – clearing up & widening (8 R.E.s 2 Infantry) of approach to "MIDLAND RLY"	
		NIGHT	R.E. only revetting entrance to fatigues in front line – revetting "ROTTEN ROW" on new Advanced Report Centre – on fatigues of Inf. onto front line – fitting trestle of foot-bomb in MASSELOT – FAUQUISSART ST." – R.E. only fitting trestle foot-bomb in "MASSELOT – FAUQUISSART St." supervising Infantry widening & deepening "INDIAN AVENUE."	
do.	5/10/15	DAY.	Supervising Infantry on new Adv. Report Centre – revetting in "FLEET ST" o "ROTTEN ROW" – widening & revetting 70 yds line – constructing Dug-outs in 70 yds line – widening "S. ELGIN ST" "LONELY ERITH", "S. EGLISE ST" – construction of specimen trenches – refacing MIDLAND RAILWAY dumbs for sine – in "LE DRUMEZ" Post excavating & work on fine trench.	

Army Form C. 2118.

WAR DIARY
or
INTELLIGENCE SUMMARY.

(Erase heading not required.)

Instructions regarding War Diaries and Intelligence Summaries are contained in F. S. Regs., Part II. and the Staff Manual respectively. Title pages will be prepared in manuscript.

Place	Date	Hour	Summary of Events and Information	Remarks and references to Appendices
RUE DE PARADIS. LAVENTIE	5/10/15	DAY	R.E. only revetting entrances to galleries in front line – on galleries & dug-outs in front line – laying trestles & foot-boards in "MASSELDT".	
		NIGHT	Supervising Infantry widening & revetting "INDIAN AVENUE". R.E. only laying foot-boards on "MASSELDT" trench south of "RUE TILLELOY."	
do.	6/10/15	DAY.	Supervising Infantry on new Adv. Report Centre – excavating "NORTHUMBERLAND AVENUE" widening & revetting 70 yds line – constructing firestep near "ROAD BEND" do. – cleaning up "LONELY ERITH" & "ELGIN ST." – widening "S. EGLISE ST." – on Bn.'s dug-outs & on "LE DRUMEZ" – on 70 yds line – on "LE DRUMEZ" do. – revetting "ROTTEN ROW" – relaying entrance to galleries in front line – on galleries & dug-outs in front line – laying trestles & foot boards in "MASSELDT" – FAUQUISSART ST." – repairing MIDLAND RAILWAY – getting out details for hutting requirements for 3 au Battalions.	
		NIGHT	R.E. 15 Infantry Carpenters in workshops. Superintending Infantry widening & deepening "INDIAN AVENUE" – thickening earth behind revetting frames in "INDIAN AVENUE" – repairing "ELGIN ST." R.E. only revetting "INDIAN AVENUE".	
do	7/10/15	DAY	Supervising Infantry on new Adv. Report Centre – revetting "ROTTEN ROW" – excavating "NORTHUMBERLAND AVENUE" – widening, deepening & revetting 70 yds line – cleaning up "ELGIN ST." & "S. EGLISE ST." – on firestep trench near "ROAD BEND" – widening "LONELY ERITH" – getting on "LE DRUMEZ" dpt.– R.E. only laying trestles & foot-boards in "MASSELDT" trench, Job RUE TILLELOY – repairing "MIDLAND RLY." – repairing numerous Infantry Billets & working on Abutments – preparing Stables & stand for numerical section of 96th Coy. R.E. 9 to 12 Infantry Carpenters in workshops.	
		NIGHT	Supervising Infantry widening & deepening INDIAN AVENUE & working on known trenches. R.E. only erecting hutch from Loop-hole at M. 18. d. and M. 24. b.	

WAR DIARY
or
INTELLIGENCE SUMMARY.

(Erase heading not required.)

Army Form C. 2118

Instructions regarding War Diaries and Intelligence Summaries are contained in F.S. Regs., Part II. and the Staff Manual respectively. Title pages will be prepared in manuscript.

Place	Date	Hour	Summary of Events and Information	Remarks and references to Appendices
RUE DE PARADIS LAVENTIE	8/10/15	DAY	Supervising Infantry on new Bde Adv Report Centre – widening & deepening "STRAND" – widening & revetting 70 yds Line – on specimen Trenches near "ROAD BEND" Post – widening "S. EGLISE St" – cleaning up "ELGIN St" & "LONELY ERITH" – on "LE DRUMEZ" Post. – R.E. only revetting "RIFLEMANS AVENUE" – on Dug-outs & Galleries in front-line – on gun emplacement. No. 6 Infantry Carpenters on "MIDLAND RLY." – reps & improving Infantry Billets & preparing material for huts, & working on erecting hutments. No. 6 Infantry Carpenters in Workshops.	R.E.
		Night	Supervising Infantry widening "INDIAN AVENUE" & working on Barrow Ditch – revetting "S. ELGIN St". R.E. only on Dug-outs in front-line.	R.E.
ditto	9/10/15	DAY.	Lieut WITUCH-JONES wounded. Supervising Infantry on new Bde. Adv. Report Centre – widening, deepening and revetting 70 yds Line – on specimen trenches near ROAD BEND Post – widening "S. ELGIN St" & "S. EGLISE St" & "LONELY ERITH" – repairing MIDLAND RAILWAY. – working on LEDRUMEZ Post. R.E. only revetting "RIFLEMANS AVENUE." – on Galleries & Dug-outs in front-Line – R.E. & Infantry Carpenters on Billets and Materials for hut shelters. R.E. & Infantry Carpenters in Workshops.	R.E.
		NIGHT	Supervising Infantry widening & deepening "INDIAN AVENUE" & revetting "S. ELGIN St" R.E. only on Dug-outs in front-line & on gun emplacements.	R.E.
ditto	10/10/15	DAY	(Sunday) No Infantry Carpenters on preparing material for hut shelters & in Workshops making materials.	R.E.
		NIGHT	NIL.	

1577 Wt. W10791/1773 500,000 1/15 D.D. & L. A.D.S.S./Forms/C. 2118.

WAR DIARY
or
INTELLIGENCE SUMMARY.
(Erase heading not required.)

Army Form C. 2

Instructions regarding War Diaries and Intelligence Summaries are contained in F. S. Regs., Part II. and the Staff Manual respectively. Title pages will be prepared in manuscript.

Place	Date	Hour	Summary of Events and Information	Remarks and references to Appendices
RUE DE PARADIS, LAVENTIE	9/10/15	DAY	Supervising Infantry on Bde. Adv. Report Centre. — No 1. Battn. Adv. Report Centre — Cleaning up "NORTHUMBERLAND AVENUE" — working on "MASSELOT" Post — working on "WANGERIE" Post — widening 70 yds Line — widening "S. ELGIN St" — Cleaning up "LONELY ERITH" — working on "LONELY Post" — working on "ROAD BEND" Post. — R.E. only — on Bgy — onto 1 fallen in front line — on field gun emplacements — erecting Barricade on RUE MASSELOT. R.E. Infantry Carpenters repairing M.G. Gun Billets, extras preparing material for hut shelters and in Workshop.	
		NIGHT	Supervising Infantry on wire entanglements a revetting on right side of "NORTHUMBERLAND AVENUE." — erecting Barricade on RUE MASSELOT a revetting "S. ELGIN St"	
do.	10/10/15	DAY	Supervising Infantry on Bde. Adv. Report Centre — on No 2. Battn. Adv. Report Centre — working on "MASSELOT" Post — working on "WANGERIE" Post — on "ROAD BEND" Post — on "LONELY Post" — widening 70 yds Line — revetting revetment of 70 yds Line — on Bgy — onto "Enemy step in 70 yds Line — revetting "S. EGLISE St" — widening "S. ELGIN St" — on " LE BRUMEZ " Post — R.E. only — revetting "ROTTEN ROW" — on fallens in front line. — on frais foot-board trestles in "MASSELOT — FAUQUISSART St" — repairing M.G. Ry a G.E. Ry. R.E. Infantry Carpenters repairing infantry Billets, extras preparing material for hut shelters and in Workshop.	
		NIGHT	Supervising Infantry, excavating NORTHUMBERLAND AVENUE — on Barricade in RUE MASSELOT — revetting "S. ELGIN St" R.E. only — preparing "ROTTEN ROW" for defence. — on Gun emplacement in front line.	

Army Form C. 2118

WAR DIARY
or
INTELLIGENCE SUMMARY.
(Erase heading not required.)

Instructions regarding War Diaries and Intelligence Summaries are contained in F.S. Regs., Part II. and the Staff Manual respectively. Title pages will be prepared in manuscript.

Place	Date	Hour	Summary of Events and Information	Remarks and references to Appendices
RUE DE PARADIS, LAVENTIE	13/10/15	DAY	R.E. only. – on Rde. Adr. Report Centre – preparing screens for Rue Masselot and Rue Tilleloy. – on shield gun emplacement in front line – sandbag revetment of "S. ELGIN St". – ROAD BEND Post. – on repairs to MIDLAND RLY & C.C. RLY. R.E's Infantry Carpenters on Billets. – a material for Ant. Shelters – and in Workshops.	
		NIGHT	R.E. only.	
do.	14/10/15	DAY	R.E. & GRANT Brigade on RUE MASSELOT & revetting "S.ELGIN St". Supervising Infantry on Rde. Adr. Report Centre. – on No 2 Battn Adr. Report Centre. – wiring etc on "STRAND" – cleaning up 70 yds line near "RIFLEMANS AVENUE" – widening & revetting 70 yds line left of "MASSELOT" Trench – widening & deepening "S.ELGIN St" – widening & deepening "LONELY ERITH" & "EGLISE St" – on dug outs in 70 yds line left of "S.ELGIN St" – working on following Posts. – "DEAD END." – "WANGERIE" – "MASSELOT" – "ROAD BEND" – "LONELY" – working on repairs to "MIDLAND RAILWAY." – cleaning out existing Ant Shelters. R.E's Infantry Carpenters on Billets and material for Ant Shelters. – and in Workshops. R.E. only superintending galleries in front line left of "S. ELGIN St".	
		NIGHT	Supervising Infantry wiring along ROTTEN ROW. – excavating "NORTHUMBERLAND AVENUE" – widening & deepening "INDIAN AVENUE". – on gun emplacement in front line – revetting "S. ELGIN St".	
do.	15/10/15	DAY	R.E. & GRANT Brigade. Supervising Infantry. – on Rde. Adr. Report Centre – on No. 2 Battn. Adr. Report Centre. – cleaning up 70 yds line near "NORTHUMBERLAND AVENUE" – wiring along "ROTTEN ROW" – cleaning up "RIFLEMANS AVENUE" – Capper's french Parade – on gun emplacement in front line at N.15/I. – Capper's 9'0" Parade in "MASSELOT" Trench – Capper's 9'0" Parade between "WANGERIE St" & "MASSELOT" Trench – on dug-outs & sandbag revetment of 70 yds line left of "S. ELGIN St" – cleaning up & revetting "S.ELGIN St" – revetting "EGLISE St" – cleaning up "LONELY ERITH" – on repairs to "MIDLAND RAILWAY" & "GT CENTRAL RLY" – erection of screens for CENTRAL RLY and its extension to front. – working on following Posts. – "DEAD END" – "MASSELOT" – "WANGERIE" –	

WAR DIARY
or
INTELLIGENCE SUMMARY.
(Erase heading not required.)

Army Form C. 2118.

Instructions regarding War Diaries and Intelligence Summaries are contained in F. S. Regs., Part II. and the Staff Manual respectively. Title pages will be prepared in manuscript.

Place	Date	Hour	Summary of Events and Information	Remarks and references to Appendices
RUE DE PARADIS. LAVENTIE	15/10/15	DAY.	"ROAD BEND" – "LONELY" – "LE DRUMEZ". R. & a Infantry Carpenters in Workshops & on Billets for Sq/m Bde. Infantry & sorting & preparing material for hut shelters & working in construction.	KZ
		NIGHT	Superintending Infantry wiring etc along "ROTTEN ROW" – excavating "NORTHUMBERLAND AVENUE" – filling in behind revetting frames in "INDIAN AVENUE" – revetting in "S. ELGIN ST."	KZ
ditto	16/10/15	DAY	Superintending Infantry on Bde. Advanced Report Centre – on No. 2 Battn. Adv. Report Centre – cleaning Dyke line near "ROTTEN ROW" – wiring etc along "STRAND" – laying foot-boards in "RIFLEMANS AVENUE" – wiring etc reserve line near ROTTEN ROW – revetting & preparing MASSELOT ST. for transomes – on gun emplacement in front line – reps parapet in front line at N.13/1 – on Emplac. & firing step in Dyke line left of S. ELGIN ST. – cleaning up "S. ELGIN ST." & laying foot-boards. "MIDLAND RLY" & "GT CENTRAL RLY" – revetting "LONELY ERITH" – on repairs to follanny Posts. "DEAD END" "WANGERIE" MASSELOT, "ROAD BEND" "LONELY" "LE DRUMEZ" – cleaning out existing ditches. R. & a Infantry Carpenters in Workshops & on Billets for Sq/m. Bde. & sorting & preparing material for hut shelters & working in construction. R & & only on fatigues in front Line.	
		NIGHT	Superintending Infantry wiring etc along "ROTTEN ROW" – excavating "NORTHUMBERLAND AVENUE" – revetting "INDIAN AVENUE" & Enlarging cover for same – on gun emplacement & in front Line – reps parapet of front line at N.13/1 revetting S. ELGIN ST.	KZ
ditto	17/10/15 Sunday	DAY.	Infantry Carpenters on Hutting material, and in Workshops on Dug-out frames & foot Boards etc.	KZ

1577 Wt. W10791/1773 500,000 1/15 D. D. & L. A.D.S.S./Forms/C. 2118.

WAR DIARY
or
INTELLIGENCE SUMMARY.

(Erase heading not required.)

Army Form C. 21

Instructions regarding War Diaries and Intelligence Summaries are contained in F. S. Regs., Part II. and the Staff Manual respectively. Title pages will be prepared in manuscript.

Place	Date	Hour	Summary of Events and Information	Remarks and references to Appendices
RUE DE PARADIS LAVENTIE	18/10/15	DAY	Supervising Infantry on Barricade at Tweedy end of "DRURY LANE" – on Bde. Adv. Report Centre – wiring etc on "STRAND" – clearing 70 yds line near "ROTTEN ROW" – clearing "RIFLEMANS AVENUE" & laying foot-boards – wiring fwing parapet in front line at N 13/1. – on N tees firing emplacements in front line reporting on "FAUQUISSART ST" as a wired avenue – on Brig. onto a firing step in 70 yds line left of "S. ELGIN ST" – revetting "S. ELGIN ST" – revetting "MIDLAND RLY" & "GT CENTRAL RLY" – erection of screens for "GT CENTRAL RLY" & its extension towards the front – working on following Pets "DEAD END" "WANGERIE" "MASSELOT" "ROAD BEND" "LONELY" R.B. & Infantry Carpenters etc. & improving Bullet accommodation for Sq. Inf. Bde. & on material for hut shelters – in Wd shops on material	Ref
		NIGHT	Supervising Infantry wiring etc on "ROTTEN ROW" – excavating "NORTHUMBERLAND AVENUE" – on "INDIAN AVENUE" borrow pit & revetting "INDIAN AVENUE" – on field firm emplacements in front line – revetting "S. ELGIN ST."	
ditto	19/10/15	DAY	Supervising Infantry hopping up "STRAND" "FAUQUISSART ST" "ROAD BEND AVENUE" on united avenues – on Bde Adv. Report Centre – clearing 70 yds line near "ROTTEN ROW" – wiring along "STRAND" & "ROTTEN ROW" – laying foot boards in "RIFLEMANS AVENUE" – on Barricade in "DRURY LANE" & "MASSELOT AVENUE" – fillers in front line – on 70 yds line left of "S. ELGIN ST – revetting "S. ELGIN ST" & "G. EGLISE ST" – clearing "LONELY ERITH" – repairs to "MIDLAND RLY" & "G.C. RLY" – on erection of screens for "GT CENTRAL RLY" & its extension towards the front. N.B. only on parapet in front line at N 13/1. A.6.9 Infantry Carpenters etc & improving Bullet accommodation for Sq. Inf. Bde. & on material for hut shelters – in workshops on material for same.	
		NIGHT	Supervising Infantry wiring "ROTTEN ROW" – excavating "NORTHUMBERLAND AVENUE" – on borrow ditch & revetting "INDIAN AVENUE" – revetting "S. ELGIN ST" – excavating "ROAD BEND" AVENUE – realignment of same.	Ref

WAR DIARY or INTELLIGENCE SUMMARY

(Erase heading not required.)

Army Form C. 2118

Instructions regarding War Diaries and Intelligence Summaries are contained in F. S. Regs., Part II. and the Staff Manual respectively. Title pages will be prepared in manuscript.

Place	Date	Hour	Summary of Events and Information	Remarks and references to Appendices
RUE DE PARADIS, LAVENTIE	20/10/15	DAY	Supervising Infantry working in "STRAND" – clearing "STRAND" "FAUQUISSART ST" & "ROAD BEND AVENUE" as winter avenues – laying foot boards in "RIFLEMANS AVENUE". On dug-out in front line left of "S. ELGIN ST" (firing step & dug-outs in "O" line left of "S. ELGIN ST" – "INDIAN AVENUE" – on cleaning LONELY ERITH – to drain to "MIDLAND RLY" & "G.T. CENTRAL RLY" revetting & preparing for tramway. G.E.R. to its extension towards the front – cleaning out & drain from M10 to M17.7M.12. R.G.A. Batteries in front line (superintending Infantry) R.E. Infantry Carpenters in Workshops & repairing Billets, and working in Arts Shelters.	R/E
		NIGHT	Supervising Infantry working on along "ROTTEN ROW" – revetting "INDIAN AVENUE" & "INDIAN AVENUE" – revetting & "S. ELGIN ST" – communication trench, ditch draining. "ROAD BEND AVENUE" R.E. – alignment of "ROAD BEND AVENUE" R.E. only on Vicker gun emplacement in front line	R/E
do	21/10/15	DAY	Supervising Infantry working in "STRAND" – preparing "STRAND" – "FAUQUISSART ST" – "ROAD BEND AVENUE" & "S. ELGIN ST" as winter avenues – laying foot-boards in "RIFLEMANS AVENUE" – on repairs to "G.T. CENTRAL RLY" (preparing siding & erecting screens) R.E. on Batteries in front line (superintending Infantry) R.G.A. Infantry Carpenters in Workshops & repairing Billets & working on Arts Shelters.	R/E
		NIGHT	Supervising Infantry working "ROTTEN ROW" – deepening & revetting "DRURY LANE" – revetting "S. ELGIN ST" – revetting "INDIAN AVENUE" & working on lower ditch – revetting "S. ELGIN ST". R.E. only on Vicker gun emplacement in front line	R/E
do	22/10/15	DAY	Supervising Infantry working "STRAND" – preparing "STRAND" "FAUQUISSART ST" "ROAD BEND AVENUE" & "S. ELGIN ST" as winter avenues – laying foot-boards in "RIFLEMANS AVENUE" – repairs to "G.T. RLY" & screens along extension of line towards front. R.E. on dug-outs & gun emplacements in Workshops & repairing Billets. R.E. Infantry Carpenters in Workshops & repairing Billets and working on Arts Shelters.	R/E

Army Form C. 2

WAR DIARY
or
INTELLIGENCE SUMMARY.

(Erase heading not required.)

Instructions regarding War Diaries and Intelligence Summaries are contained in F. S. Regs., Part II. and the Staff Manual respectively. Title pages will be prepared in manuscript.

Place	Date	Hour	Summary of Events and Information	Remarks and references to Appendices
RUE DE PARADIS, LAVENTIE	22/10/15	NIGHT	Supervising Infantry wiring "ROTTEN ROW" — revetting "DRURY LANE" — revetting "INDIAN AVENUE" & trench ditch for same — revetting "S. ELGIN. St." R.E. only on Gun emplacements.	yes
do.	23/10/15	DAY.	R.E. only on gun emplacements. A.E. and Infantry Carpenters in Workshops — and on repairs to "G. CENTRAL RLY", and preparing bedding & sheeting. Infantry Carpenters on preparing material for Strut Shelters & working on construction.	yes
		NIGHT	R.E. only on Gun emplacements.	
do.	24/10/15 (Sunday)	DAY	Supervising Infantry on trench wiring "STRAND" – "FAUQUISSART ST" & "S. ELGIN. ST" as winter avenue — on Brigade Gen. Reports Centre - Clearing new part of "ROAD BEND AVENUE" in front of Posn — on repairs to G.C. RLY & Screed along extension of line towards front. R.E. & Infantry Carpenters in Workshops & on material for Strut Shelters. R.E. only from temporary Bridge for Artillery from RUE TILLELOY to front line.	yes
		NIGHT	Supervising Infantry revetting "DRURY LANE" — wiring "RIFLEMANS AVENUE" - Clearing Reserve line at "ROTTEN ROW" — revetting "INDIAN AVENUE" & making broken ditch - & revetting S. ELGIN. St. R.E. on Gun emplacements at N.13.c.3.0 – 2.5 & N.13.C.4.5 – 7.0.	
do.	25/10/15	DAY	Supervising Infantry on "FAUQUISSART St" & "S. ELGIN. St" preparing as winter avenue — Clearing new part of "ROAD BEND AVENUE" — on repairs to "G.C. RLY" & Screed along extension of line towards front. R.E. & Infantry Carpenters in Workshops & on material for Strut Shelters.	yes
		NIGHT	Supervising Infantry revetting "DRURY LANE". R.E. only on bridges for Artillery.	yes

WAR DIARY
or
INTELLIGENCE SUMMARY.
(Erase heading not required.)

Army Form C. 2

Instructions regarding War Diaries and Intelligence Summaries are contained in F. S. Regs., Part II. and the Staff Manual respectively. Title pages will be prepared in manuscript.

Place	Date	Hour	Summary of Events and Information	Remarks and references to Appendices
RUE DE PARADIS. LAVENTIE.	26/10/15	DAY.	Supervising Infantry on "STRAND" - "FAUQUISSART ST" & "S. ELGIN. ST" - preparing for winter avenues - filling & carrying sandbags - A Coy on Punt Shelter at RED LAMP Corner. - on G.C. RLY & Sarsens for same. B Coy Infantry Carpenters in workshops making materials & repairs to beds.	
		NIGHT	Supervising Infantry revetting "DRURY LANE" - wiring "RIFLEMANS AVENUE" - excavating Advanced Communication trenches - revetting "INDIAN AVENUE" & a "Borrow ditch" for same - on "FAUQUISSART ST" & "S.ELGIN ST" - preparing as winter avenues. A Coy on Punt-shelter at RED LAMP Corner. 2/L HARRISON proceeded.	H.R.
do	27/10/15	DAY	Supervising Infantry filling & carrying sandbags - on "FAUQUISSART ST" - preparing as a winter avenue - on "S. ELGIN. ST" - preparing as a winter avenue - on "GORY" & Sarsens for same - B Coy Infantry Carpenters in Workshops.	
		NIGHT	Supervising Infantry filling & carrying sandbags - working on & awaiting Advanced Comm. trenches - revetting "INDIAN AVENUE" & thickening parapet from Comm ditch cleaning Willow ditch - on "S. ELGIN. ST" revetting & preparing as a winter avenue. A Coy on Punt shelter at "RED LAMP" Corner.	H.R.
do	28/10/15	DAY.	2/Lt HARRISON died of wounds. A Coy only filling & carrying sandbags. No. 3 Infantry Carpenters in Workshop making materials. B Coy Infantry Carpenters on G.C. RLY - preparing beds, & creating Sarsens.	
		NIGHT	B.R. only laying part - tracks in "INDIAN AVENUE"	H.R.

WAR DIARY
or
INTELLIGENCE SUMMARY.
(Erase heading not required.)

Army Form C. 2118

Instructions regarding War Diaries and Intelligence Summaries are contained in F.S. Regs., Part II. and the Staff Manual respectively. Title pages will be prepared in manuscript.

Place	Date	Hour	Summary of Events and Information	Remarks and references to Appendices
RUE DE PARADIS, LAVENTIE	29/10/15	DAY	Supervising Infantry carrying up & filling Sandbags on "S. ELGIN St." preparing as a winter avenue. - on "Gt. RLY" preparing siding & erecting Screens - wiring along "Gt. NORTH ROAD" R.E. Infantry Carpenters in Workshops making Special hurdles etc.	R.E.
		NIGHT	Supervising Infantry carrying up & filling Sandbags - excavating Adv. Comm. trenches - carrying up Special hurdles etc - revetting "S. ELGIN St".	
	30/10/15	DAY	Supervising Infantry carrying up & filling Sandbags on "S. ELGIN St" & "FAUQUISSART St" & "G.C.RLY" preparing siding a revetting screens - working on "STRAND" - BOW" - on "G.C.RLY" (repairing a winter avenue - revetting "ROTTEN ROW" R.E. Infantry Carpenters in Workshops making Special hurdles etc - wiring along "Gt NORTH RD".	R.E.
		NIGHT	Supervising Infantry carrying up & filling Sandbags - excavating Adv. Comm. trenches - cleaning "INDIAN AVENUE" - on which gun emplacement - on "S. ELGIN St" preparing as a winter avenue.	
	31/10/15	DAY	R.E. Infantry Carpenters in Workshops making materials. 1 Officer & 10 N.C.O's were on duty with 60th Brigade.	R.E.

Not to be taken into the trenches

SECRET.

G 380 K

TRENCH FORTIFICATION.

Lecture to Officers and N.C.O's, 96th Coy.R.E., 20th Division.

The frontage and area occupied by Divisions is liable to constant change. During the past 5 months the area now held by the 8th Division has been held by no less than 5 Divisions. Much confusion of idea, waste of labour, and even harmful work, from the fortification point of view, is directly traceable to the tendency of new comers to reject the partially completed schemes of their predecessors in favour of some new scheme. The result is not infrequently chaos. It is most desirable, therefore, that the R.E. should realize how the existing fortifications have arrived at their present form and the lines upon which future developments should proceed.

2. The line of the front breastwork has grown from the original fire trenches dug by infantry in the course of the fighting in the early part of the war. Originally there were doubtless support and reserve trenches and all were in short lengths. The communication trenches were nearly always the natural ditches of the country.

3. As time went on, the front trenches were gradually joined up for convenience of lateral communication and rough dug-outs and shelters were built.

4. At a later stage when the rain came all these trenches, communications, etc., were flooded out. Recourse to breastworks became a necessity. Patches were built on the dryer spots, and by degrees these have been joined up, parados added, shelters built, etc. Most of the communications had to be abandoned and relief of the trench garrison had to be effected at night over the open.

5. Similarly the support trenches and reserve trenches were flooded out and there arose on the dryer spots small supporting works.

6. In the meantime, in rear of the front line trenches and supporting points a continuous trench line had been dug under the direction of G.H.Q. as a 2nd line of defence to be held in case of a "break through". This line was similarly flooded out and in its place arose at intervals what are known as "G.H.Q.Posts" or "2nd Line Posts".

7. It should be noticed that so long as our defences were organized on the foregoing lines, counter attacks to recover lost trenches could be, and were usually, made over the open, though where communication trenches existed, and bombs were available, counter attacks were also made by bombing down the communications and laterally along the trenches. It will be seen that later developments have rendered counter attacks over the open impracticable and that counter attack must now be by bombing and bayonet parties.

8. When an attack upon the enemy's position was contemplated, "assembly trenches" had to be dug as the front breastwork could obviously not hold enough troops to assault. These assembly trenches had to be dug as far as possible in orchards or wherever some concealment was possible and in the process there was great

danger

danger of giving away the point of attack. The new system provides much better facilities for assault.

9. Some time ago the danger of having one line only to hold, under heavy bombardment, was realised and orders were issued that there must be a second or support trench close in rear of the breastwork to which the trench garrison could retire leaving only look-outs and machine guns in the front line. In the 8th division it was decided that 40 yards distance from the breastwork would be suitable. It was thought that this distance would avoid "overs" from shots fired at the front line, and that the German artillery would not be likely to "lift" 40 yards only. More recent opinion is that 60 to 70 yards would be a better distance and the latter distance has been taken in the greater part of the 8th division front.

10. Later developments are a 3rd line known as the "Reserve Trench", numerous main communication trenches known as "avenues" and the arrangement of wiring supporting points, etc, etc, shown in the accompanying diagram (A). It will be seen at once that counter attack over the open is no longer possible so that an adequate supply of bombs at the intersections of avenues and bombers' trenches, with the support trench and reserve trench is essential. If they are not there the whole theory of the defence very largely falls to the ground as the "bird cage" system of wiring precludes counter attack over the open and necessitates bombing down the avenues and trenches.

11. For attack on the enemy it is obvious that much greater accommodation exists than formerly for the assembly of troops behind any point in the line and that there are much greater facilities for increasing this accommodation, unknown to the enemy than was formerly the case.

It may be noted here that formerly troops issued from their breastworks by ladders placed every yard or two apart, but this would not be done in future, sally ports taking their place to reduce exposure. The "trench of departure", i.e., that from which the 1st line of stormers starts, would also be made in front of the breastwork, as was done at NEUVE CHAPELLE in March and at ROUGES BANCS in May last.

12. The wire in front of the breastwork is usually the chevaux de frise type. The framework was originally made of wood. It is now being gradually replaced by angle steel framework. This type of obstacle has the advantage of being easy to place in position and lends itself to cutting the wire in front of any portion of our line which may be selected as suitable to assault from. The old rule that an obstacle must be seen from the fire position holds good and it must be at such a distance that bombs cannot be thrown from it into our front line. Repairs to and replacements of chevaux de frise are normally carried out by the trench garrison. Normally R.E. do not put out such obstacles. Their responsibility ends with supplying the materials required.

13. Breastworks vary in section all along the line according to the depth at which the subsoil water level stands. Essential features are that :-

(1).

(i). the top of the parapet must not be more than 4' 6" above the fire step,

(ii) the top must be at least 4' thick,

(iii) there must be not less than 6' of cover above the "gangway"

14. A point which must be specially guarded against as likely to occur when newcomers take over trenches, is raising the height of the breastwork by adding sandbags one or two stretchers thick. This not only renders it impossible for the men to fire over the top but it is dangerous, as the insufficient thickness cannot be detected from inside.

If sufficient cover is not given by the parapet, care must be taken to raise and thicken it and to re-adjust the fire step to the proper height. This is often a matter of some difficulty as the outside borrow pit will often be found too close to the breastwork.

15. Loopholes are used only for observation and for sniping. They are not used to repel an attack. This is met by fire over the top. They must never fire directly to the front.

There should be two loopholes at least in each bay.

16. Machine guns also fire obliquely across the front flanking salients, wire, etc., and never straight to the front

17. There should be frequent sally ports. These are useful for patrols and also in case it is desired to attack. If they do not exist, the point of attack may easily be given away by putting them in.

18. There should be frequent listening posts carried out in front of our wire and wired in.

19. The design approved for the 8th division support and reserve trenches is as sketched in Diagram B. In criticizing them it must be borne in mind that these lines have had to be built against time, that materials for revetting some 18,000 yards of trench and for roofing 1800 dug-outs are not easy to obtain and that carriage, depth of subsoil water and other factors must be taken into consideration. The dotted lines show how these trenches should be improved as time goes on as in their present form they undoubtedly do not give good facilities for "command" and are not well suited for habitation by the greater part of the trench garrison, and it is most desirable that they should be.

20. The wire in front of the 70 yards shelter trench (support trench) is two lines of French wire with a certain amount of barbed wire and standards. This type was selected for rapidity in fixing and can be added to as time goes on.

The wire in front of the reserve trench will be 18" high and 10 yards deep. This type was selected because being low it will be concealed by the corn and grass and will not be shot away by fire from the 18" parapet to any great extent as it might be if higher.

21. The "run up" communication trenches at 50 yards intervals are straight to allow of fire down them. The arrangement at the point they enter the support trench is as sketched in diagram B. Unless carefully laid out errors occur as shown.

22. Bombers trenches are to be spaced every 125 yards apart as far as local conditions allow and should have a bombers' emplacement as shown in diagram B.

23. The location and design of avenues requires careful consideration. Unless their location is carefully considered they are liable to interfere seriously with fire from posts and trenches, especially if allowed to be dug obliquely. In the 8th division, trench garrison or brigades have to submit any proposals for a new avenue or communication trench to div h.q., before putting work in hand, to obviate mistakes of this kind.

Avenues should be dug on the highest ground available and not on the lowest as would at first sight seem more natural. The reason is that in winter the hollows will be full of water and drainage impossible. They should also be given high parapets in summer so that when winter comes their floor levels may be raised and sufficient cover still remain without having to raise the parapets and so attract undesirable attention to them.

It is well to have a standard design of trace. That which is thought to be suitable in 8th division is as shown. The advantages claimed are :-

    (a) Ease in laying out.
    (b) passing places.
    (c) Ease in building traverses and rapidity.

24. Care must be taken to make satisfactory arrangements for the passage of avenues and trenches through supporting points. Unless this is attended to there will be covered bombing approach up to the work. The arrangements approved in 8th division are as shown in diagram C.

25. G.H.Q. posts provide fire all round without being "closed works" in the ordinary sense of the word. They usually extend over a considerable area of ground. Their machine gun emplacements should never fire direct to the front but to cover the ground in front of the next post. This point is frequently overlooked and machine gun emplacements will be found altered to shoot down a road to the front. This is quite wrong as a rifle or two would cover the road equally well. Infantry garris garrisons are forbidden to make alterations in G.H.Q. posts. Work on them is to be carried out only under the orders of the Corps Commander.

7/8/15.

ORGANIZATION OF A SECTOR OF DEFENCE

Diagram A

Support & Reserve Trenches

Diagram B

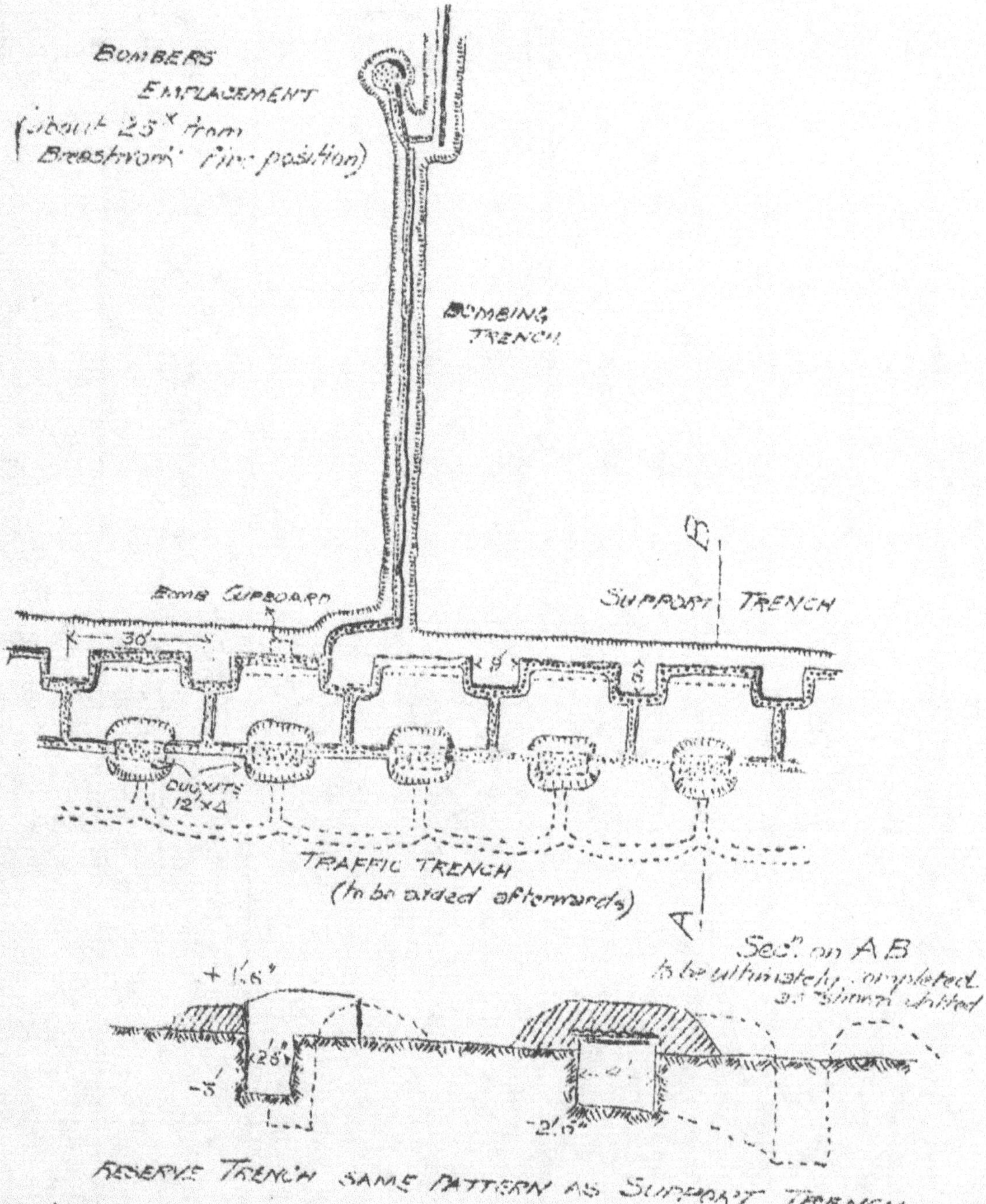

BOMBERS EMPLACEMENT
(about 25' from Breastwork fire position)

BOMBING TRENCH

BOMB CUPBOARD — SUPPORT TRENCH

DUGOUTS 12'×4'

TRAFFIC TRENCH
(to be added afterwards)

Section on AB
to be ultimately completed
as shown dotted

RESERVE TRENCH SAME PATTERN AS SUPPORT TRENCH

Note

Common errors in laying out trenches from SUPPORT LINE to FRONT LINE, are:—

(i) 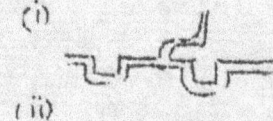 Fire blocked by Traverse

(ii) 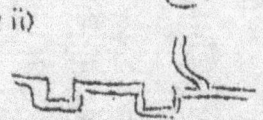 Only a left hand shot can be fired down trench & interior of Support trench is exposed

AVENUES

Diagram C

SECTION FOR AVENUE

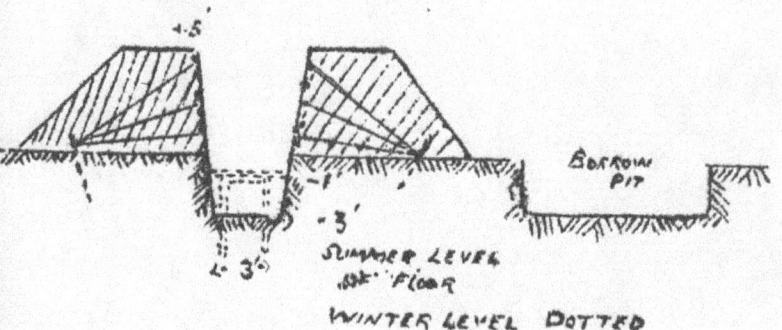

Summer level at floor
Winter level dotted

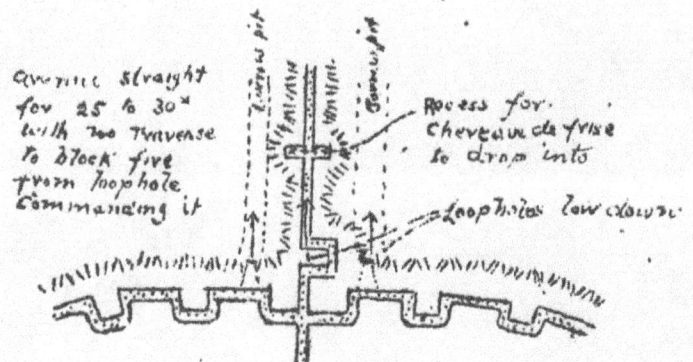

Avenue straight for 25 to 30 yds with no traverse to block fire from loophole commanding it

Recess for Cheveaux de frise to drop into

Loopholes low down

PASSAGE OF AVENUE THROUGH A. WORK.

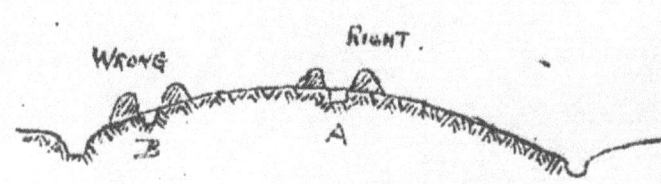

WRONG — B
RIGHT — A

Sketch to show correct siting of an Avenue. i.e. on highest part of turtle backed field
A may be usable in Winter
B will generally be under water

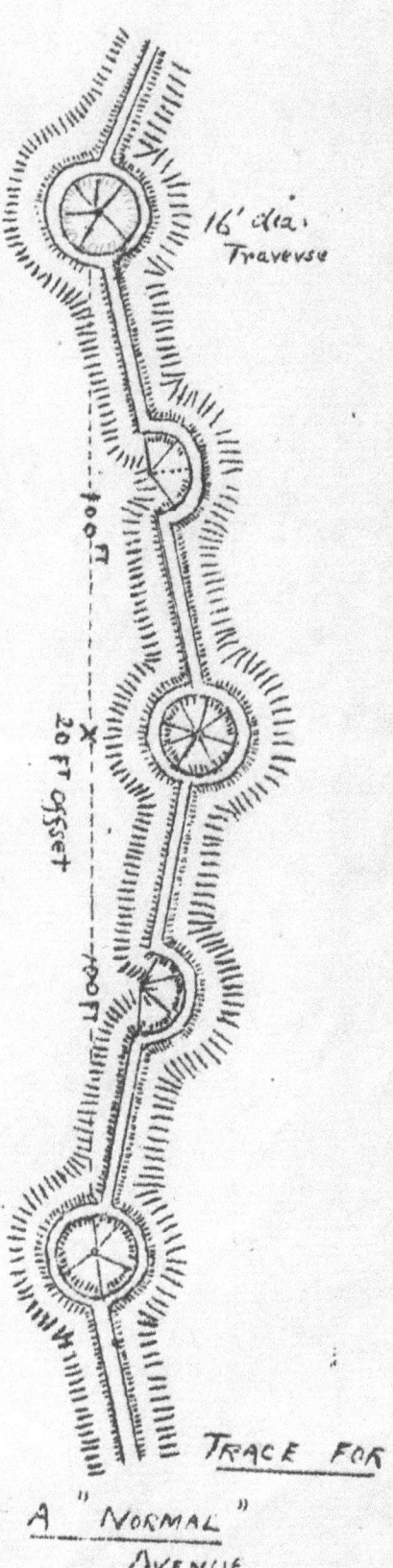

16' dia. Traverse
100 ft
20 ft offset
100 ft

TRACE FOR A "NORMAL" AVENUE

96th F.C. R.E.
Vol: 2
Captain Jones

121/7656

30th Hussars

Nov. 15.

CONFIDENTIAL

WAR DIARY
OF
96TH FIELD COY R.E.

Nov. 1st 1915 to Nov. 30th 1915.

VOLUME No. II

WAR DIARY
or
INTELLIGENCE-SUMMARY.

(Erase heading not required.)

Army Form C. 2118

Instructions regarding War Diaries and Intelligence Summaries are contained in F. S. Regs., Part II. and the Staff Manual respectively. Title pages will be prepared in manuscript.

Place	Date	Hour	Summary of Events and Information	Remarks and references to Appendices
RUE DE PARADIS, LAVENTIE	1/11/15	DAY	Strength of Company:- 6 Officers, 224 Rank & File, 27 Horses, 51 Mules. Major A.C. SCOTT, and 7 men in Hospital. No. 1 Section of Company attached for duty at School of Mortars, 1st Army. 24 Carpenters from 59th Bde. Brigade attached for duty. Work:- Supervising Infantry carrying up & filling sandbags, revetting "ROTTEN ROW", deepening "STRAND", tightening up a winter avenue, cleaning "S. ELGIN ST", carrying up special hurdles and repairs to "G.C. Rly", & repairing siding & erecting screens wire along "GT NORTH ROAD". R.E. only on "FAUQUISSART ST" preparing to a winter avenue. R.E. & Infantry Carpenters in Workshop making materials. R.E. & Infantry on experimental work at 59th Inf. Bde. Bombing School.	RE/
ditto	2/11/15	NIGHT	Strength of Company:- 6 Officers, 223 Rank & File, 27 Horses, 51 Mules. Major A.C. SCOTT and 7 men in Hospital. No. 1 Section of Company attached for duty at School of Mortars, 1st Army. 24 Carpenters from 59th Brigade attached for duty.	
		DAY	Work:- Supervising Infantry carrying up & filling sandbags, draining & revetting "ROTTEN ROW",- on "FAUQUISSART ST", preparing as a winter avenue, - on repairs to "G.C. Rly", & repairing siding & erection of screens. R.E. & Infantry Carpenters in Workshop making materials.	RE/
		NIGHT	No work owing to very bad weather.	

Army Form C. 2118.

WAR DIARY
or
INTELLIGENCE SUMMARY.
(Erase heading not required.)

Place	Date	Hour	Summary of Events and Information	Remarks and references to Appendices
RUE DE PARADIS, LAVENTIE	3/11/15		Strength of Company:- 6 Officers, 225 Ranks & File. 27 Horses, 51 Mules. Major A.C. Scott and 1 men in Hospital. No.4 Section of Company attached for duty at School of Mortars, 1st Army. 24 Carpenters from 59th Brigade attached for duty.	
		DAY	Work:- R.E. only on "FAUQUISSART ST" repairing as a winter avenue. – on Gun emplacement at head of "INDIAN AVENUE" – on experimental work at 59th Bde Bombing School – R.E. R.E. & Infantry Carpenters in Workshops making materials, & on repairs to "G.C.R." & erection of cisterns.	
		NIGHT	R.E. only on Barricade at TILLELOY end of "FAUQUISSART ST" – on Gun emplacement at head of "INDIAN AVENUE"	
ditto	4/11/15		Strength of Company:- 5 Officers, 223 Ranks & File. 27 Horses. 51 Mules. Major A.C. Scott taken off strength of Company. 1 men in Hospital. No.4 Section of Company attached for duty at School of Mortars 1st Army. 24 Carpenters from 59th Brigade attached for duty.	
		DAY	Work:- Supervising Infantry carrying up & filling sandbags – revetting "ROTTEN ROW" on "FAUQUISSART ST" & "STRAND" – repairing as winter avenues – on repairs to "G.C. RLY" – repairing sides & erecting Cheveaux – clearing out ditches for drainage. R.E. & Infantry Carpenters in Workshops making materials.	R.E.
		NIGHT	Supervising Infantry excavating Adv. Comm. Trenches – erecting Barricade opposite RUE MASSELOT on RUE TILLELOY – clearing "FLEET ST" & preparing as a winter avenue.	R.E.

Army Form C. 2118

WAR DIARY
or
INTELLIGENCE SUMMARY.
(Erase heading not required.)

Instructions regarding War Diaries and Intelligence Summaries are contained in F.S. Regs., Part II. and the Staff Manual respectively. Title pages will be prepared in manuscript.

Place	Date	Hour	Summary of Events and Information	Remarks and references to Appendices
RUE DE PARADIS. LAVENTIE	5/11/15		Strength of Company :- 6 Officers. 222 Rank & File. 27 Horses. 51 Mules. 2/Lt. BAZELEY.H. joined Company. 6 men in Hospital. No.4 Section of Company attached for duty at School of Mortars. 1st Army. No.4 Carpenters from Sqdn. Infy. Bde attached for duty.	
		DAY	Work:- Supervising Infantry revetting "ROTTEN ROW" working on "FLEET ST" preparing as a winter avenue. - working on "G.C. RLY" preparing siding & erecting Screens along extension of line towards front, joining "Gt NORTH RD". R.E. & Infantry Carpenters in Workshops.	R.E.
		NIGHT	Supervising Infantry working on Barricade on RUE TILLELOY opposite RUE MASSELOT.	
do.	6/11/15		Strength of Company :- 6 Officers. 221 Rank & File. 27 Horses. 51 Mules. 2 men in Hospital. No.4 Section of Company attached for duty at School of Mortars. 1st Army. No.4 Carpenters from Sqdn Infy Bde attached for duty.	
		DAY	Work:- Supervising Infantry revetting "ROTTEN ROW" — on preparing "FAUQUISSART ST" as a winter avenue. - repairing "G.C. RLY" - preparing sidings & erecting Screens. R.E & Infantry Carpenters in Workshops.	
		NIGHT	Supervising Infantry revetting "ROTTEN ROW" — on field gun emplacement in front line to right of "INDIAN AVENUE".	R.E.
do	Sunday 7/11/15	DAY	Strength of Company :- As before. Work:- R.E. & Infantry Carpenters in Workshops.	
		NIGHT	NIL.	

1577 Wt.W10791/1773 500,000 1/15 D.D.&L. A.D.S.S./Forms/C. 2118.

Army Form C. 2118.

WAR DIARY
or
INTELLIGENCE SUMMARY.
(Erase heading not required.)

Place	Date	Hour	Summary of Events and Information	Remarks and references to Appendices
RUE DE PARADIS. LAVENTIE	8/11/15	DAY	Strength of Company :- As before. Work :- Supervising Infantry on repairs to a drainage of "ROTTEN ROW" on general improvements in front line. - Laying fascines & trench covers in "DRURY LANE" - No 1 Battn. Section - on "G.C. RLY" preparing siding & erecting screens. R.E. only a Infantry - a specimen trench at Company H.qrs. As a Infantry Carpenters in Workshops	R.E.
do.	9/11/15	NIGHT	NIL	
		DAY	Strength of Company :- As before. Work :- R.E. Pioneers & Infantry reptg "ROTTEN ROW" & cleaning out ditch to the front - working on drg - ado in front line. - pumping & cleaning "MASSELOT" trench from front line 5 to TILLELOY - cleaning ditches from front line to RUE TILLELOY. - draining "DRURY LANE" a laying fascines & trench boards - R.E. only in construction of specimen trench at Company H.qrs. a No 1 Battn Section - on "G.C. RLY" preparing siding & erecting screens. R.E. a Infantry Carpenters in Workshops	R.E.
do	10/11/15	DAY	Strength of Company :- As before. Work :- R.E. Pioneers & Infantry reptg "ROTTEN ROW" - on Drg - ado in "front Line. - cleaning ditches from front line to TILLELOY - cleaning "MASSELOT TRENCH" on "DRURY LANE" draining, carrying fascines & trench boards - on No 1 Battn Section - on "G.C. RLY" preparing siding & erecting Screens. R.E. a Infantry Carpenters in Workshops.	R.E.

Army Form C. 21

WAR DIARY
or
INTELLIGENCE SUMMARY.
(Erase heading not required.)

Place	Date	Hour	Summary of Events and Information	Remarks and references to Appendices
RUE DE PARADIS. LAVENTIE	11/11/15	DAY	Strength of Company:- As before. R.E. Infantry on erecting Aug-outs in front line - carrying up stores - laying trench boards in "DRURY LANE" & "STRAND" - on h.o.1 Battn Shops - constructing Store at Rail-head - on repairs to "MIDLAND RLY" - on "G.C. RLY" preparing & doing a erecting canteen. R.E. & Pioneers repg. & cleaning "ROTTEN ROW" a cleaning out ditches from front line to FILLELOY - laying foot Boards in MASSELOT in trench. R.E. & Infantry Carpenters in Workshops. R.E. & Infantry revetting "DRURY LANE".	R.E.
do.	12/11/15	NIGHT DAY	Strength of Company:- As before. R.E. & Infantry on erection of Aug-outs in front line - working & repairs to firing step - fixing loose drains & trench Boards in front line - draining & cleaning "ROTTEN ROW" - on "DRURY LANE" & "STRAND" laying trench Boards - constructing Store at Rail head "G.C.R." - on h.o.1 battn Shops - on "G.C. RLY" preparing & erecting Canteen. R.E. & Pioneers on drainage from front line to FILLELOY - clearing out "MASSELOT" trench & laying foot Boards. R.E. & Infantry Carpenters in Workshops. R.E. & Infantry revetting "DRURY LANE".	R.E.
		NIGHT		

Army Form C. 2118

WAR DIARY
or
INTELLIGENCE SUMMARY.
(Erase heading not required.)

Place	Date	Hour	Summary of Events and Information	Remarks and references to Appendices
RUE DE PARADIS. LAVENTIE	13/11/15	DAY	Strength of Company :- As before. Work :- R.E. Infantry on erection of new Eng. onto in front line - on laying trench Boards in "DRURY LANE" & "STRAND" - constructing cut and head "G.A." - on hot Batth Hdqrs - on "G.C. RLY" Infantry Siding & erecting Screens. N.Z. Pioneers on drainage in front line - clearing drainage "ROTTEN ROW" - on drainage from front line to TILLELOY - on MASSELOT trench, laying foot boards.	R.E.
		NIGHT	a. only constructing A.E. Stone in front line. b. R.E. Infantry revetting "ROTTEN ROW" - revetting "MASSELOT" trench - clearing & revetting "DRURY LANE"	
do.	14/11/15	DAY	Strength of Company :- As before. Work :- R.E. Infantry on erection of new Eng. onto in front line. R.E. Pioneers clearing "ROTTEN ROW" - laying foot boards in "MASSELOT" trench - on drainage from front line to RUE TILLELOY - clearing & draining "DRURY LANE" & laying trench Boards. R.E. Infantry Carpenters in Workshops. R.E. Pioneers excavating new winter avenue.	R.E.
do.	15/11/15	NIGHT	Strength of Company :- As before. Work :- R.E. Infantry on construction of Eng. onto in front line - erection of Stone in front line - laying trench Boards in front line - laying foot Boards in MASSELOT trench - on construction of new winter Avenue - on "G.C. RLY".	

Army Form C. 2118

WAR DIARY
or
INTELLIGENCE SUMMARY.
(Erase heading not required.)

Instructions regarding War Diaries and Intelligence Summaries are contained in F. S. Regs., Part II. and the Staff Manual respectively. Title pages will be prepared in manuscript.

Place	Date	Hour	Summary of Events and Information	Remarks and references to Appendices
RUE DE PARADIS LAVENTIE	15/11/15	DAY (contd)	R.E. Pioneers & Infantry working on "ROTTEN ROW" A.B. & Infantry Carpenters in Workshops.	
		NIGHT	R.E. Pioneers & Infantry working on construction of new winter avenue. The Company handed over Line west of "FAUQUISSART" and took over portion of Line from "RIFLEMAN'S AVENUE" N.u.a.2.3k to "PICANTIN AVENUE" N.8.C.7.5. Strength of Company :- as before.	R.E.
do	16/11/15		Work :-	
		DAY	R.E. & Infantry on construction & erection of Aug- ents in front line – on construction of new R.E. Store in front line – laying trench Boards in front line – revetting "ROTTEN ROW" – on "C.G.R." preparing siding & erection of Guavers. A.B. & Pioneers draining front line – on drainage from front line to TILELOY. R.E. & Infantry Carpenters in Workshops.	
		NIGHT	R.E. Pioneers & Infantry on construction of new winter avenue. R.E. & Infantry laying foot-Boards in "MASSELOT" trench – a revetting ROTTEN ROW. Strength of Company :- as before.	R.E.
do	17/11/15	DAY	R.E. Infantry on construction & erection of Aug-ents in front line. R.E. & Pioneers on drainage of front line – laying foot Boards in front line – making dam for sap & pumping out water – drainage at RED LAMP – also on "MASSELOT" trench – on new winter avenue – on G. CRy.	
		NIGHT	R.E. & Infantry Carpenters in Workshops. Pioneers on new Comm. trench	R.E.

WAR DIARY
or
INTELLIGENCE SUMMARY.

(Erase heading not required.)

Army Form C. 2118

Instructions regarding War Diaries and Intelligence Summaries are contained in F. S. Regs., Part II. and the Staff Manual respectively. Title pages will be prepared in manuscript.

Place	Date	Hour	Summary of Events and Information	Remarks and references to Appendices
RUE DE PARADIS. LAVENTIE	18/11/15	DAY	Work:- Strength of Company:- As before. - B C° Infantry on general improvements in front line, Dug-outs, Drainage, laying foot-boards etc. - clearing & revetting "ROTTEN ROW" - new Winter Avenue - Barricade for same - an "G.C.R." - repairing M.G. Guns & erecting Screens. A.S. Pioneers & Infantry working on new Avenue. N.S. only draining MASSELOT trench.	R2
do.	19/11/15	NIGHT	Strength:- Work:- As before.	
		DAY	B C° Infantry on Dug-outs etc in front-line, draining & laying foot-boards - laying foot-boards in "ROTTEN ROW" - draining MASSELOT trench - cleaning out ditches from front Line to TILLELOY - an construction of new winter Avenue - on "G.C.R." Q C° Pioneers on "ROTTEN ROW" - cleaning out ditches from front-Line to TILLELOY. R C° Infantry Carpenters in Workshops. R C° Infantry on "ROTTEN ROW".	R2
		NIGHT	26 men of No4 Section returned from St VENANT.	
do	20/11/15	DAY	Strength of Company:- As before. Work:- No1 Pioneers & Infantry working on new Avenue. No2 do. do. renewing Cantoons. No3 do. Pioneers on new Avenue.	
do SAILLY	21/11/15	NIGHT	Strength of Company:- As before. Company moved into fresh Billets at SAILLY.	P.S.

Army Form C. 2118

WAR DIARY
or
INTELLIGENCE SUMMARY
(Erase heading not required.)

Instructions regarding War Diaries and Intelligence Summaries are contained in F. S. Regs., Part II. and the Staff Manual respectively. Title Pages will be prepared in manuscript.

Place	Date	Hour	Summary of Events and Information	Remarks and references to Appendices
SAILLY	22/11/15	DAY	Strength of Company :- As before. Works :- Erecting Pontoon Bridge at BAC ST MAUR. Working on Anthuis, Cleaning & improving new Billets & Tents, making roadway for Horse Lines & working on erection of new Workshop.	R&S
		NIGHT	NIL.	
do.	23/11/15	DAY	Strength of Company :- As before. Works :- Erecting Pontoon Bridge at BAC ST MAUR. Working on Anthuis, working, cleaning & improving new Billets, making roadway for Horse Lines & on erection of new Workshop. Working on foundations for Circular Saw Engines, & on foundations for Dynamo at SAILLY Empire.	R&S
		NIGHT	Strength of Company :- As before. Sappers & 2 or 3rd Divnl R.E. attached to Company for Rations & Administration. NIL.	R&S
do.	24/11/15	DAY	Works :- Erecting Pontoon Bridge at BAC ST MAUR. Working on Anthuis, working & improving Billets, making roadway for Horse Lines & on erection of new Workshop. Working on foundations for Circular Saw Engines & foundation for Dynamo at SAILLY Empire.	R&S
		NIGHT	NIL.	

Army Form C. 2118

WAR DIARY
or
INTELLIGENCE SUMMARY
(Erase heading not required.)

Instructions regarding War Diaries and Intelligence Summaries are contained in F.S. Regs., Part II. and the Staff Manual respectively. Title Pages will be prepared in manuscript.

Place	Date	Hour	Summary of Events and Information	Remarks and references to Appendices
SAILLY	25/11/15	DAY	Strength of Company:- As before. Work:- Guarding erection of Pontoon Bridge at BAC St MAUR. Working on Shutters. 96th Coy informing 59th Bde Sigs. Billets making roadway for 96th Coy. Working on foundations for Circular Saw Engines	RLS
		NIGHT	NIL.	
do	26/11/15	DAY	Strength of Company:- As before. Work:- Working on construction & erection of Huts - repairs to 59th Bde Sigs Billets - making roadway for 96th Coy Store Lines - repairs to Anne Battn Battn Billets.	RLS
		NIGHT	NIL.	
do	27/11/15	DAY	Strength of Company:- As before. Working on construction & erection of Huts & Anne Sigrs & 59th Bde Sigrs Billets - making roadway for 96th Coy Store Lines. Starting Pontoon Bridges.	RLS
		NIGHT	NIL	
do	28/11/15	Sunday. Strength of Company:- As before.		RLS
do	29/11/15		Strength of Company:- 6 Officers 223 Rank & File (1 man joined Coy from ROUEN) Signaler Anne R.E. ceased to be attached. Work:- (Day only) Shutters, erecting Screens to Pontoon Bridge - Repairs to Anne Sigrs Battn Billets on construction of magazine. 59th Bde Sigrs Billets - making roadway for 96th Coy Store Lines	RLS

1875 Wt. W593/826 1,000,000 4/15 J.B.C. & A. A.D.S.S./Forms/C. 2118.

Army Form C. 2118

WAR DIARY
or
INTELLIGENCE SUMMARY
(Erase heading not required.)

Place	Date	Hour	Summary of Events and Information	Remarks and references to Appendices
SAILLY	30/11/15	DAY	Strength M Company :- As before. Erecting Screens for Pontoon Bridge at BAC ST MAUR. - on Railway work. NOUVEAU MONDE - Shutting construction & erection. - Repair to Railway at Billets of 59th Bde. 59th Bde 3rd gp. Billets A. 59/ 13 Bde. - Making roadway for 96th Coy Stores Limes - on foundation for Engine & am.	(P.T.)
		NIGHT	Nil.	

96th FCSE.
Vol 3

151/7910

30/4/62

CONFIDENTIAL.

WAR DIARY

OF

96TH FIELD COMPANY. R.E.

from DEC. 1ST 1915 to DEC 31ST 1915.

(VOLUME 3).

WAR DIARY
or
INTELLIGENCE SUMMARY
(Erase heading not required.)

Army Form C. 2118

Place	Date	Hour	Summary of Events and Information	Remarks and references to Appendices
SAILLY	1/12/15	DAY	Strength of Company:- 6 Officers, 222 Rank & File. 17 Horses, 47 Mules. (5 men in Hospital.) 1 Officer & 15 N.C.Os & men detached at School of Mortars. 1st Army. 24 Carpenters from 59th Sqn. R.E. attached to Company for duty. Work:- Construction & erection of huts & accessories – making magazine for 96th Coy – Repairs to Divnl. Baths – erecting Bynne steam Bench – repairs to 59th Fd Coy Billets – on Railway at NOUVEAU MONDE – making roadway for 96th Coy. Horse Lines.	RZ
		NIGHT	NIL.	
do	2/12/15	DAY	Strength of Company:- As before. Work:- Construction & erection of huts & accessories – magazine & incinerator for 96th Coy – Dly. at NOUVEAU MONDE – 30 – Stone Lime & Wagn. standing for 96th Coy – Stable at Capts Stables – making Bonjour – repairs to softs hut. Pole Billets.	RZ
		NIGHT	NIL.	
do	3/12/15	DAY	Strength of Company:- As before, except that Dvr Limmett is in s/s strength. 1 Horse & 3 Mules received. Work:- Construction & erection of huts & accessories – offs sqrs Pole Billets – Repair to Divne Baths – on Railway at NOUVEAU MONDE – magazine for 96 Coy – Stone Lime & Wagn standing for 96 Coy – Vacuum – making Bonjour:- Stable at Opts Stables.	RZ
		NIGHT	NIL.	

WAR DIARY
or
INTELLIGENCE SUMMARY

(Erase heading not required.)

Army Form C. 2118

Place	Date	Hour	Summary of Events and Information	Remarks and references to Appendices
SAILLY 4/12/15			**Strength of Company:** As before — 2 Officers & 54 NCOs & men (proceeded to CROIX BLANCHE to be billetted, for work in front line area —	P.S.
		DAY	**Work:** Construction & erection of huts & accessories — repairs to Divnie. Baths — repairs to s.g.m Bde Billets — Welding Brayiers — mining experiments — Workshops & Engine Shed for 96th Coy.	
		NIGHT	NIL	
SAILLY	5/12/15		**Strength of Company:** As before	
		DAY	**Work:** A.O. on "CELLAR FARM" Comm. Trench making dam — A.O. Infantry on "V.C. AVENUE", cleaning & pumping, laying foot boards & revetting — A.O. on 91st Bde Detachment Billets — on Divne Baths — on s.g.m Bde Bdqrs — making Brayiers — mining experiments. A.O. Infantry Carpenters in workshops.	P.S.
		NIGHT	NIL	
do	6/12/15		**Strength of Company:** 2 NCO's & 13 men from 59th Inf Bde attached to Company for Grand Gateyne As before.	
		DAY	**Work:** A.O. shifting Dumps in front Line at N. 16/4 — Jumping water at SP. CELLAR FARM AVENUE — on CELLAR FARM AVENUE making dams at R. LYS. — Pumping & cleaning V.C. AVENUE — repairing Railway — A.O. & Infantry threshering parapet in front Line — Jumping trench for R. LYS — A.O. on s.g.m Bde Design Billets — on Divne Baths — mining experiments — A.O. & Infantry Carpenters in workshops — R.O. & Infantry getting up material to front end of CELLAR FARM AVENUE.	P.S.
		NIGHT		

WAR DIARY or INTELLIGENCE SUMMARY

Army Form C. 2118

(Erase heading not required.)

Place	Date	Hour	Summary of Events and Information	Remarks and references to Appendices
SAILLY	7/12/15	DAY	Strength of Company :- as before. Work. R.E., Pioneers & Infantry repairing Railways & making CELLAR FARM AVENUE Parades - thickening parapet in front Line - on V.C. AVENUE, pumping out water, damming PINNEY AVENUE & R. LYS - laying trench boards & cleaning - sq.oak/bde dugs - mining experiments - making Traverses - shutting. N.S. Infantry Carpenters in Workshops.	RE
do.	8/12/15	DAY	Strength of Company :- as before. Work. R.E. Pioneers & Infantry thickening & revetting Parapet in front Line - on CELLAR FARM AVENUE laying trench boards, making dams & pumping out water - repairing Railway - pumping water out of V.C. AVENUE & laying trench boards - Revetting V.C. AVENUE - damming R. LAIES & pumping it dry - on sq/m Pole dugs - on Divne Baths - erecting Latrine for Billets - mining experiments - making Traverses. R.E. Infantry Carpenters in Workshops.	RE
		NIGHT	R.E. Infantry carrying up material for CELLAR FARM & V.C. AVENUES.	
do.	9/12/15	DAY	Strength of Company :- as before. Work :- R.E. Pioneers & Infantry on CELLAR FARM AVENUE - pumping out water, making dams, laying trench boards - cleaning out ditch on right of CELLAR FARM AVENUE to R. LAIES - thickening parapet & paradoes in front line - pumping water out V.C. AVENUE, making trench boards - damming R. LAIES & pumping it dry on sq/m 10 ft dugs - on Divne Baths - erecting Latrines for Billets - mining experiments - making Traverses. N.S. Infantry Carpenters in Workshops.	RE
		NIGHT	R.E. Infantry carrying up material for CELLAR FARM & V.C. AVENUES	

WAR DIARY or INTELLIGENCE SUMMARY

Army Form C. 2118

Place	Date	Hour	Summary of Events and Information	Remarks and references to Appendices
SAILLY	10/12/15	DAY	**Strength of Company:** As before. **Work:** R.E. Pioneers & Infantry thickening & revetting parapet in front line, and laying front foot-boards – revetting CELLAR FARM AVENUE & making dam in steam Railways – pumping CELLAR FARM AVENUE & frans foot-boards on craters at N.10½ & N.10/5 making entrance for working parties – cleaning V.C. AVENUE & raising foot-boards – damming & laying foot-boards – carrying up material – damming Sap & laying foot-boards – R.E. only on 59th Bde Steps – Bund Baths – Erecting Latrines for Billets – on mining experiments – in shops in progress N.C.O.s & Infantry Carpenters in Workshop. N.C.O.s & Infantry carrying up material for CELLAR FARM AVENUE & Front Line.	PRS
do.	11/12/15	NIGHT		
		DAY	**Strength of Company:** As before. **Work:** R.E. Pioneers & Infantry thickening & revetting Front Line parapet and traverses, lifting foot-boards – making dam for CELLAR FARM AVENUE – revetting CELLAR FARM AVENUE – laying trench boards & pumping out water – leveling up at N.10/1 & N.10/3 & making entrance to crater on V.C. AVENUE – raising foot-boards & clearing away fallen earth – on dam for R. LAIES – repairing Railways – R.E. only on 59th Bde Steps – Bund Baths – Erecting Latrines for Billets – repairs to 59th Bde Billets – mining experiments – making Bomb-jars N.C.O. & Infantry Carpenters in Workshop. N.C.O. & Infantry carrying up material for front parapet & V.C. AVENUE.	PRS
		NIGHT	13 men from No 4 Section returned to Company from St VENANT.	

Army Form C. 2118.

WAR DIARY
or
INTELLIGENCE SUMMARY.
(Erase heading not required.)

Instructions regarding War Diaries and Intelligence Summaries are contained in F. S. Regs., Part II. and the Staff Manual respectively. Title pages will be prepared in manuscript.

Place	Date	Hour	Summary of Events and Information	Remarks and references to Appendices
SAILLY	12/2/15	DAY	Strength of Company :- As before. R.E. Pioneers & Infantry in front line, revetting parapet, sandbagging traps, firesteps, pumping out water, moving old & making new fort-boards, revetting sides of trench, pumping out water & then fort-boards - levelling ground at N. 107 & cleaning away to make an approach to water - repairing Railways - on V.C. AVENUE running fort-boards etc. No. 1 on sq. 3A Mole Shyps - erecting Latrine & on Billets - on Observation Post at V.C. Corner - taking over section (5 R.L.A.E'S - well sinking - mining etcetera - making ironworks for pumps - making trangers - making Railway trollies. R.E. Infantry Carpenters in Workshops.	P.S.
		NIGHT	R.E. & Infantry carrying up stones for CELLAR FARM & V.C. AVENUE'S.	
do.	13/2/15	DAY	Strength of Company :- As before. R.E. Pioneers & Infantry thickening and parapet in front line, making firing steps, laying fort-boards etc - on CELLAR FARM AVENUE making dams revetting sides, pumping out water, laying fort-boards - on Railway - making fort-boards - on V.C. AVENUE - fort-boards on new front line & parapet near R.L.A.Y.E.S. No. 1 on sq. 3A Mole Shyps - erecting Latrines for Billets - sinking new well - making trangers - R. Pumps - making Railway trollies - wire revetment etcetera No. 2 mining etcetera - No. 3 Infantry Carpenters in Workshops.	P.S.
		NIGHT	R.E. & Infantry carrying up stones for CELLAR FARM & V.C. AVENUE'S.	

Army Form C. 2118.

WAR DIARY
or
INTELLIGENCE SUMMARY.
(Erase heading not required.)

Place	Date	Hour	Summary of Events and Information	Remarks and references to Appendices
SAILLY	14/2/15	DAY	Strength of Company:- As before. Work:- R.E. Pioneers & Infantry in Front Line. N.C.O's revetting Parapet, making Sally Ports, sandbags & fixing foot boards. On CELLAR FARM AVENUE making dams bumpers & head.— Laying foot boards. ety Railway — mens foot boards in V.C. AVENUE — Shoring up bridge at R. LAIES. N.C. only on sysn role steps — sinking well — making Parapiers — on various experiments — making Ry shelter — on experimental mine revetment. — & pumps. N.C.O. Infantry Carpenters in Workshops. N.C.O. revetting Parapet at R. LAIES. N.C. Infantry company up material to CELLAR FARM AVENUE & Front Line.	[sig]
		NIGHT	30 additional N.C.O's men sent to Billets at CROIX BLANCHE.	
do	15/2/15	DAY	Strength of Company:- As before. Work:- R.E. Pioneers & Infantry making Sally Ports in Front Line. rep parapet, revetting, raising trench boards — Lifting trench boards in CELLAR FARM AVENUE — rely Railway — a new bridge at R. LAIES. N.C. only on mining experiments — making traverses — making ironwork &c for Grenades. N.C. Infantry in Workshops. R.E. arranging up material for Front Line CELLAR FARM AVENUE an additional 6 N.C.O's men sent to Billets at CROIX BLANCHE.	[sig]
		NIGHT		

WAR DIARY or INTELLIGENCE SUMMARY.

Army Form C. 2118.

(Erase heading not required.)

Place	Date	Hour	Summary of Events and Information	Remarks and references to Appendices
SAILLY	16/2/15	DAY	**Strength of Company :-** As before. Work :- No 1 Pioneers Infantry, getting Sally-ports in front line - on general work in front line. No 2 Cmy Pnrs Corpt - bombs in CELLAR FARM AVENUE - on/rs CELLAR FARM Railway - building bridge to carry parapet over stream in front line - front bridge for parapet at R.LAIES. No 3 only on 57pdr Rifle & hypo - joining up exchange - Bullets - making stores - running experiments - framework for R.LAIES. Catapult to support side - fitting up pumps. No 4 Infantry Carpenters in Workshops - No 5 Infantry carrying up material to front line.	yes
do.	17/2/15	NIGHT		
		DAY	**Strength of Company:-** As before. Work :- No 1 Pioneers Infantry making Sally-ports in front line - General work in front line - on CELLAR FARM AVENUE - pumping out water, lifting foot-bridge. No 2 Cmy CELLAR FARM Railway - on Bridge at R.LAI @ 3. No 3 only on pumps - running experiments - making stores - erecting frame for Bullets - No 4 Infantry Carpenters in Workshops. No 5 Infantry carrying up material to front line.	yes
do.	18/2/15	NIGHT		
		DAY	**Strength of Company :-** As before. One addition 2 M.Us received. Work :- No 1 Pioneers Infantry on gas-cert & Sally-ports & General work in front line - making Aug-abo at CORDONNERIE Post - on CELLAR FARM AVENUE making foot boards - No 2 Cmy FARM Rly - on Bridge for R.LAIES. No 3 only on pumps - running experiments - making stores -. No 4 Infantry Carpenters in Workshops. No 5 Infantry carrying up material to front line.	yes
		NIGHT		

Army Form C. 2118.

WAR DIARY
or
INTELLIGENCE SUMMARY.

(Erase heading not required.)

Instructions regarding War Diaries and Intelligence Summaries are contained in F.S. Regs., Part II. and the Staff Manual respectively. Title pages will be prepared in manuscript.

Place	Date	Hour	Summary of Events and Information	Remarks and references to Appendices
SAILLY	19/12/15	DAY	Strength of Company :- As before No 1 & 2 Infantry thickening strengthening front line parapet - in Dug-outs in front line - making Sally-ports - pumping water out of front line - raising foot-boards - relaying duckboards in CELLAR FARM AVENUE - making Dug-outs at CARBONNERIE Post - on bridge for R. LAIES - fixing expanded metal on foot-boards in V.C. AVENUE. No 3 only in accessories for Billets - running experiments - making Sporting up Stores - ironwork for Trump Catapults. No 3 Infantry Carpenters in Workshops. No 4 Infantry carrying up material for front line & CELLAR FARM AVENUE.	
		NIGHT		
do	20/12/15	DAY	Strength of Company :- As before No 1 Proirs G. Infantry - making Sally ports in front line - on Dug-outs in front line - raising foot-boards in CELLAR FARM AVENUE - repairing CELLAR FARM AVENUE Railway - revetting demolished dug-outs & pumping water out front line - making bridge over RIVER LAYES No 2 only accessories for Billets - incinerator - running experiments - making and fitting Stores - ironwork for Catapults & Pumps. No 3 Infantry Carpenters in Workshops No 4 Infantry - Sally ports front line - carrying up material for CELLAR FARM AVENUE & front line No 4 only. Dug outs front line - unloading material for CELLAR FARM AVENUE.	
		NIGHT		

WAR DIARY
or
INTELLIGENCE SUMMARY.

(Erase heading not required.)

Army Form C. 2118.

Place	Date	Hour	Summary of Events and Information	Remarks and references to Appendices
SAILLY	21/12/5		Strength of Company :- ao before - Sap. Walton R.E. admitted to Hospital with injury to foot.	JHS
		DAY	WORK :- R.E. & Pioneers :- on H.Q. Dug outs in front line R.E. only ordering material & tools for special operation - Dug outs for 65th T.M. Battery - Bridge & Grafet over R.VBR LAYES. R.E. moving experiments - Workshops for Catapults - Infantry Carpenters in Workshops.	
		NIGHT	NIL	
do	22/12/5		Strength of Company :- ao before	RE
		DAY	WORK :- R.E. & Pioneers :- on H.Q. Dug outs in front line - Ventilating ovens of CELLAR FARM AVENUE R.E. only ordering material & tools for special operation. Dug outs for 65th T.M. Battery. Fitting up Dumps & Stoves - Slings for Catapults - meeting Bayers, now Latrine at Artillery Wille, making Fireplaces for billet - Laying drain at Bde H.Q. R.E. & Infantry Carpenters in Workshops. R.E. Infantry on Bridges over R. LAYES.	
		NIGHT		

Army Form C. 2118.

WAR DIARY
or
INTELLIGENCE SUMMARY.
(Erase heading not required.)

Instructions regarding War Diaries and Intelligence Summaries are contained in F. S. Regs., Part II. and the Staff Manual respectively. Title pages will be prepared in manuscript.

Place	Date	Hour	Summary of Events and Information	Remarks and references to Appendices
SAILLY	23/9/15		Strength of Company :- 6 Officers. 220 Rank & File. 21 Horses. 50 mules (1 new in hospital) Sap. Cumming struck off strength as from 4/12/15	
		DAY	Work :-	
			Pl. 1. Infantry - Sally ports & Shelters Front Line - revetting firing trench bays Front Line	
			Pl. 2. Pioneers - revetting sides of CELLAR FARM AVENUE :- repairing V.C. RAILWAY - Opening Expanded metal to trench boards. Straining, Dumping. Cleaning ditches & Keeping bn drains in V.C. AVENUE	
			Pl. 3. H.Q. August - Laying tramlines & repairing Curators at N/10/2 revetting parados at N/10/4 & N/10/5 - repairing CELLAR FARM RAILWAY - building Bridge over Bulge near V.C. RAILHEAD - erecting Buying Forms. Cutting & Shelters into C dugs. C/90, B/90, & B/93 - Accessories for billets. Boards for emergency roads - Strops for Catapult for Bomb - Fitting up Stores dumps	Ref.
		NIGHT	Pl. 4 Infantry Carpenters in workshops Pl. 5 unloading R.E. materials at CELLAR FARM DUMP.	
SAILLY	24/12/15	DAY	Strength of Company :- as before.	
			Work - Pl. 1. Infantry - erecting temporary accessories for Artillery Billets - fittings for Stores & trenches - Fitting up pumps - Straps for catapults for Bomb. Boards for Emergency roads.	
			Pl. 2. Infantry Carpenters in workshops	
			All N.C.Os & men returned from billets at CROIX BLANCHE to Head Qrs. at SAILLY Company in Brit Reserve from this evening	Ref.
		NIGHT	NIL	

1577 Wt.W10791/1773 500,000 1/15 D. D. & L. A.D.S.S./Forms/C. 2118.

Army Form C. 2118.

WAR DIARY
or
INTELLIGENCE SUMMARY.
(Erase heading not required.)

Instructions regarding War Diaries and Intelligence Summaries are contained in F. S. Regs., Part II. and the Staff Manual respectively. Title pages will be prepared in manuscript.

Place	Date	Hour	Summary of Events and Information	Remarks and references to Appendices
SAILLY	25/12/15		Strength of Company :- as before. Work:- Cleaning up billet & Christmas Celebrations	RG
do	26/12/15		Strength of Company :- as before except that Lgt-Cpl William R.S. is off strength from 10/12/15. Work:- Cleaning up billet & Equipment. Clothing & Necessaries Inspection	RG
do	27/12/15		Strength of Company :- as before. Work:- Pte Infantry - Breastwork CROIX MARCEHAL - PRESERVED CROIX BLANCHE to CROIX MARCEHAL - Repairing CROIX MARCEHAL - Earthing up Bomb Dug out at CROIX BLANCHE - Dug out at Rde BIACHE - Dug out at 60 B10 Jn. Pte Inty - Revetting & Earthing up Bomb Dug out at WINDY - Repairing Brickwork Belth & accessories for Billets - Carrying road at Coy yard - Draining of Coy Billets - Obtaining tools, coal, collecting material after enemy movements, cleaning up of yard - Escorts from Lothian at CROIX BLANCHE - Boards to Infantry Crafts to R.E. & Infantry Carpenters in Workshops - Netting -	RG

Army Form C. 2118.

WAR DIARY
or
INTELLIGENCE SUMMARY.
(Erase heading not required.)

Instructions regarding War Diaries and Intelligence Summaries are contained in F. S. Regs., Part II. and the Staff Manual respectively. Title pages will be prepared in manuscript.

Place	Date	Hour	Summary of Events and Information	Remarks and references to Appendices
SAILLY	28/12/15	DAY	Strength of Company increased by 1 man + 1 mule.	
		WORK:-	R.E. Infantry - Breastwork between CROIX BLANCHE & CROIX MARECHAL - Bomb Bay out at CROIX BLANCHE - Dump at CROIX MARECHAL - Bay out at RUE de BIACHE - Bay out at 60 yds H.Q. - Bomb Bay out at WINTER'S NIGHT - Bomb Bay out at WINDY - Bomb Dugouts at JUNCTION - Bomb Bay out at new H.Q. ROUGE de BOUT. R.E. envy. - Accessories for Fort Belour - C/93, C/90, D/90, D/93 + for D Coy 11th R.W. - Boards for Temporary Church B+C ST MAUR - Boards for Bridges R22 - Bridge Main, Cordwry Rds at C/93 BULLET - Bracing Sery BIGOT. Collecting Mining Plant Gear - Overhauling tools + tool carts - Iron Clips for trench covers.	P.T.S.
			R.E. Infantry Carpenter in Workshop - Hutting &c.	
do.	29/12/15	DAY	Strength of Company. - As before.	
		WORK:-	R.E. Infantry on Bay-works at RUE de BIACHE - Breastwork between CROIX BLANCHE - CROIX MARECHAL - Refuses to CROIX MARECHAL - on Bay-works at CROIX BLANCHE - on Bomb Bay-out at JUNCTION - on Bomb Bay-out at ROUGE DE BOUT - Bomb Bay-out at WINTERS NIGHT - at Bomb from Store at SAILLY. R.E. Artillerymen on D.P. at V.C. Corner. R.E. Infantry - Assistance to Billets - St Vincents work - Training Company Sapper - on Ordway Road at 9th Coy - overhauling Tool Carts, tools yoga etc. R.E. Infantry Carpenters in Workshop - Hutting etc.	P.T.S.

WAR DIARY or INTELLIGENCE SUMMARY.

Army Form C. 2118.

Place	Date	Hour	Summary of Events and Information	Remarks and references to Appendices
SAILLY	30/12/15		**Strength of Company:-** As before. **Work:-** R.E. & Infantry on Bng-ents at 60th Rd. Style – on Bng-ents at RUE DE BIACHE – on Ramparts at CROIX MARECHAL Post – on Banquets at BAC ST MAUR – on Bng-ents at ROUGE DE BOUT WINTER NIGHT & JUNCTION Posts – on Rival Bomb store at SAILLY. R.E. & Artillerymen on O.P. at V.E. Corner. R.E. only on Excessive to Billets – on Bridge N° 61 & Field Ambulance – on Cinder Road at 96 Cay yard – making & reviving Safes – cleaning up yard – drawing Company yard – erecting ammunition (style) – on glass Cloth for trench covers – overhauling & oiling tool Carts – Timber Carts – overhauling motor lorries – Shutters etc. R.E. & Infantry Carpenters in Workshops.	Rec?
do.	31/12/15		**Strength of Company:-** As before, and an additional force received. **Work:-** R.E. & Infantry on Bng-ents at RUE DE BIACHE – on parapet at CROIX MARECHAL Post – on new Breastwork at CROIX BLANCHE – on Bng-ents at ROUGE DE BOUT JUNCTION & WINTER NIGHT Posts – on Prime Bomb store at SAILLY – putting in Loose to Strata. R.E. Artillerymen on O.P. at V.E. Corner. R.E. only on Bridge N° 61 & Field Ambulance – on accessories for Billets – on Cinder & Rapid for Company yard – cleaning up mine & drainage – on Rifle Range at BAC St MAUR – erecting & fixing – stone – making & repairing grommets for O.P. – overhauling lorries – trailers – overhauling tool Carts & Limber Carts – Shutters etc. R.E. & Infantry Carpenters in Workshops.	Rec?

(P F Stacey?)
Capt R.E.
COMDG. 96th Fd. COY. R.E.

96th F.C.R.E.
1st: 4
January 1916

25th Div.

CONFIDENTIAL

WAR DIARY

of

96th FIELD COY. R.E.

VOLUME IV

Army Form C. 2118.

WAR DIARY
or
INTELLIGENCE SUMMARY.
(Erase heading not required.)

Place	Date	Hour	Summary of Events and Information	Remarks and references to Appendices
SAILLY	1/1/16	DAY	Strength of Company. 6 Officers. 220 Rank & File. 26 Horses. 52 Mules. On detachment at School of Mortars 1st Army – 1 Officer & Well's gunners, and 1 Stone. & men in Hospital. 8 men in Hospital. Attached:– 41 Infantry from Sqn. Work:– R.E. 1 Infantry on Dug-outs at RUE BIACHE – 10hrs Bde Hqrs – on CROIX MARECHAL Dout – on Precautional at CROIX BLANCHE – on Dug-outs at ROUGE DE BOUT – on Bomb Dug-out at WINTER'S NIGHT & JUNCTION. R.E. 2 Artillerymen on O.P. at V.C. Corner. R.E. 3 only on accessories to Billets – making Ordway Road for 96 Coy – cutting expanded metal – erecting Armstrong Huts – grounds for O.P. & hauling Tool Carts & Lumber & sinking Carts – repg Bicycles. R.E. 4 Infantry Carpenters in Workshops.	RE2
	2/1/16		Strength of Company:– As before Work:– NIL	
	3/1/16	DAY	Strength of Company:– As before Work:– R.E. 1 Infantry on Dug-outs at RUE BIACHE – 10hrs Bde Hqrs – on CROIX MARECHAL Post – on Precautional at CROIX BLANCHE – on Dug-outs at ROUGE DE BOUT – on Dug-outs at WINTER'S NIGHT & JUNCTION. R.E. 2 Artillerymen on O.P. at V.C. Corner R.E. 3 only on accessories to Billets – 10hrs SAILLY Bridge – 10hrs Dump – making groundsels – erecting Armstrong Huts – cleaning up yard – overhauling Tool Carts & Lumber – repg Bicycles – cutting expanded metal – painting waterings. R.E. 4 Infantry Carpenters in Workshops.	RE2

Place	Date	Hour	Summary of Events and Information	Remarks and references to Appendices
SAILLY	4/1/16	DAY	Strength of Company:- as before. Work:- A.p. a Infantry - on Emg. subs at RUE BIACHE - on Breastworks at CROIX BLANCHE - on Parapet at CROIX MARECHAL - on adv. H.Q. at ROUGE DE BOUT - Front Eng. subs at JUNCTION TWINTERS NIGHT. - A.2. Artillery - on V.C. Corner O.P. A.3. only dismantling Pontoon Bridge at G.16.b.5.4 - on Bank Stores at SAILLY - accessories to Billets - making trackways - on Armoury Huts - making roadway, cleaning up yard - overhauling one Carts, Limbers, wagons - refg. Bicycles - cutting expanded metal - painting wagons - cleaning refg. well R.E. a Infantry Carpenters in Workshops.	R.E.
do	5/1/16		Strength of Company:- as before. Work:- A.p. a Infantry refg. Bde H.Q. Eng-subs - on Eng-subs at RUE BIACHE - Bank Store at JUNCTION a WINTERS NIGHT - on adv H.Q at ROUGE DE BOUT - A.2. a Artillery - on O.P. at V.C Corner. R.3. only accessories to Billets - Ammunition Store at SAILLY - making tramways - making tramways on Armoury Huts - making roadway, cleaning up yard. - overhauling Horse Carts & Limber wagons - refg. Bicycles - painting wagons. R.E. a Infantry Carpenters in Workshops.	R.E.

WAR DIARY or INTELLIGENCE SUMMARY

Army Form C. 2118.

Place	Date	Hour	Summary of Events and Information	Remarks and references to Appendices
SAILLY	6/1/16		Strength of Company :- As before. Leo 1 Riding Horse.	
			W.O's :- As before.	
			R.E.: Infantry on Eng-arts at Dumt Stops - Eng-arts at Adv. Stops at RUE BIACHE - Bomb Store at CROIX BLANCHE - WINTER NIGHT SMITH'S VILLA ELBOW FARM - Adv. Stops at ROUGE DE BOUT - Bomb Store at CROIX MARECHAL.	R.E.
			A.S.C.: Artillery on O.P. at V.C. Corner.	
			R.A.S.C.: only repr. Ammunition Shop at ESTAIRES - accessories to Billets - collecting explosives - washing & painting Carts/Wagons - making harness - on Ammunition Carts - washing & patching Tool Carts & Limber wagons.	
do	7/1/16		Strength of Company :- As before.	
			W.O's :- As before.	
			R.E.: Infantry on Eng-arts at Dumt Stops - Eng-arts at Adv Stops at RUE BIACHE - Bomb Store at CROIX BLANCHE, WINTER NIGHT, SMITH'S VILLA, ELBOW FARM, CROIX MARECHAL - Adv Stops at ROUGE DE BOUT.	R.E.
			A.S.C.: Artillery on O.P. at V.C. Corner - FLEURBAIX.	
			R.A.S.C.: only repr. Ammunition Shop at ESTAIRES - accessories to Billets - washing & painting Carts/Wagons - collecting explosives - making harness - Repairing Carts, Limber wagons.	
			Strength of Infantry - Carpenters in Shops.	
do	8/1/16		Strength of Company :- As before.	
			R.E.: Infantry on Eng-arts at Dumt Stops - Eng-arts at RUE BIACHE - Bomb Store at ELBOW FARM SMITH'S VILLA, CROIX MARECHAL, CROIX MARECHAL & Dugouts at ROUGE DE BOUT, FLEURBAIX.	
			A.S.C.: Artillery on O.P. at V.C. Corner & FLEURBAIX.	
			R.A.S.C.: only repr. Ammunition Shop at ESTAIRES - accessories to Billets - washing & painting Carts, Limber wagons - collecting explosives - making harness & patching Tool Carts.	R.E.
			39 attached 2nd Canby. C/N Company to rejoin their Units.	

Army Form C. 2118.

WAR DIARY
or
INTELLIGENCE SUMMARY.
(Erase heading not required.)

Instructions regarding War Diaries and Intelligence Summaries are contained in F. S. Regs., Part II. and the Staff Manual respectively. Title pages will be prepared in manuscript.

Place	Date	Hour	Summary of Events and Information	Remarks and references to Appendices
SAILLY	9/1/16		Strength of Company :- do before. Work :- Cleaning up Billets etc for move. Night of 9th/10th :- O.C. Extra officer, Hells, and 96th Company (No 2 Section) joined 15th DLI in front line at 2 a.m. for gas attack.	RE
do	10/1/16		Strength of Company :- do before. Nothing done however after the gas attack.	RE
GRAND SEC BOIS	11/1/16		Strength of Company :- do before. Company left SAILLY & marched to billets at GRAND SEC BOIS. R.E. Billets or quartered over to 1st Home Counties Coy. R.E.	RE
MORBECQUE	12/1/16		Strength of Company :- do before. Company left GRAND SEC BOIS & marched to Billets at MORBECQUE occupied by 15th Company R. & 1st Home Counties Coy. R.E.	RE
do	13/1/16		Strength of Company :- do before. Drill & rifle exercise etc. Alarm, repairing & improving new Billets.	RE
do	14/1/16		Strength of Company :- do before. Drill & rifle exercise etc. Altering, repairing & improving new Billets. & working on new Rifle Range	RE
do	15/1/16		Strength of Company :- do before. Drill & rifle exercise etc. Altering, repairing & improving new Billets. & working on new Rifle Range	RE
do	16/1/16 Sunday		Strength of Company :- do before. Drill & rifle exercise etc. 2/Lt Ayley admitted to Hospital. Lt Thurnder joined Company for temporary attachment.	RE

WAR DIARY
or
INTELLIGENCE SUMMARY
(Erase heading not required.)

Army Form C. 2118

Place	Date	Hour	Summary of Events and Information	Remarks and references to Appendices
MORBECQUE	17/1/16		Strength of Company:- 6 Off/icers. 220 Rank & File. 29 Horses. 49 Mules. Cap. Glenn taken off strength of Company on from 27/12/15. Lt. Laing & 2 NCOs & men on detachment at School of Mortars 1st Army.	R2
			Work:- 8 men in Hospital. Rifle & rifle exercise. Work on Rifle Range & Field Work training.	
	18/1/16		Strength of Company:- as before. Work:- Drill & rifle exercise. Work on Rifle Range & Field Work training.	R2
	19/1/16		Strength of Company:- as before. Work:- Drill & rifle exercise. Work on Rifle Range & Field Work training.	R2
	20/1/16		Strength of Company:- as before, and 2/Lt. Jopling joined Company. Work:- Route March.	R2
	21/1/16		Strength of Company:- as before. Inspection of Company by G.O.C. 3rd Corps & C.E. 3rd Corps.	R2
	22/1/16		Strength of Company:- as before. Company left billets at MORBECQUE marched to fresh billets at OUDEZEELE.	R2
OUDEZEELE	23/1/16 Sunday		Strength of Company:- 6 Off. 2nd Lt. 7 (Sunday) to join 2nd Army. Company in reserve.	R2

1875 Wt. W593/826 1,000,000 4/15 J.B.C. & A. A.D.S.S./Forms/C. 2118.

WAR DIARY
or
INTELLIGENCE SUMMARY

(Erase heading not required.)

Army Form C. 2118

Place	Date	Hour	Summary of Events and Information	Remarks and references to Appendices
OUDEZEELE	24/1/16		Strength of Company: As before. Work: Cyclonius. Outdoorsing. Drill & Rifle Exercises etc.	R.L.
	25/1/16		Strength of Company: As before. Work: Ditto. Outdoor instruction, Drill & Rifle Exercises etc.	R.L.
	26/1/16		Strength of Company: As before, except that Lt Norman left Company after temporary attachment. Work: Ditto. Outdoorsing. Drill & Rifle Exercises etc.	R.L.
	27/1/16		Strength of Company: As before. Work: Ditto. Outdoorsing. Drill & Rifle Exercises etc.	R.L.
	28/1/16		Strength of Company: As before. 3 Officers, 95 N.C.O.'s men & 39 horses. Middle left Company for attachment for special work at A.22.d.8.4 (Sheet 28) for 2 platoons. Outdoorsing. Drill & Rifle Exercises etc.	R.L.
	29/1/16		Strength of Company: As before. Work: Outdoorsing. Drill & Rifle Exercises etc.	R.L.
	30/1/16		Strength of Company: As before. Work: Outdoorsing. Drill & Rifle Exercises etc.	R.L.
	31/1/16		Strength of Company: As before. Company inspected with 56th Infty Brigade by G.O.C. 2nd Army	R.L.

P. L. Smith

96th F.C.R.E.
vol: 5

CONFIDENTIAL.

WAR DIARY

OF

96TH FIELD Coy. R.E.

from 1st February to 29th February, 1916.

(VOLUME V)

WAR DIARY or INTELLIGENCE SUMMARY

Army Form C. 2118

Place	Date	Hour	Summary of Events and Information	Remarks and references to Appendices
OODEZEELE	1/2/16		Strength of Company: 6 Officers 212 Rank & File. 76 horses & Mules. 3 men joined Company from ROUEN in afternoon. In Walks allotted.	RL
			Lt Fairy & 3 OR. men on detachment at School of Mortars at Army & Corps School. 3 Officers 95 NCO. men & 39 Horses & Mules detached from Company on special work.	
	2/2/16		Work: Entrainer & detraining. Drill & Rifle exercises etc.	RL
			Strength of Company: as before	
	3/2/16		Work: Deployment & Bartering. Drill & Rifle exercises etc.	RL
			Strength of Company: as before	
	4/2/16		Work: 2 Platoons entrained. Drill & Rifle exercises etc.	RL
			By Regt & Capt Company (now attached to 39th Field Company from 1/2/16 to 31/3/16 for inspection of new line at HOUTKERQUE (E.25.b.4.2. Sheet 27).	
HOUTKERQUE	4/2/16		Strength of Company: as before.	RL
	5/2/16		Work: Drill & Rifle exercises. Knotting & Lashing etc	RL
			Strength of Company: as before.	
	6/2/16 Sunday		Lt Williams & Capt Colwell attached to 39th Field Coy R.E. from 4/2/16 to 4/2/16 for inspection of new line.	RL
	7/2/16		Strength of Company: as before	RL
			Work: Drill & Rifle exercises. Knotting & Lashing etc	
	8/2/16		Strength of Company: as before	RL
			Work: Drill & Rifle exercises. Lectures on Field Works.	

1875 Wt. W593/826 1,000,000 4/15 J.B.C. & A. A.D.S.S./Forms/C. 2118.

Army Form C. 2118

WAR DIARY
or
INTELLIGENCE SUMMARY
(Erase heading not required.)

Instructions regarding War Diaries and Intelligence Summaries are contained in F. S. Regs., Part II. and the Staff Manual respectively. Title Pages will be prepared in manuscript.

Place	Date	Hour	Summary of Events and Information	Remarks and references to Appendices
HOUTKERQUE	9/7/16		Strength of Company:- As before. Work:- Drill, Rifle Exercises etc. Smoke Helmet Drill.	App.
	10/7/16		Strength of Company:- As before. Work:- Drill & Rifle Exercises etc. Smoke Helmet Drill etc.	App.
	11/7/16		Strength of Company:- As before. Work:- Packing up Wagons & cleaning up Billets.	
	12/7/16		Strength of Company:- As before. Company marched to Camp (Huts) & (Barn) at A.23.a.2.b. Sheet 28. O.C. 9 noo 1 & 3 Sections went up to Dug-outs on Canal Bank at C.25.a.59 for work in line. Levi, (3 N.C.O's men) No 5 (37 N.C.O's men) —	App.
A.23.a.2.b C.25.a.59 Sheet 28	13/7/16		Strength of Company:- As before. a 2nd Infantry Carpenters joined Company. Work:- Front line:- Inspecting line.	App. 2
			Camp:- Working on Anvil Stone, Office Magazine, Workshop ablution Hut etc. making material for front line	
do	14/7/16		Strength of Company:- As before + 7 men joined Company from ROUEN Front Line:-	App.
			Camp:- Working material for trenches, working on improvements to Toilets.	

WAR DIARY
or
INTELLIGENCE SUMMARY
(Erase heading not required.)

Army Form C. 2118

Place	Date	Hour	Summary of Events and Information	Remarks and references to Appendices
A.23.a.2.6 C.25.a.s.9 Sheet 28	15/7/16		Strength of Company :- As before. Work :- Front Line. R. & a. Infantry on E 23, D 22, D 21, C 10 – thickening parapet & cleaning trenches. N.O.a. Infantry strengthening parapet – VICARS LANE & DAWSONS CITY – strengthening parapet & draining trench in front to the WILLOWS. a. & a. Infantry moving & carrying up Stores. a. & a. repairing Railway. Miners working on BOAR LANE. Making Revetting hurdles, a 3'6" wide trench boards arranging water tanks. Dumps. Reps camp pathways. Erecting Shoeing Smiths Shelter & erecting Hut frames. Washing Repatorial bovcies, transporting unloading.	RZ
do	16/7/16		Strength of Company :- As before. Work :- Front Line. R. & a. Infantry carrying stores & strengthening parapet C Line east of AILE KEM Rd. strengthening parapet & DAWSONS CITY, cleaning trench VICARS LANE, thickening parapet, cleaning & draining trenches B 23, D 22, D 21 on C Line to right of KNARESBORO CASTLE removing butts cutting new trench & broken ditch – on various work on X 10 Line. R. & a. Infantry moving & carrying up Stores. a. & a. repairing Railway. Pioneers on improvements to CONEY St. & BOAR LANE. Adpte. Making Revetting hurdles etc for front line. Working on Workshop ablution hut. Office etc. Handling material, loading, transporting, unloading.	RZ

WAR DIARY or INTELLIGENCE SUMMARY

Army Form C. 2118

Place	Date	Hour	Summary of Events and Information	Remarks and references to Appendices
A.23, a.2.b C.25.a.5.9 Sheet 28	17/9/16		**Strength of Company**: as before. **Work**: Front line - R.S.of Infantry on VICARS LANE - working on CLIFFORDS TOWER - working in front line at D.19, S.16a, cleaning trench & constructing x.10 - working in front line at D.19, S.16a, B.17a, B.16, S.23, D.22, D.21, C.11 & C.10 — on DAWSONS CITY — on VICARS LANE. R.E. near Railway dugouts on connecting line D.20 : working on BOAR LANE. Sappers: Making trench boards. Revetting shingles etc. Erecting magazine. O.M.S Store. Workshop. Alteration Stnt. Officers Shoeing Smiths Shelter. Unloading material, loading, transporting & unloading.	ref²
do.	18/9/16		**Strength of Company**: as before. **Work**: Front line - R.S.of Infantry thickening parapet, cutting new trench & draining etc. C line VICARS LANE to CLIFFORDS TOWER - on new Dugouts in X.1.D line & the WILLOWS: thickening parapet - thickening parapet & cleaning trench S.16a — revetting & cleaning trench B.17a B.16 - draining trench & revetting parapet in front line E.2.5 - cleaning trench & building parapet in front line D.21 - on VICARS LANE & line, removing broken wire thickening parapet & draining trench. - carrying up stores & collecting material from damaged dugouts. R.S.: draining trench & revetting parapet in front line D.22, every Railway Pioneers on front line trench D.20 & cleaning lines BOAR LANE. Sappers: Making wide trench boards & draining lines. Completing O.M.S Store. Cutting angles in Cook house & working on magazine. Alteration Stnt Officers Shoeing Smiths Shelter. Unloading material, loading, transporting & unloading.	ref²

WAR DIARY
or
INTELLIGENCE SUMMARY

Army Form C. 2118

Place	Date	Hour	Summary of Events and Information	Remarks and references to Appendices
A13.a.2.b.6 C.25.a.5.9 Sheet 28	19/3/16		**Strength of Company:** As before. **Work:** **Front Line:** R.E. & Infantry on Dugouts. In THE WILLOWS — strengthening parapet VICARS LANE — working on 6 line VICARS LANE & CLIFFORDS TOWER — thickening parapet between B16, B17a, B17a, B16a — on Dug outs X10 — sawing & carrying up stores. R.E. reclaiming trenches & draining D21 & D22 — on repairs to Rly. Pioneers working on D22 & BOAR3 LANE. **Base:** Making Revetting frames & Dugouts. Working on Ablution hut, Workshop, Pumphed, Office, Magazine & Cookhouse in Camp. Unloading material, loading, transporting, unloading.	R.E.
do	20/3/16		**Strength of Company:** As before. **Work:** **Front Line:** R.E. & Infantry carrying up Stones. Pioneers on D20 & BOAR3 LANE. **Camp:** Making Revetting frames & Dugouts. Completing Ablution Hut & Office. Unloading material, loading, transporting, unloading.	R.E.
do	21/3/16		**Strength of Company:** As before. **Work:** **Front Line:** R.E. & Infantry cleaning out trench connecting D21 — drawing trench, making up parapet D21, — thickening parapet & forming trenches at D20, WILLOW WALK, S16a, B17a, B16 — on VICARS LANE; draining; thickening parapet, — on CLIFFORD3 TOWER — thickening forming parapet, — on Dugouts at THE WILLOWS, — R.E. Dugouts draining at X10 — relaying & carrying up Stores. R.E. very Railway. Pioneers cleaning D20 — draining sumppump BOAR LANE & CONEY St.	R.E.

Place	Date	Hour	Summary of Events and Information	Remarks and references to Appendices
A.23.a.2.6 C.25.a.5.9 Sheet 28	21/9/16	(contd)	Strype: Making dugouts & revetting frames. Completing Magazine, working on Workshop Engine Bed & repairing pathway in castle. Unloading material, loading, transporting & unloading	K2
do	22/9/16		Strength of Company:- as before Work:- H.Q. & Infantry thickening parapet & laying trench boards at WILLOW WALK - revetting & thickening parapet S16a & S17a on dugouts & thickening parapet at R16 - D21 revetting & making up parapet - revetting trench & making up trench at C line VICARS LANE - on dugouts at THE WILLOWS - on dugouts & thickening parapet at X10 dugouts & carrying up stores. H/B working on CLIFFORDS TOWER, on Rly Railway. Pioneers on new trench D22 & BOAR LANE Strype: making dugouts. Laying traverses for roadway, drainage of stables, working on roadway. Unloading material, loading, transporting & unloading	K2
do	23/9/16		Strength of Company:- as before Work:- NIL Infantry Relieving. Strype making dugouts. Laying traverses for roadway & working on tramway. Unloading Material, loading, transporting & unloading	K2

WAR DIARY
or
INTELLIGENCE SUMMARY
(Erase heading not required.)

Army Form C. 2118

Place	Date	Hour	Summary of Events and Information	Remarks and references to Appendices
A, 2, B a, b C, 15 a, 5, 9 Sheet 28	24/7/16		**Strength of Company**: As before. **Wo/h**: 18 men Thos Sector joined part of Company in Canal Bank (night) front line: R.E. & Infantry working on D 20 & WILLOW WALK reclaiming trench – reclaiming trench B16 – on new trench VICARS LANE & CLIFFORDS TOWER – building parapet at X10 – reclaiming trench x 9 – thickening parapet B13 – reclaiming trench B14 – strengthening parapet & draining trench S13 – leaving scarping up stores R.E. revetting trench S16 A – reclaiming trench B17 a – refg Railway. **Ang/o**: making dugouts – giving up ordinating Huts to NCO's – firing up Engine – unloading material, loading, transporting, unloading.	K 2
do	25/7/16		**Strength of Company**: As before. **Wo/h**: front line: R.E. & Infantry on WILLOW WALK reclaiming trench – revetting S 16 A – reclaiming trenches B16 & B17 a – on VICARS LANE & CLIFFORDS TOWER, B on A12h, thickening parapet revetting – on X10 strengthening parapet & draining – clearing & revetting trenches B14 & B15 – strengthening parapet B13 – reclaiming trenches S13 & S14 – on X 9 strengthening parapet – making Dugouts – scarping up stores – R & M repairs to Railway. – building dugout at LA BELLE ALLIANCE – Pioneers working in THREADNEEDLE St, CONEY St & BOARS LANE. **Ang/o**: making dugouts – Pom – completing Engine House – unloading material, loading, transporting, unloading	K 2

WAR DIARY or INTELLIGENCE SUMMARY

Army Form C. 2118

Place	Date	Hour	Summary of Events and Information	Remarks and references to Appendices
A.23.a.2.6 C.25.a.5.9 Sheet 28	26/7/16		Strength of Company: as before. Work:— Front Line: R. & 2 Infantry working on D21, D20, B16, WILLOW WALK, reclaiming trenches & constructing dugouts — on VICARS LANE & CLIFFORDS reclaiming trenches & constructing dugouts — erecting dugouts at THE WILLOWS — TOWER, dugouts, Bomb Pitch & revetting — thickening parapet & drawing — reclaiming trenches B14 & B13 — on X10, thickening parapet & drawing — reclaiming trenches B14 & B13 — carrying up stores. R/E on D20, reclaiming trench & constructing dugout — on dugout at LA BELLE ALLIANCE — reclaiming trenches B16 & B20 dugouts at X9 — repairs to tramway. Dismounted on reclaiming trenches BOAR LANE, CONEY ST & THREADNEEDLE ST. Hays making dugouts. Working on Nuel Globe extension to Wakehop, loading, transporting, unloading material for Yprench.	R₂
do.	27/7/16		Strength of Company: as before. Work:— Front Line: R. & 2 Infantry reclaiming trenches & laying Company revetting at D21, D20, WILLOW WALK, SIFA, B17a & B.16 — on BOAR'S LANE & CLIFFORDS TOWER, thickening parapet & revetting — cleaning trenches. & making revetting B13 & B14 — carrying & carrying up stores R/E working on BOARS LANE & CLIFFORDS TOWER — wiring B13 — cleaning & making revetting B15 & B13. — on dugouts at X9, LA BELLE ALLIANCE & CANAL BANK — repairs to tramway. Dismounted reclaiming THREADNEEDLE St, CONEY St & BOARS LANE. Revetting frames & trenches. Hays. Machine gun dugouts. Completing Nuel Globe & working on extension to Wokehop. Mending material, loading, transporting, unloading.	R₂

WAR DIARY or INTELLIGENCE SUMMARY

Army Form C. 2118

Place	Date	Hour	Summary of Events and Information	Remarks and references to Appendices
A.23.a.2.6 C.25.a.5.9 Sheet 28	28/9/16		**Strength of Company:-** As before. **Work:- 9hour time:-** Relief - No Working parties available. **Staffe:-** Making Revetting frames. Augmts. tickets & Wooden Rails. Completing entrance to Workshop. Unloading material, loading, transporting, unloading.	
do	29/9/16		**Strength of Company:-** As before. **Work:- 9hour time:-** R.E. on O.P. at LA BELLE ALLIANCE. R.E. on S18.a, D.20, D.21, D.17.a, B.16 draining, revetting, laying trench boards. Augmts:- Revetting VICARS LANE - wiring CLIFFORD'S TOWER - on Augmts. breadening trench X9 - wiring S13 - repairs to Highway - carrying up stores. A.2. Infantry reclaiming trenches. draining B13, B14 Bis, S13. Pioneers working on THREADNEEDLE St. CONEY St & BOARS LANE. Making Revetting frames Augmts. French Decauville Railway. Working on extra sink & experimental roadway. Unloading material, loading, transporting, unloading. **Staff:-**	

P.F. Story
Capt. R.E.
O.C. 96 Coy. R.E.

96 FCRE Vol 6

CONFIDENTIAL

WAR DIARY

OF

96TH FIELD COY. R.E.

FROM. MARCH 1st to 31st 1916

(VOLUME VI)

Place	Date	Hour	Summary of Events and Information	Remarks and references to Appendices
A.23.a.2.b C.25.a.5.q Sheet 28	1/3/16		Strength of Company: 6 Officers. 220 Other Ranks. 9 men joined Company from ROUEN. 27 3rd entry attached to Company. 9 men in hospital. Work:- Section (minus Carpenters q No3) at CANAL BANK. Nos 1, 2 q 3 Front Line:- A.8. drawing, revetting, making trench boards at D11, D20 q WILLOW WALK — ditto B17a. — revetting, drawing, making VICARS LANE — at S13 q x9 drawing, revetting, reclaiming trenches — refg Railway. R.8. Infantry on S18 q B15. drawing, revetting, making trench boards — on B13, B14, B15. drawing, revetting, reclaiming trenches — reaving scantlings M.G. store. R.G. R.9.a on O.P at LA BELLE ALLIANCE. Stypo: Making Notice Boards Dugouts q Revetting BOAR LANE q THREADNEEDLE St. Bar Lane q Revetting France. Pioneers working on CONEY ST, BOAR LANE q THREADNEEDLE St. (Day q night work) Erecting Armoured Shelters Hut over q Armoured Hut q working on roadway. Unloading material, loading, transporting unloading.	PS
do	2/3/16		Strength of Company: As before. No 3 Section returned to Anzio q now went into CANAL BANK (nights of 2nd q 3rd March) RE. Front Line:- R.8. on S18a. WILLOW WALK, D20 q D21, revetting, making dugouts q making trench boards — on VICARS LANE revetting, drawing — on sites for dugouts at x9 — drawing refy parapet B15. — drawing, laying trench boards S13 — roads to Railway. R.8. q Infantry on B16 q B17a, revetting, drawing, dugouts, drawing trench boards — on A.514. clearing trench, laying foot boards, refy parapet B13 — revetting, reaming up stores. Pioneers on THREADNEEDLE St, CONEY St q BOAR LANE (Day q night work)	RE

WAR DIARY or INTELLIGENCE SUMMARY

Army Form C. 2118

Place	Date	Hour	Summary of Events and Information	Remarks and references to Appendices
A.23 a 6 C.25 a 5.9 Sheet 28	3/3/16 (cont)		HdQrs:- Making Angare, Window Box, Stand for M.G. Officer + an artillery O.P. Completing Drivers Hut + working on Roadway. Unloading material, loading, transporting, unloading.	A2
do	3/3/16		Strength of Company:- As before. Work:- ynant Rune. No Work owing to relief. HdQrs:- Making M.G. Angare, Special large V frame artillery O.P. Refrigerator Meat Room, making Army Table, unloading material + loading, transporting, unloading.	
do	4/3/16		Strength of Company:- As before. Work:- ynant Rune. (with 60th Infantry Brigade.) R.E. on D.1, D.21, D.20 + WILLOW WALK, raising trench boards + drawing - on S.169, B.17a, B.16, repairing trench + drawing - drawing + revetting VICAR'S LANE - drawing B.13 - preparing site for Angarts at X.9 - rtg Railway R.E. Infantry on B.14, cleaning trench + laying trench Boards - on B.15, rtg dugouts + drawing - drawing S.13 - raising + carrying up Stone R.E. a D.9 + on O.P at LA BELLE ALLIANCE. HdQrs:- Making Revetting frames, Notice Boards, Trench Boards, Pickets + frames. Unloading material, loading, transporting, unloading.	R2
do	5/3/16		Strength of Company:- As before. Work:- ynant Rune. R.E. on B.16, S.16a, D.20, D.21, WILLOW WALK, laying trench Boards + revetting - revetting trench B.17 - drawing VICAR'S LANE - laying trench Boards in B.14 - preparing steps for Angarts at X.9 - repairs to Railway R.E. Infantry drawing B.13, B.15 & S.13 - loaning + carrying up Stone. Dugouts on CONEY St & BOAR LANE, revetting + drawing trenches (Angworks)	R2

1875 Wt. W593/826 1,000,000 4/15 J.B.C. & A. A.D.S.S./Forms/C. 2118.

WAR DIARY or INTELLIGENCE SUMMARY

Army Form C. 2118

Place	Date	Hour	Summary of Events and Information	Remarks and references to Appendices
A.23.a.2.b C.26.a.5.9 (Sheet 26)	5/3/16 (Contd)		Hqrs:- Making Sign Boards, Window Frames & Office Furniture for Front Line. Working on Annexe Mess Room. Unloading material, loading, transporting, unloading	
do	6/3/16		Strength of Company:- as before. Work:- Front Line:- R.G. draining B13 — retg Parapet & draining B15 — on draining Dugouts at X9 — draining D21 — VICARS LANE — laying trench boards & netting D20, D16a, WILLOW WALK, B17a & B16 — retg Railway R.E. & Infantry on B14, clearing trench boards — on S13 draining & cleaning trench — on BUFFS ROAD, clearing drain — wiring screwing up Stores Pioneers on CONEY ST & BOAR LANE ditto Hqrs:- Making Trench Boards, Office Furniture for Front Line & wooden huts for Engine Working on alteration to Annexe Mess Hut Unloading material, loading, transporting, unloading	
do	7/3/16		Strength of Company:- as before + 2 Annexes joined Company from ROUEN. Work:- Front Line:- R.G. on D21, D20, WILLOW WALK, S16a, B17a, B16 VICARS LANE, draining & laying trench boards and retg parapets — draining Dugouts X9 — draining trench boards B14 — draining retg parapet B15 — Infantry retg trench S13 — draining B13 — on M.G. emplacement at WILSON'S FARM — retg Railway — moving Stores R.E.: R17a on O.P. at LA BELLE ALLIANCE Pioneers on CONEY ST, BOAR LANE & THREADNEEDLE St. do on CONEY ST & BOAR LANE (Dugouts) Hqrs:- Making Trench Boards, Pickets & Annexes working on Brynn Byon, Annexe Mess hut & Roadway, Unloading material, loading, transporting, unloading	

Army Form C. 2118

WAR DIARY or INTELLIGENCE SUMMARY

(Erase heading not required.)

Instructions regarding War Diaries and Intelligence Summaries are contained in F.S. Regs., Part II. and the Staff Manual respectively. Title Pages will be prepared in manuscript.

Place	Date	Hour	Summary of Events and Information	Remarks and references to Appendices
A 23 a 2 6 C 25 a 5 9 Shot 28	8/3/16		**Strength of Company :-** As before. **Work :- Front Line :-** R.E. laying trench boards in D.20. — revetting WILLOW WALK — retg B.17a trench — delaying trench boards in B.16 — drawing VICARS LANE — drawing & laying trench boards in B.14 — drawing WILSONS POST. — M.G. Emplacement at WILSONS FARM — drawing POND FARM Salient — setting at CANAL BANK — retg Railway. N.G. Infantry drawing D.21 — laying trench boards in S.18a — drawing drawing B.13, S.13, X.9 — on B.15, clearing retg parapet — laying trench boards — on BUFFS ROAD, clearing drain — issuing & carrying up stores. R.B. R.B.R.B.Ja on O.P. at LA BELLE ALLIANCE. Pioneers on CONEY St., BOAR LANE & THREADNEEDLE St. " " on CONEY St. (Raynock). Appx: Making trench boards. Noticeboards, pickets & Yarrowmes — working on drying room & ammo. Mess Hut — including material, loading, transporting, unloading.	Pat2
do	9/3/16		**Strength of Company :-** As before. **Work :- Front Line :-** R.E. in B.13 cleaning trench & revetting. — B.14 cleaning trench & laying trench boards — on B.13 revetting & draining — drawing X & TWILSONS POST. — on M.G. emplacement at WILSONS FARM — laying trench boards retg parapet — drawing VICARS LANE. — on D.20, laying trench boards retg parapet — retg Railway. R.B. Infantry on B.15, clearing trench, laying trench boards — drawing BUFFS ROAD & POND FARM SALIENT — working D.21, S.18a TWILLOW WALK — on B.17a & B.16 revetting parapet — issuing & carrying up stores. Pioneers on CONEY St. BOAR LANE & THREADNEEDLE St. do " on CONEY St. & BOAR LANE (Raynock) Appx: Making trench boards. Noticeboards, Yarrowmes pickets & chloride paint for completed drying room — working on drying Mess Hut — including material, loading, transporting, unloading. Material.	Pat2

WAR DIARY
or
INTELLIGENCE SUMMARY

(Erase heading not required.)

Army Form C. 2118

Place	Date	Hour	Summary of Events and Information	Remarks and references to Appendices
A.23.a.6 C.25.a.9 Sheet 28	10/3/16		**Strength of Company :-** As before. No 1 Section returned to Strijpe. No 3 Section went into Canal Bank (right of 10/11 May) **Work :-** Front Line. R.B. on B14, laying trench Boards - revetting B13 - draining x 9. 7 BUFFS ROAD - on Dugouts & M.G. tunnel at CANAL BANK - laying trench boards at Pole 110 - draining & revetting VICARS LANE - retg Railway R.B. & Infantry revetting B13 - laying trench boards in B15 - draining POND FARM Salient - wiring on D1, S16a. WILLOW WALK - thickening parapet B16 - draining & revetting D10da B17a - laying & cleaning up stores Tunnels on M.G. tunnel at CANAL BANK. do on CONEY ST & BOAR LANE (Dugouts) Strijpe: Making mining frames. M.G. Steelel/notice boards artillery O.P. notices Aircra Wire Shut. Working on Aircra Wire Shut. Unloading material, loading, transporting, unloading	R.S.
do	11/3/16		**Strength of Company :-** As before. **Work :-** Front Line. No Working Parties owing to relief. R.D. on Railway & M.G. emplacement at WILSONS FARM Strijpe :- Making mine frames, gunnery Artillery O.P. & M.G. emplacement working on Aircra, three Shut Unloading material, loading, transporting, unloading	R.S.
do	12/3/16		**Strength of Company :-** As before. **Work :-** Front Line. R.B. on M.G. emplacement at WILSONS FARM. - on Dugouts at x.9. - on S13.9 S16a draining & cleaning trenches. - on D.21. draining at D.20. wiring trench boards & revetting - on B.16. revetting & laying trench boards - on WILLOW WALK thickening parapet - return to Railway	R.S.

WAR DIARY
or
INTELLIGENCE SUMMARY.

(Erase heading not required.)

Army Form C. 2118.

Place	Date	Hour	Summary of Events and Information	Remarks and references to Appendices
A.23.a.2.b C.25.A.5.9 Sheet 28	10/3/16 (contd)		R.S. Infantry revetting B13. – digging trenches on Canal Bank. – on B17a o VICARS LANE drawing & revetting – whitewashing French CLIFFORDS TOWER – loading & carrying up Stores. Pioneers working on Canal Bank (Anywork).	R.E.
			Attps:- Making mine frames, Artillery O.P. shelters & transoms M.G. emplacement. Working on Armco Mess Hut. Unloading material, loading, transporting, unloading.	
do	13/3/16		Strength of Company:- As before. Works:- Infantry:- Front line:- R.S. on O.P. at Canal Bank. – on M.G. emplacement at WILSONS FARM. – R.S. on SISA WILLOW BANK, B17a drawing & revetting. – R.S. on WILLOW WALK, D21, D20, revetting. Carpys French Bombs – drawing B16 – retg Railway R.S. & Infy digging trenches on CANAL BANK – on VICARS LANE & CLIFFORDS TOWER drawing & revetting – loading & carrying up Stores. (Pioneers working on CANAL BANK (in 6 hour shifts from 1 noon 13/3/16). Attps:- Making Mine frames Duckets, transoms, Wooden tramway, revetment for Bgde Hqrs. Making material, loading, transporting, unloading.	R.E.
do	14/3/16		Strength of Company:- As before and 1 man joined Company from ROUEN. Works:- Front line:- R.E. on M.G. emplacement & drawing at WILSONS FARM. – on O.P. at CANAL BANK – drawing POND FARM Salient – drawing B16 – on D20. WILLOW WALK, B17a, laying & drawing French Bombs – retg Railway. R.S. & Infantry digging & drawing trenches at CANAL BANK – revetting along French Boards on VICARS LANE – drawing SISA VICARS LANE & CLIFFORDS TOWER – on X.10 wiring & thickening parapet. – revetting D21 – loading & carrying up Stores. Pioneers working on CANAL BANK (in 6 hour shifts).	R.E.

WAR DIARY
or
INTELLIGENCE SUMMARY

(Erase heading not required.)

Army Form C. 2118

Place	Date	Hour	Summary of Events and Information	Remarks and references to Appendices
A.23.a.1.b C.25.a S.9 Sheet 28	14/3/16 (contd)		Steps:- Making running repairs tramway signals, transporting & unloading material & ordering, transporting & unloading.	
do.	15/3/16		Strength of Company:- As before. Trench Line:- No 3 on front line WILLOW WALK S.16.A. B.17a draining & revetting - on M.G.E at WILSON'S FARM - No 3 supply on B.16 draining revetting - revetting CORNHILL ? THREADNEEDLE St. - No 4 Supply on B.16 draining revetting - revetting VICARS LANE ? CLIFFORDS TOWER - on BOAR LANE & CONEY St draining, cleaning out parapet. - revetting dugouts. Trenches at "CANAL BANK" Steps:- Making running repairs, trollier, dickets, tramways. Repair dit-drake tramways, making material, loading, transporting, unloading	R
do	16/3/16		Strength of Company:- as before. Trench Line:- No 3 Company trench boards in WILLOW WALK - draining S.16a - revetting B.17a - on M.G.E. at WILSON'S FARM - on R.de Steps - repairs to Railway. No 4 Infantry on FOCH FARM felling sandbags cleaning & revetting VICARS LANE & CLIFFORDS TOWER. - Draining CONEY St supply parapet - on BOAR LANE draining & cleaning trench - on THREADNEEDLE St & CORN HILL reply trench boards revetting - on CANAL BANK digging trench - carrying & carrying up Stones. Dugouts on CANAL BANK in L-horn shafts. Steps:- Making running repairs dickets, tramways, abutments for dugouts, artillery O.P & M.G. Emplacements, unloading material, loading, transporting, unloading	R

1875. Wt. W593/826 1,000,000 4/15 J.B.C.&A. A.D.S.S./Forms/C. 2118.

Army Form C. 2118.

WAR DIARY
or
INTELLIGENCE SUMMARY.
(Erase heading not required.)

Place	Date	Hour	Summary of Events and Information	Remarks and references to Appendices
A.13 a,b C.25 a,c,q Sheet 28	17/3/16		Strength of Company: As before. Work: Front Line. R.B. revetting D.21 - laying trench Boards in WILLOW WALK - draining S18a ?B.16 - on R.9, draining, slaying, trench Boards - on CORNHILL & THREADNEEDLE St, revetting - laying trench boards - on RLY. W., infantry on D.20, revetting strengthening parapet - drawing BOAR LANE - on CONEY St, draining trench - on R de H.Q. - on M.G & Y WILSONS FARM - on trench at CANAL BANK - carrying material for revetting CANAL BANK - draining POTY FARM SALIENT - draining trench VICARS LANE x CLIFFORDS TOWER - filling sandbags at FOCH FARM - laying tramway up to Area. Pioneers on CANAL BANK (known as N/5) making M.G. emplacements. Pioneers, Abutments for dugouts 9 dug making Tramway sheets, tramway, loading, transporting, unloading tramway material.	Rec.
do	18/3/16		Strength of Company: as before. 2/Lt WIMBY joined (on temporary attachment) Work: Front Line. R.B. No 3 Section relieved No 2 in CANAL BANK in night of 18/19th. Front Line R.B, on Front line WILLOW WALK, S18a B16, revetting, retaining - R.B, draining CONEY St, ? BOAR LANE - R.B. Infantry draining strengthening parapet, B17a - revetting, draining VICARS LANE - on M.G.& E at FOCH FARM, WILSONS FARM - on CANAL BANK digging revetting trenches - constructing dugouts at X.10. Pioneers on CANAL BANK (known as N/5) Repto: Tramway M.G.E abutments for dugouts, Artillery O.P., wire trench Boards, tickets, Tramway tramway material, loading, transporting, unloading	Rec.

Army Form C. 2118.

WAR DIARY
or
INTELLIGENCE SUMMARY.
(Erase heading not required.)

Instructions regarding War Diaries and Intelligence Summaries are contained in F. S. Regs., Part II. and the Staff Manual respectively. Title pages will be prepared in manuscript.

Place	Date	Hour	Summary of Events and Information	Remarks and references to Appendices
A.23.a.2.6 C.25.a.5.9 Sheet 28	19/3/16		Strength of Company: as before. Work: — Front Line: — R.E. on CANAL BANK digging & revetting trenches — wiring — supports to expect dugouts. — on M.G.E. at FOCH FARM & WILSON'S FARM — on dugouts at X10. Artys: — Making M.G.E. Improvers for M. Guns. French & Bavaros dischets & — Gunners Artillery O.P. Loading material, loading, transporting & unloading	Re
do	20/3/16		Strength of Company: as before. Work: — Front Line: — R.E. on M.G.E. at FOCH FARM & WILSON'S FARM & Artillery O.P. Killing: Gunner EWING killed by shrapnel. R.E. & Infantry revetting & draining B13, B14, B15. — on S13, X10, X9, on dugouts & thickening parapets — digging & revetting VICARS LANE & CLIFFORD'S TOWER — digging & revetting CANAL BANK — Artys: Making M.G.E. Gunning frames, & French Boards	Re
do	21/3/16		Strength of Company: as before. Work: — Front Line: — R.E. on M.G.E. at WILSON'S FARM, FOCH FARM, PLONELY WILLOW R.E. & Infantry on B13, B14, B15, revetting, thickening parapets, draining — on dugouts at X9, X10 & S13 — on VICARS LANE & CLIFFORD'S TOWER — digging revetting CANAL BANK R.E. Artillery on O.P. at LA BELLE ALLIANCE & WIELTJE Artys: — Making French Boards, Gunning frames, M.G.E. & Gunners Loopholes. Loading material, loading, transporting & unloading	Re

WAR DIARY
or
INTELLIGENCE SUMMARY.

Army Form C. 2118.

(Erase heading not required.)

Place	Date	Hour	Summary of Events and Information	Remarks and references to Appendices
A.23.a & b C.25.a & 9 Sheet 28	21/3/16		Strength of Company:- As before Work:- Front Line:- R/o Infantry on B.13, B.14, T.B.15, drawing revetting - on S.13, X.9, X.10, VICARS LANE & CLIFFORDS TOWER revetting revenning - on Dugouts on M.G.E. at FOCH FARM, WILSONS FARM - excavating revetting trenches at CANAL BANK. R/o Tactillery on O.P. at LA BELLE ALLIANCE & WIELTJE. Mojo:- Making M.G.E. having frames Uprands dichets Pyramones knuckling material loading, transporting, unloading.	Rg
do	23/3/16		Strength of Company:- As before Work:- Front Line:- R/o on M.G.E. at FOCH FARM - on Cyprus Dugout at WILSONS FARM - revetting CANAL BANK. R/o artillery on O.P. at WIELTJE. Mojo:- Making frames Uprands Abutments for Dugouts, M.G.E. etc knuckling material loading, transporting, unloading.	Rg
do	24/3/16		Strength of Company:- As before Work:- Front Line:- R/o Infantry on Dugouts at X.10 & X.9 drawing - revetting & draining VICARS LANE & CLIFFORDS TOWER - on M.G.E. at FOCH FARM, WILSONS FARM & LONELY WILLOW - digging revetting trenches at CANAL BANK. R/o Tactillery on O.P. at WIELTJE. Style:- Making M.G.E. Uprams frames french Ronds dickets Pyramones knuckling material loading, transporting, unloading.	Rg

WAR DIARY or INTELLIGENCE SUMMARY
Army Form C. 2118.

Place	Date	Hour	Summary of Events and Information	Remarks and references to Appendices
A22.a26 C25a5q Sheet 28	25/9/16		Strength of Company :- as before. WDM :- No.1 Sap. R.G. on M.G. Emplacements at WILSON'S FARM, FOCH FARM & LONELY WILLOW - R.S.9 Infantry revetting & draining PICARD LANE, CLIFFORD'S TOWER - on dugouts & draining at X9 and X10 - digging & revetting trenches at CANAL BANK. R.E. Battalion on O.P. at WIELTJE. Sgts. Madden & Bergant :- Mining & Frames, Bomb boxes, Pickets & Frames. Infantry (Borders) 90 Frames. loading, unloading material, transporting, unloading	RE
do	26/9/16		Strength of Company :- as before. WDM in strong wind :- No.9 on M.G. Emplacements at SOUTHORPS ROAD, LONELY WILLOW, FOCH FARM. R.E. Infantry on dugouts at X10 and X9 and draining revetting CLIFFORD'S TOWER & VIGAR LANE, selection. Still revetting trench and post. No.2 Artillery on O.P. at WIELTJE. Sgts. Madden Mining & Frames, Bomb boxes, knifrests & frames & Picksta. Loading transporting & unloading mining material. No.2 section relieved No.4 section in CANAL BANK on night of 26/27th. Sapper Wade & No.1.5557 wounded.	RE
do	27/9/16		Strength of Company :- as before. WDM :- strong Wind :- R.E. only on M.G.E. at R.H. and LONELY WILLOW - no Infantry available owing to reliefs. put. O.P. at LA BELLE ALLIANCE. no work on CANAL BANK and no Infantry abutments for dugouts, ahead M.G. Sgts. :- Making Mining & Frames. Sgts. Bergant & Madden, Pickets & Frames & Brgm Boards. Mining material. loading, transporting, unloading.	RE

Army Form C. 2118.

WAR DIARY
or
INTELLIGENCE SUMMARY.
(Erase heading not required.)

Instructions regarding War Diaries and Intelligence Summaries are contained in F. S. Regs., Part II. and the Staff Manual respectively. Title pages will be prepared in manuscript.

Place	Date	Hour	Summary of Events and Information	Remarks and references to Appendices
Area 2.6 C 7&a. S. 9 Sheet 28	28/3/16		Strength of Company :- As before. Work :- Front Line :- R.E. Carpenters on M.G. Emplacements at B14, FOCH FARM, LONELY WILLOW, GOWTHORPE RD, WILSONS FARM – cleaning & draining VICARS LANE & CLIFFORDS TOWER – on dugouts & draining at X10 X 9, LA BELLE ALLIANCE – tunnels for M.G. Emplacements in CANAL BANK – digging & revetting CANAL BANK defences – on dugouts for signallers at WILSONS FARM. Strps :- Making M.G. dugouts, abutments for dugouts, mining frames, U frames etc.	AE
do	29/3/16		Strength of Company :- As before. R. WINBY left Company after temporary attachment, went into hospital. The 66th Brigade relieved the 59th on night of 29/30. Mch. Work :- Front Line :- R.E. Infantry digging & revetting trenches at CANAL BANK – on tunnels in trenches in CANAL BANK – setting frames for tunnel heads & for M.G. Emplacements at B14, WILSON FARM, FOCH FARM, LONELY WILLOW & GOWTHORPE RD – draining and revetting VICARS LANE & CLIFFORDS TOWER – on dugouts & draining at X10 X 9, FRASCATI & WILSON FARM. R.E. & D.H.D. made the Shaft tunnel at CANAL BANK. Strps :- Making M.G. dugout, mining frames, dugout torpedoes, U frames etc.	KE
do	30/3/16		Strength of Company :- as before. Work :- Front Line :- R.E. Infantry on M.G. Emplacements at B14, FOCH FARM, & WILSON FARM – on dugouts & draining at X10 – dugout for signallers at FRASCATI – on LA BELGE Trolley Line – revetting & tunnelling at CANAL BANK. R.E. Artillery on O.P. at WEILTJE Strps :- Making M.G. Emplacements, Loopholes, Mining Frames, Wooden Floor etc.	KE

Army Form C. 2118.

WAR DIARY
or
INTELLIGENCE SUMMARY.
(Erase heading not required.)

Place	Date	Hour	Summary of Events and Information	Remarks and references to Appendices
A 23 a 2 b C 15 a 5.9 Sheet 28	21/3/16		Strength of Company :- As before W D/a :- Work Line :- R.E. on M.G. Emplacements on Signallers Dugout at FRASCATI - Dugout at B14, FOCH FARM, WILSON FARM - Dugout at X 16 - revetting CANAL BANK trenches - tunnelling at CANAL BANK - on LA BRIQUE RLY. Infantry :- making M.G. Emplacements, mining frames, scrub & trench ones etc.	R.

[signature]
MAJOR, R.E.
COMDG. 96TH Fd. COY. R.E.

96 FRZ
Vol 7

CONFIDENTIAL.

WAR DIARY

OF

96TH FIELD COY. R.E.

FROM APRIL 1ST TO 30TH, 1916.

(VOLUME VI)

Army Form C. 2118

WAR DIARY
or
INTELLIGENCE SUMMARY
(Erase heading not required.)

Place	Date	Hour	Summary of Events and Information	Remarks and references to Appendices
A.23.a.2.6 C.25.a.5.9 Sheet 28	1/4/16		Strength of Company: 6 Officers. 215 Other Ranks. 26 Infantry from 59th Brigade attached. Work: Front Line: R.E. & Infantry on M.G. Emplacements at B14. Wilson's FARM & FOCH FARM. — on tunnelled dugouts at FRASCATI — repairing trench & tunnelling at CANAL BANK — on laying heavy Trolley Lines at LA BRIQUE, BUFFS ROAD & LA BELLE ALLIANCE. R.E. & artillery OP at WIELTJE Support: Making M.G. Emplacements, trenches, drains & tramways.	RE
do	2/4/16		Strength of Company: — as before. OP.2 Section relieved No.4 Section in Canal Bank. Work:— Front Line: R.E. and Infantry on all M.G. Emplacements. FOCH FARM, WILSONS FARM, McGREGORS POST CONEY STREET — on wireless dugouts dug-out at FRASCATI. R.E. and artillery on OP at WIELTJE. R.E. and Infantry netting trenches at CANAL BANK & on tunnelling at CANAL BANK — on trolley line BUFFS ROAD. Support:— Making M.G. Emplacements, Redoubts and trenches, drawing trench, netting fire step, dug-out	RE
do	3/4/16		Strength of Company: — as before. Work:— Front M.G. and Infantry on M.G. Emplacements. WILSONS FARM, CONEY STREET, FOCH FARM. Line: on netting and drawing VICARS LANE, CLIFFORDS TOWER. — on netting and thickening parapet THREADNEEDLE STREET. — on wireless dugouts dug-out FRASCATI. — on netting trenches and tunnelling CANAL BANK — on railway BUFFS ROAD. Supp: Making drainage trenches, facades and tramways, M.G. Emplacements, T. posts dumps for infantry stores	RE

WAR DIARY or INTELLIGENCE SUMMARY

Army Form C. 2118.

Place	Date	Hour	Summary of Events and Information	Remarks and references to Appendices
A23.a.2.b. C15.a.5.9 Sheet 28	4/4/16		**Strength of Company:** 6 Officers, 215 Other Ranks. 26 Infantry from 59th Brigade attached. **Instrns:—** R.E. and artillery completing O.P. loop-hole dug-out at WIELTJE. R.E. working in two shifts on dying of CANAL BANK. Inf: 2 shifts completed 20 yds running track 10 yds filling in. R.E. and Infantry Tunnelling East track for M.G. emplacements fixed 10 frames 6ft by 3ft by 6 inches.— on dug-trenching (M) gallery to 60th B.de Hqrs. 6ft by 4 ft deepened from 9ft to 13ft. R.E. and reached on 115ft revived laid BUFFS ROAD 110 yds packed and closed.	h.E.
do.	5/4/16		**Strength of Company:** as before. **Works:—** R.E. and. Infantry thickening parapet for M.G. emplacements 50yds WILSONS FARM, on laying 60 trench boards THREADNEEDLE STREET. On end and floor in dug-out TRASCATI. R.E. on CANAL BANK dugouts finishing completed. 13 yds running track 11yds filling in. R.E. and Infantry Tunnelling East track fixed 15 frames much subsidence. On deepening trench for gallery to 60th B.de Hqrs 2ft. cleaning and setting gallery frames, running sand, particular for ghost. On M.G. emplacement and lagging road FOCH FARM. On erecting 18 yards CONEY STREET and dug 10 yds 11 yds in on BEAR LANE, cleared 200 yards WILLOW BROOK, drainage trench inspected. Clearing 300ft BUFFS ROAD. R.E. and Infantry drawing and transporting. **Eyre:** Making Mining Frames, 18 frames, wire trench boards, crackets, pickets and tramway.	h.E.

WAR DIARY or INTELLIGENCE SUMMARY

Army Form C. 2118.

Place	Date	Hour	Summary of Events and Information	Remarks and references to Appendices
A.23.a.2.6. C.25.a.5.9. Sht 28	1/4/16		**Missing A/B Companys.** 6 Officers. 215 Other Ranks. 26 Infantry from 59th Bde attached. **Work:** Front line:- N3 and Infantry raising and thickening 50 yard parapet crossing 15 yards cleared. WILSON FARM. N1 completing dugouts work on signallers dug-out. FRASCATI. N1,2 and Infantry clearing 50 yards of drain near L.13 thickening parapet 20 yards THREADNEEDLE STREET - on ovoing on G. Emplacement work Vickers. Cutting up and laying girders. CONEY STREET - on laying infantry road and BUFF'S ROAD - on road repairing soft ground and filling in shell hole L.9 BELLE-ALLIANCE - on M.G. Emplacement VIEW FARM. N.R. or M.G. Emplacement FOCH FARM, just nth of road frame fix well of gunners dugout. Infantry carrying: N.2 and Infantry on Canal Bank M/fence 22 yards revetment - units and filled in. - on revetting 20 yards done VICARS LANE placing T frames BDE hqrs. On M.G. tunnel placing 5 frames Coal Bunk. First ground timber at parapec. **Lgrs:** Making Boot chains, trench Boards, W. frames, M.G. Emplacement, Pickets & Gammons.	✓
C10	7/4/16		**Missing A/B Company.** 6 Officers. 220 Other Ranks. 26 Infantry from 59th Bde attached. 5. Sapper joined. LtCol. M Rouse(?). Lieuts And visited. **Work:** Front line N2. Lumbered and small TOCH FARM. N3 and Infantry on CANAL BANK defences widely lowest coat and thickener parapet 12ft by 7ft by 3ft. 11ft Traverse (Bde HQ). Shafter T frame 6ft by 3ft. by 8 inches on M.G. Tunnel all scales CANAL BANK such entrance. On revetting 20 yards VICARS LANE on clearing 20 yards drain and erecting M.G. Emplacement 50 yds cont. WILSON FARM. on clearing 20 yards main laid 30 yards Boards THREADNEEDLE STREET. N.1 and Artillery road and front trolley line BUFF'S ROAD. On M.G. Emplacement VIEW FARM. N.2 and Infantry repaired 20 yards BURNT FARM. Ground filled in, ashes on finish BURNT FARM. **Engineers:-** Starting Trench BOAT LANE & TOCH STREAM. Making BOAT LANE, Frames, Duckboards grain, BOAT LANE, 150 drains, Picket and Gammons.	✓

WAR DIARY or INTELLIGENCE SUMMARY

Army Form C. 2118.

Place	Date	Hour	Summary of Events and Information	Remarks and references to Appendices
A 23.a.2.6. C.25.a.5.9. Nieu[port]	3/4/16		**Strength of Company:** 6 Officers. 220 Other Ranks. H. Infantry from 5 pt. Bde attached. **Work:** *Front Line:* R.E. completing M.G. Emplacement covering Lock Gates and cash also cleared 30 yards drainage WILSON FARM. an fifty scrim and shutters, about-jogged 3/6 c.ft. of well-space built (special) Reinforced passage way, FOCH FARM. R.E. and attached Infantry 50 yards filling (Line). LA BELLE ALLIANCE road. R.E. and Pioneers clearing 100 yards drain at BURNT FARM. Pioneers erect 10 inches h. new track to WILLOW 3'6" by 3'. Pioneers deepens 2'; 50 yards. Pioneers dug 65 ft. new track to WILLOW 3'6" by 3'. Pioneers deepens 2', 2' two rows of cross drains BOAR LANE. A.P. erecting M.G. Emplacements at NEW FARM. **Lyon:** Making Bayonetins, 4 Frames, Pickets and Frameworks.	RES
do	4/4/16		**Strength of Company:** as before. **Work:** *Front Line:* R.E. on M.G. Emplacements repairing supported passage completed and 200 sandbags placed FOCH FARM. R.E. and Infantry emplaced and sample for a box used sandbag dugout and 20 c.ft. also filled bayonets whole regime funnel used after at 14 cam. CANAL BANK DEFENCES. M.G. Tunnel at 14 frames much subsidence, driving second tunnel for work. R.E., attached and Infantry hand 50 ft. LATRIG railway line 20 yards drain filled 50 sandbags which truck suited WILSON FARM. M.G. Emp. Dugouts dugout at and temporarily covered. gutters carried 50 c.ft. night, removed, or roof would have been finished. R.E. and Pioneers filled 300 sandbags and dug 50 yards of drain. BURNT FARM. R.E. and Pioneers thickened parapet 50 yards by 1ft. by 1 yd 13ft. Pioneers BOAT LANE 90 yards of drain cleared. 50 yards cleared of obstruction FOCH STREAM. **Lyon:** Making M.G. Emplacements, Mine Frames, filling Wedges, Pickets and handrails, Windlass for Giant Shaft.	RES

WAR DIARY
or
INTELLIGENCE SUMMARY

Army Form C. 2118.

(Erase heading not required.)

Place	Date	Hour	Summary of Events and Information	Remarks and references to Appendices
U.23.a.2.b. C.23.a.5.a. Sheet 28.	10/4/16		**Strength of Company** 6 Officers. 220 Other ranks. 26 Infantry from 13th Regina returned from 4 Section relieved No 3 Section in CANAL BANK.	
			Front line: N.Z. and Infantry cleared 30 yards drain. Thickened parapet 150'x2'x1'. Filled 50 sandbags with trash. WILSON FARM. – on thickening parapet 10'x2'x1'. Laying 20 trench boards. THREADNEEDLE STREET. – on excavating & repairing trench and revet M.G. Emplacement. HILLTOP FARM. – on carrying material for M.G. Emplacement and during 30 yards drain for same N.G. – on carrying M.G. Emplacement and drawing 10 yards WILSON FARM. – on thickening parapet and revetting 30 yards. – on fixing 16 luminous sign boards on right sub sector. CONEY STREET. N.Z. completed the unfinished passage covert emplacement and passage with two layers rubble, filled sandbags over top & covered and trip and painted for concealment. FOCH FARM. N.Z. working two night shifts and daily from 3am – till 8pm. N.Z. and Infantry 15 yards of parados filled and thickened to 10 12ft by 4ft, 10 yards parapet filled in and coast line twilled. CANAL BANK DEFENCES. 14 frames at started on dug-out Brigade Hqrs Tunnel. NY frames at Wig N.Z and Pioneers Nº5 frames set by N.Z and Pioneers. CANAL BANK M.G. Tunnel by 5pc by N.Z. N.Z and Pioneers filled 200 sandbags. Thickened parapet by 5pc by N.Z for 20 yards. BURNT FARM. N.Z. and Pioneers 150 yards trench 15 July 2'6" revetted 30 yards cleared 150 yards of drain. **Note:** Making 15th Arrivo, 16 Frames, 16 Emplacements, others Frames.	

Place	Date	Hour	Summary of Events and Information	Remarks and references to Appendices
a23.a.1.6. 6.25.a.5.9. Sheet 28	1/14/16		**Strength of Component:** 6 Officers. 220 Other Ranks. 26 Infantry from 59th Brigade attached. **Works:** **Front Line:** R.E. and Infantry thickening parapet and raising parapets 1'0" × 3' × 1'6" drawing 50 yards WILSON CRATER. — on carrying material thickening parapet and laying up Track towards THREADNEEDLE STREET. R.E. thickening walls of shelter, and packing parapet up with trench rubble filled in sandbags 500 bags. Making up shell hole in front and not with peat-moss places and slab slabs. Leaving white with iron matts to make Machine trotting layer. Fitting emplacement with platforms to carry gun mounts. M.Infantry filling sandbags FORT FARM. R.E. and Infantry revived two new 12 ft. Mine Shafts complete with portable sandbagging filling and cutting 90 craters to get right if advanced filled in on other bays and thickened parapet 110 (CAMEL BACK DEFENCES). R.E. and Pioneers on M.G. Tunnels East bank. In filled 6 coats South filled screen. — one Bde Agra Tunnel filled (approx HH4 by 3ft 3in R.E and Infantry widening D20 and WILLOW WALK. R.E. and Pioneers 110 yards new trench 3'×2'. Thickening parapet 1'×3'. 20 yards revetted BOATLANE. Deepened drain 30 yards 1'×2'. Thickened parapet by 3'×1' 10-20 yards BURNT FARM. **Mine:** Making Mining Frames, M.G. Emplacement, loophole, Frames and Framework, N. Frames, cutting grass.	R.E.

Army Form C. 2118.

WAR DIARY
or
INTELLIGENCE SUMMARY.
(Erase heading not required.)

Place	Date	Hour	Summary of Events and Information	Remarks and references to Appendices
A.23.a.2.b. 6.15.a.5.g. Shot 28	12/4/16		**Strength of Company:** 6 Officers 220 Other Ranks. 26 Infantry from 29th Bde attached. **Work:** Front line: N.Z. laying 600 sandbags filling 200 with earth. Two tramway trucks of shelter repairs to square post Guthrie pits and tramway bays. FOUNTON & F. line infantry by day filter and tank trenches parapet. Three two feet bays. M.G. emplacement timber cover at frames front at infiltrates. N.Z. and Pioneers at T. frames held up by new delivery of material got the M.G. gallery. CANAL BANK DEFENCES. N.Z. revetting roof 20 paps viala & clearing drain 30 yards new drain 30 yards. M.G. emplacement filling and laying sandbags of iron trench and covering roof. WILSON FARM. N.Z. and Pioneers filled 500 sandbags. BURNT FARM. Pioneers carrying material for new trench on MARK LANE. N.Z. and attached relaying 25 yds of trolley line LABELLE ALLIANCE N.Z. fixing loophole and securing M.G. emplacement HILLTOP FARM. Batallion relief no infantry at night. Gas Alarm. M.G. emplacement, loophole, Mining Frames, Trolleys, cutting garden.	V.G.
do	13/4/16		**Strength of Company:** 6 Officers 222 Other Ranks. 26 Infantry 29th Bde attached. 2 other ranks from Reserve. **Work:** Front line. N.Z. and Infantry prepared 20 yards of trench for revetting drew 20 yards of drain 100 sandbags with trestle bridges completed. M.G.E. WILSON FARM. — On thickening parapet worked 9 o.c. ft. laid 30 french strokes. THREADNEEDLE STREET N.Z. and Pioneers 50 yards of trench slapped 1'6" x 3'0". 50 yards of new trench drug 2'1 by 3'1 trench put 20 yards dug 3'1 x 2'1 BOAR LANE. — on thickening parapet. 3'16', x 10' long. BURNT FARM. N.Z. thickening walls of shelter with rubble filled sandbags repairing 229 yds of tramway with pit props and covering with iron trench improving loophole screen and shelter. Infantry filling sandbags. FORT FARM. N.Z. and infantry finished sandbagging and thickening. 2 bays filling and thickening parapet and parados. N.Z. Pioneers tunnelling east. Bank. N.Z. Pioneers 5.10 filling N.Z. and Pioneers 1500 MGs at Yarnco. CANAL BANK DEFENCES. N.Z. Pioneers 150 ax M.G. emplacement. Trenches, Firm steps.	V.G.

1577 Wt. W10791 H730 500009 9/15 D.D. & L. (A D55) Forms C2118 (10)

WAR DIARY
or
INTELLIGENCE SUMMARY
(Erase heading not required.)

Army Form C. 2118

Place	Date	Hour	Summary of Events and Information	Remarks and references to Appendices
A.23.a.2.6. C.25.a.5.9. Neuve'28	1/4/16		**Strength of Company:** 6 Officers 223 Other Ranks. 16 Infantry from 5th Brigade attached. 1 Officer joined Coy from TOUTEN. LT. W.E. LAING evacuated to Base sick. **Works: Front Line:** No 1 and Infantry: 150 new sandbags over old 30 monitoring frames, cleared 45 yards of trench 20 yards drain, shelter over 10 yards filled and 50 sandbags used taken. Refilled and repaired all the foot gangways, WILSON FARM — on clearing 130 x 3 x 1 feet layer 20 trench boards THREADNEEDLE STREET, in trenching layer of tracks on new 140 sandbags [illegible] thick trench nettle traverse, over 5"— on digging new trench from BOOT LANE to the WILLOW [illegible] 15 yds 3 x 16" by 3 ft dug and laid 15 ft trench boards. FOCH FARM. 2 traps made up and to tell with the same parapet, sanitary arrangement over fire steps. CANAL BANK. M.G. Emmt. N six frame set in 5 trench. M.G. Emmt. B hands at B.o. H.O tunnel, framed set, LA BELLE ALLIANCE, 20 200 ft revetted and 15 yards laid and cleared N.O new trench hoarding, LA BELLE ALLIANCE, 20 BRIDGE Railway. N.2 and Infantry: improving drain system from VIK to SAP. BOAR LANE. the revetting parapet VIX by 15 for 30 yds. 30 yds revetted. VAN's V. STREET. N.2 clearing 50 yards of deck X.Q. MG. Emplacements. Relieved R.E. placing and covered in WILSON FARM. **Loss:** Mining Frames, Fascing steps, Duck board, M.G. emplacement	RH
do	2/4/16		**Strength of Company:** 6 Officers. 1 other attached. 5/1st CANAL BANK. LT LAING evacuated to Base sick. **Works: Front Line:** N. 1 and Infantry: 40 yards concrete sent in 580 M.G. Emplacement erecting frame for new sap to cellar revetting 30 yards revetted forepart 100 x 3 x 1 feet, WILSON FARM. — on thickening [illegible] 150 x 4 x 1 laying 30 trench boards THREADNEEDLE STREET. 1x clearing [illegible] and repairing trench replaces. [illegible] land layer on BOUNDARY — BOSS ROAD. BRIDGE No 6 LA BELLE ALLIANCE. R.2 and Infantry: thickening parapet 4 on 10 sandbags laid FORY. N.S. on tracking M.G. Emplacement, QUINCY STREET. — on sitting around to step. No 3 N Sunday. Wilson made and sanitary between separate outside communication trench of van BOOR LANG. G.R. WILLOWS. N.3 and N.S. Nelson 150 yards 3" to 3" and laid trench boards the whole way. 15 yards Nechloch across tunnel and 25 yards BOOT LANE will complete the trench. POCK FARM two trunks filled sandbagged and 100 yards over reverted to current into (2)en. M.G. Emplacement funnel. N. Sap. 3 frames. Q. Sap. 3 frames. B. d. frames. CANAL DEFENCES. R. 2 and Rowers 10 yards disposed of MG, 100 yards of bullet cleared. Machine gun for his own work, BOOR LANE.	RH

Signed: Making Special Bridge.

WAR DIARY
or
INTELLIGENCE SUMMARY.
(Erase heading not required.)

Army Form C. 2118.

Place	Date	Hour	Summary of Events and Information	Remarks and references to Appendices
23.a.2.6. 25.a.5.9. Sheet 28	1/16/16		**Strength of Company:** 6 Officers. 223 Other Ranks. 26 Infantry from 39th Brigade attached. Remainder of Company afternoon. 1/2 Company off Headquarters. Attached Infantry left Company.	
			Work. Front line. Guide ways in other and opening out in wall for entrance, concrete slab in M.G. Emplacement started. WILSON FARM. M.G. Emplacement 1/2 thickened trench eaves. FOCH FARM. New Communication Trench from BROOKLANE 6 to the WILLOWS. 1/2 cleared 30 yards. 1/2 boarded flood arch opening off TUNNEL 13A H.Q. on cleaning M.G. Emplacement in sylla x.9 arming M.G. Emplacement reported. HILLTOP FARM. On thickening parapet at 3 M.G. Emplacement. COTMILL FM. cutting clearing trench, M.G. Emplacement, packets and traverses.	R.E.2
			Eqpt. cutting clearing trench, as before.	
	17/4/16.		**Strength of Company:** as before. Company marched into fresh billets at HERZEELE for period of training equal.	R.E.2
HERZEELE	18/4/16.		**Strength of Company:** as before. Physical Drill. Rifle Exercises etc.	R.E.2
do	19/4/16.		**Strength of Company:** as before. Physical Drill. Drill & Rifle Exercises etc.	R.E.2
do.	20/4/16.		**Strength of Company:** as before. Detail as on 19th inst.	R.E.2

WAR DIARY
or
INTELLIGENCE SUMMARY

(Erase heading not required.)

Army Form C. 2118

Instructions regarding War Diaries and Intelligence Summaries are contained in F.S. Regs., Part II. and the Staff Manual respectively. Title Pages will be prepared in manuscript.

Place	Date	Hour	Summary of Events and Information	Remarks and references to Appendices
HERZEELE	21/4/16		Strength of Company :- As before. Drill & Rifle Exercises & Physical Drill. Held W/who Lecture & Instruction to 10th R.I.R.	RR
do	22/4/16		Strength of Company :- As before. Drill etc as on 21st. Held W/who Lecture & Instruction to 10th R.I.R.	RR
do	23/4/16		Strength of Company :- As before. Drill etc as on 22nd. 2 Officers, 95 N.C.Os & men left Company for work on L. Defences	RR
do	24/4/16		Strength of Company :- As before. Drill etc as before. Held W/who Lecture & Instruction to 11th R.I.R. Lt. L.B.—	RR
do	25/4/16		Strength of Company :- As before. Drill etc as before. Held W/who Lecture & Instruction to 11th R.I.R. Lt. L.B. Defences	RR
do	26/4/16		O.C. Company proceeded to L.4. L.B. trading life waganais. Lt. L.4. L.B.	RR
do	27/4/16		Strength of Company :- As before, and 3 men joined Company from ROUEN Company marched to fresh billets at WINNIZEELE. Rev. Com yield works. Lt. L.4. L.B.	RR

1875 Wt. W593/826 1,000,000 4/15 J.B.C. & A. A.D.S.S./Forms/C. 2118.

WAR DIARY
or
INTELLIGENCE SUMMARY

Army Form C. 2118

Place	Date	Hour	Summary of Events and Information	Remarks and references to Appendices
WINNIZEELE	28/4/16		Strength of Company:- As before. Cleaning up new Billets, Hygiene arrangements, Rifle exercises etc.	Ref
	29/4/16		Strength of Coy as before. As before. Drill, Hygiene arrangements, Rifle exercises etc. Coy Ref Lt. L.G.	Ref
	30/4/16		Strength of Company:- As before. 6 men proceeded to join Cpl Edwards for work on Adv. Coy K.L.M & N Camps Yeiza works Lt. L.G. Lt. L.G.	Ref

MAJOR, R.E.
COMDG. 96TH Fd. COY. R.E.

96 FCRE
Vol 8
✗✗

CONFIDENTIAL.

WAR DIARY

OF

96TH FIELD COY. R.E.

FROM MAY 1st to 31st, 1916.

(VOLUME VII)

Army Form C. 2118

WAR DIARY
or
INTELLIGENCE SUMMARY
(Erase heading not required.)

Instructions regarding War Diaries and Intelligence Summaries are contained in F. S. Regs., Part II. and the Staff Manual respectively. Title Pages will be prepared in manuscript.

Place	Date	Hour	Summary of Events and Information	Remarks and references to Appendices
WINNIZEELE	1/5/16		Strength of Company:- 6 Officers 223 Other Ranks. 79 Horses & Mules. Field Works Instruction to 30th K.R.R Pioneers. Physical Drill, Rifle Exercises etc. Detachment of Company on L Defences rejoined Company	A2
do	2/5/16		Strength of Company:- as before. Field Works Instruction to 30th K.R.R Pioneers. 10th R/B Physical Drill, Rifle Exercises	A2
do	3/5/16		Strength of Company:- as before. Field Works Instructing to 30th K.R.R Pioneers. Physical Drill, Rifle exercises on Welder Heath. Musketry, Range finding, Field Geometry, Explosives.	A2
do	4/5/16		Strength of Company:- as before. Field Works Instruction to 30th K.R.R Pioneers. do to men who have joined Coy since January. Physical Drill, White exercises on Welder Heath. Musketry, Range finding, Field Geometry, Explosives	A2

Army Form C. 2118

Instructions regarding War Diaries and Intelligence Summaries are contained in F.S. Regs., Part II. and the Staff Manual respectively. Title Pages will be prepared in manuscript.

WAR DIARY
or
INTELLIGENCE SUMMARY
(Erase heading not required.)

Place	Date	Hour	Summary of Events and Information	Remarks and references to Appendices
WINNEZEELE	5/5/16		Strength of Company :- As before except sent to LAIN & when 1/6 strength of field Works Instruction to Infantry of 59th Bde. do do to 28 WAR Pioneers do do to recently joined men of Company. Musevee Drill & Rifle Exercises	RE/
do	6/5/16		Strength of Company :- 6 Officers 223 Other Ranks. 79 Horses & Mules. 2/Lt. H.T. ANDREW joined Company. Field Works Instruction to 28 WAR also recently joined men of Coy. Drill & Rifle Exercises Wiring on Welded Treatle Explosives Company inspected at work by XIVth Corps Commander.	RE.
do	7/5/16 (Sunday)		Strength of Company :- As before.	RE2.
do	8/5/16		Strength of Company :- As before. Company inspected on Parade by Chief Engineer, Second Army.	RE.
do	9/5/16		Strength of Company :- As before. 4 Officers 134 NCO's & men. 15 Horses & Mules with 2 G.S. Carts & 2 limbers left Company for attachment to Guards Division in forward area. Remainder of Company cleaning up two new dated Billets.	RE2
do	10/5/16		Strength of Company :- As before. (No 66857 Cpl. Stevenson wounded). Steps: Field Works Instruction to recently joined men of Company.	RE.

WAR DIARY or INTELLIGENCE SUMMARY

Army Form C. 2118

Place	Date	Hour	Summary of Events and Information	Remarks and references to Appendices
WINNIZEELE	11/5/16		Strength of Company :- As before. Steps :- Great Works General Instruction to recently joined men - firing into tent. Attached Forward party :- Canal Bank.	R.E.
do	12/5/16		Strength of Company :- As before less 3 Sappers taken off strength. Steps :- Great Works General Instruction to recently joined men. Attached Forward party. Detached Friends Dinn. Ouy-outs East Canal Bank.	R.E.
do	13/5/16		Strength of Company :- As before. Steps :- Great Works General Instruction to recently joined men Forward party. Detached Friends Dinn. Dugouts East Canal Bank.	R.E.
do	14/5/16 (Sunday)		Strength of Company :- As before. Lt ANDREW joined Steps from forward party. Forward party :- Detached Friends Dinn. Dugouts East Canal Bank.	R.E.
do	15/5/16		Strength of Company :- As before. Steps :- Great Works General Instruction to recently joined men. Forward party :- Detached Friends Dinn. Dugouts East Canal Bank.	R.E.

WAR DIARY or INTELLIGENCE SUMMARY

Army Form C. 2118

Place	Date	Hour	Summary of Events and Information	Remarks and references to Appendices
WINNIZEELE	16/5/16		Strength of Company:- As before. Sappers:- Field Works. General Instruction to recently joined men. Forward party detached from Aire. Bryants East Canal Bank	RE2
do	17/5/16		Strength of Company:- As before. Sappers:- Helping in trenches & clearing away material from gun instruction ground. Forward party:- Detached from Aire. Bryants East Canal Bank	RE2
do	18/5/16		Strength of Company:- as before. Sappers:- Clearing wagons & clearing up Anne Lines & Billets. Forward party:- Detached from Aire. Bryants East Canal Bank	RE2
do	19/5/16		Strength of Company:- As before. Sappers:- All ready to move (Infy quarter) taken off strength and marched to new Billets at H.7.a. Sheet 28. (Dismounted) A.28.c. Forward party:- Detached from Aire. Bryants East Canal Bank.	RE2
H.7.a. A.28.c. Sheet 28	20/5/16		Strength of Company:- as before. Work:- Altering, repairing & clearing up new Billets on arrival of 19/5/16.	RE2
do	21/5/16		Strength of Company:- as before. Work:- as on previous day.	RE2

WAR DIARY or INTELLIGENCE SUMMARY

Army Form C. 2118

Place	Date	Hour	Summary of Events and Information	Remarks and references to Appendices
H.7.a. A.28.c. Sheet 28	22/5/16		Strength of Company:- As before. 3u men (Carpenters) from 59th Coy R.E. joined Company. No 3 Section of Company left for YPRES to prepare billets. Work:- Making cook stoves, Dining Room, Tool Shelters etc.	
do @ YPRES.	23/5/16		Strength of Company:- As before. LT. R.W. FORMBY joined Company. Work:- No 3 Section preparing Billets at YPRES	
do	24/5/16		Strength of Company:- Company working in Camp as on 22/5/16 5 men non steamers to work on Right Regt station, WORMHOUDT. Remainder of Company joined Company. 21 man joined Company. Work:- No 3 Section preparing Billets at YPRES. Making tables etc & preparing tool Shelters etc & working on repairs etc at Thorne Since.	
do	25/5/16		Strength of Company:- As before. Work:- As on 24th	
do	26/5/16		Strength of Company:- As before, less 2 men taken off strength. M = 225. 2 Sapper Tradesmen attached to Young Major YPRES for work on Dumps	
do	27/5/16		Strength of Company:- As before. Work:- No 3 Section party of half Section on Billets at YPRES. Attgts:- Work as before on Water Supply. In addition purposes of Instruction of work at Anne School of Instruction	

WAR DIARY or INTELLIGENCE SUMMARY

Army Form C. 2118

96th FIELD COMPANY R.E.

Place	Date	Hour	Summary of Events and Information	Remarks and references to Appendices
H.7a. A.26.c. Sheet 28. YPRES	28/5/16		Strength of Company :- As before. Works :- No 3 Section Party from hos. on Billets at YPRES. Shops :- Blacksmiths Shop, Fitters etc at Horse Lines, experimented wiring on sheds for A.S.C. Dump, on work at Army School.	
do	29/5/16		Strength of Company :- As before. Works :- No 3 Section Party from hos. on Billets at YPRES. Shops :- On repairs etc to Camp at Horse Lines, making collapsible Water Supply for Ablution purposes, on sheds for A.S.C. Dump, on water troughs at POPERINGHE, on work at Divne School of Instruction. NIGHT :- A.S. Pioneers on "STRAND" cleaning reclaiming, draining, laying Trench Boards - and Trench to White Chateau Defence	
do	30/5/16		Strength of Company :- As before. (11 O.R.'s Carpenters attached) Works :- No 3 Section Party of No 4 on Billets at YPRES Shops :- On Camp at Horse Lines - making collapsible wiring - on shirt for Intelligence Officer - on Shed for A.S.C. Dump - on Stove for Dump Shops - on Divne School of Instruction - Carpenters working on shape. NIGHT :- A.S.Pioneers on "STRAND" & "FLEET ST" cleaning draining & laying Trench Boards - excavating trench for White Chateau Defence & repairing West Face.	

1875. Wt. W593/326 1,000,000 4/15 J.B.C. & A. A.D.S.S./Forms/C. 2118.

Army Form C. 2118.

WAR DIARY
or
INTELLIGENCE SUMMARY.

(Erase heading not required.)

Instructions regarding War Diaries and Intelligence
Summaries are contained in F. S. Regs., Part II.
and the Staff Manual respectively. Title pages
will be prepared in manuscript.

Place	Date	Hour	Summary of Events and Information	Remarks and references to Appendices
H.Q. a A.2 & C Sheet 28 YPRES	21/5/16.		Strength of Company :- As before. Work :- On Billets at YPRES Day :- On Camp at Thomas River - On Shed at A.S.C Dump - on Shut for Intelligence Officers - on Shelter Trenches for Camp - Carpenters in Shops etc. NIGHT :- AS 18 works excavating trench for white Chateau Defences; on sides of West Lane - on FLEET St, STRAND clearing, draining & laying trench boards.	[signature]

[signature]
MAJOR, R.E.
COMDG. 96TH F4 COY; R.E.

June
96 F.C. R.E.
Vol 9

CONFIDENTIAL

WAR DIARY

OF

96TH FIELD Coy. R.E.

FROM JUNE 1st to 30th 1916.

(VOLUME VIII)

WAR DIARY or INTELLIGENCE SUMMARY

Army Form C. 2118.

Instructions regarding War Diaries and Intelligence Summaries are contained in F.S. Regs., Part II. and the Staff Manual respectively. Title pages will be prepared in manuscript.

(Erase heading not required.)

95th FIELD COMPANY R.E.

Place	Date	Hour	Summary of Events and Information	Remarks and references to Appendices
H & a. E E A 2 & C. Coach 28 YPRES	1/6/16	DAY	Strength of Company: 7 Officers, 217 Other Ranks, 80 Horses & Mules. Works: Shops. Making Sheds for A.S.C. Dump - completing Shelter pit YPRES 3. Section to Ruyters Hut for Intelligence Officer - on new Dump Road Station at WORMHOUDT - Shelter Trenches for Camp - new Dump Steps. Carpenters in Workshops. YPRES. Strengthening Ruhmered Billets, forming air spaces, generally protecting. Defence Work. A. & B. Pioneers laying Trench Boards in FLEET St & STRAND. A & B Pioneers on WHITE CHATEAU Defences - Cleaning FLEET St & STRAND - building up parapets of HAYMARKET.	A/2
		NIGHT		
ditto	2/6/16	DAY	Strength of Company: As before. Works: Shops. As on previous day. YPRES. Works or Billets as on previous days. Defence Work. A&B Pioneers on WHITE CHATEAU Defences - on WEST LANE Trs. shell damage & revetting sides.	A/2
		NIGHT		
ditto	3/6/16	DAY	Strength of Company: As before. Works. Shops. On Water Trough at POPERINGHE - new Dump Steps - new Dump Boat Station at WORMHOUDT for Camp - Sheds for A.S.C. Dump - new Dump Boat Station at WORMHOUDT - Carpenters in Workshops.	A/2

Army Form C. 2118.

WAR DIARY
or
INTELLIGENCE SUMMARY.
(Erase heading not required.)

Instructions regarding War Diaries and Intelligence Summaries are contained in F. S. Regs., Part II. and the Staff Manual respectively. Title pages will be prepared in manuscript.

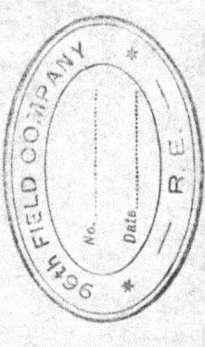
96th FIELD COMPANY R.E.

Place	Date	Hour	Summary of Events and Information	Remarks and references to Appendices
H & A 8 8 A 28. C Sheet 28 YPRES	2/6/16 (contd)	DAY	YPRES. Strengthening & protecting Billets Defence Works: R.E. & Pioneers on STRAND & FLEET St, shaping sides, sandbagging & building up parapet.	
		NIGHT	R.E. & Pioneers on WHITE CHATEAU Defence - on STRAND & FLEET St shaping trench, deepening drains & ditches & deepening main drain West of X line. R.E. Cavalry & Infantry on HORNWORKS, getting up material & wiring.	R.E.
ditto	4/6/16	DAY	Strength of Company: As before. Work: On new Annexe shops - Annexe Rest Station at WORMHOUDT - Shelter Trenches for Camp. Sundry small jobs. Carpenters in Workshops. Refuse Works. Tracing Water Tanks on RAMPARTS at YPRES - an drainage of FLEET ST. & STRAND. (R.E. & Pioneers)	
		NIGHT	R.E. Pioneers on Assembly slits at X 8 & CONGREVE WALK - forming slits at X 3 and X 4. and F 13 R.E. & Cavalry on HORN WORKS. Wiring (Infantry carrying parts) R.E.'s Infantry at ÉCOLE, preparing Billets.	R.E.

Army Form C. 2118.

WAR DIARY
or
INTELLIGENCE SUMMARY.
(Erase heading not required.)

Instructions regarding War Diaries and Intelligence Summaries are contained in F. S. Regs., Part II. and the Staff Manual respectively. Title pages will be prepared in manuscript.

96th FIELD COMPANY R.E.

Place	Date	Hour	Summary of Events and Information	Remarks and references to Appendices
H.8.a.8.8. A.28.c. Sheet 28 YPRES	5/4/16	DAY	Strength of Company:- As before. Works:- Strips. On new Pierd Strips - on Shelter Trenches for Camp - sundry small jobs. - Carpenters in Workshop. YPRES party. Revetting etc École. do Clearing cellars at École (Infantry assisting). Defence Work. R.E.'s Pioneers on Assembly slits at F.13. x 8. x 6. x 2. x 3 x 4 ft. on CONGREVE'S WALK revetting. D.D.'s Cavalry wiring at HORN WORKS (Infantry carrying party)	R.E.
do	6/4/16	DAY	Strength of Company:- 3 Other Ranks leave. Works:- Strips. On new Bund Strips, making Box drains, Boxes etc & sundry odd jobs. Carpenters in Workshop. Defence Work. R.E. & Pioneers on WEST LANE, raising parapets on South side South of ROULERS Rly. YPRES party. Preparing Cellars at École.	R.E.

T2134. Wt. W708—776. 500000. 4/15. Sir J. C. & S.

Army Form C. 2118.

WAR DIARY
or
INTELLIGENCE SUMMARY.
(Erase heading not required.)

Instructions regarding War Diaries and Intelligence Summaries are contained in F. S. Regs., Part II. and the Staff Manual respectively. Title pages will be prepared in manuscript.

96th FIELD COMPANY
No.
Date.
R.E.

Place	Date	Hour	Summary of Events and Information	Remarks and references to Appendices
H 8 & 8.8 A.26.c Sheet 28 YPRES	8/6/16	DAY	Strength of Company: As before. Work: On new Dunn Trench. – Making Box Drains – making Bench – Sundry small jobs. – Carpenters in Workshop.	
		NIGHT	Defence Work: – R.E. Pioneers & Infantry on new X line digging trenches – R.E. Pioneers repairing parapet of WEST LANE South side of ROULERS Rly.	R.W.
do	8/6/16		Strength of Company: As before. Work: As on previous day.	R.W.
do	9/6/16	DAY	Work: – Sig.n: On new Dunn Trench – making Boxes etc. – Carpenters in Shop. Defence Work: – R.E. Pioneers on new X line digging trench. – R.E. Pioneers raising South parapet WEST LANE South of ROULERS Rly. – Others digging Assembly Slits X2, X3, X4. – R.E.& Infantry preparing cellars ÉCOLE – Rifle Butts, Infantry wiring.	R.W.
do	10/6/16	DAY	Strength of Company: As before. Work: On new Dunn Trench – making Boxes for Deep Trench Mortar Stands etc.	R.W.

T2134. Wt. W708–776. 500000. 4/15. Sir J.C.& S.

WAR DIARY
or
INTELLIGENCE SUMMARY.
(Erase heading not required.)

Army Form C. 2118.

Place	Date	Hour	Summary of Events and Information	Remarks and references to Appendices
H.6.a.8.8. A.26.c. Sheet 28. YPRES.	16/6/16 (contd)		Defence Work:- R.E. on chute F13 - A.E. & Pioneers on WEST LANE - R.E. Pioneers & Infantry on new X line - Pioneers on assembly chute X3 and X4	R.E.
do	1/6/16		Strength of Company:- As before.	
		DAY	Work:- Aagr:- Making Gun Emp - Gun Recess - Trench Mortar Stands - working on new Assembly Shafts.	R.E.
		NIGHT	Defence Work:- Pioneers on chute at F13, X3 and X4 - R.E. & Pioneers & Infantry on new X line - Pioneers on WEST LANE - R.E. & Infantry wiring at HORN WORKS - Preparing Billets at ECOLE - Laying water pipes & fixing tanks in RAMPARTS	
do	17/6/16	DAY	Strength of Company:- As before.	
		DAY	Work:- Aagr:- On new Gun Emps:- Making Trench Mortar Stands - Dinner small jobs - Carpenters in Workshop. No work in Line.	R.E.

Army Form C. 2118.

WAR DIARY
or
INTELLIGENCE SUMMARY.
(Erase heading not required.)

Instructions regarding War Diaries and Intelligence Summaries are contained in F. S. Regs., Part II. and the Staff Manual respectively. Title pages will be prepared in manuscript.

96th FIELD COMPANY
No. ....
Date ....

Place	Date	Hour	Summary of Events and Information	Remarks and references to Appendices
H.6.a.8.8 A.28.c. Sheet 28 YPRES	13/6/16	DAY	**Strength of Company**: As before. **Work**: Stiff: On new Dunn Steps. Collection school A.E.S. Baths at YPRES. Making Trench Mortar Stands. Sgn. Boards etc. Carpenters in Workshop. Forward parties: R.E. preparing billets at ECOLE. R.E. on water tanks at Sally Port near LILLE GATE.	R.E.
		NIGHT	**Defence Work**: R.E. Pioneers on new X line. Pioneers on assembly slits at X3.	
do	14/6/16	DAY	**Strength of Company**: As before. **Work**: Stiff: On new Dunn Steps. Making Bee Drains. Bomb Area. Trench Mortar Stands. Sgn. Boards etc. Forward party: R.E. Pioneers on new X line. Pioneers raising earth parapet of WEST LANE. R.E. on WHITE CHATEAU Defences. Pioneers revetting Assembly slits X4. Erecting tanks at Sally Port near LILLE GATE.	R.E.
do	15/6/16	DAY	**Strength of Company**: As before. **Work**: Stiff: On new Dunn Steps. Making Bee Drains. Bomb Area. Trench Mortar Stands. Sgn. Boards etc.	R.E.

T2134. Wt. W708—776. 500000. 4/15. Sir J. C. & B.

WAR DIARY
or
INTELLIGENCE SUMMARY.

(Erase heading not required.)

Army Form C. 2118.

Place	Date	Hour	Summary of Events and Information	Remarks and references to Appendices
H.2 a.3.c. A.2.b.c. Sheet 28. YPRES	15/6/16 (cont)	DAY	Forward party: — R.E. fitting up Water Tanks. — Preparing ECOLE as Billet	
		NIGHT	R.E. & Pioneers on new X line. digging draining revetting. — Pioneers	R.E.
			on KNIET Salient, thickening parapet. Pioneers & clearing trench. — Pioneers	R.E.
			digging revetting extension of XE. — Pioneers raising parapet of	
			GARDEN STREET. — R.E. & Cavalry wiring HORN WORKS (Infantry carrying)	
do	16/6/16		Strength of Company: — As before except Capt Chapman taken ill strength	
		DAY	Stage: — Making beds for ECOLE. Wire Brims for Bomb trough, fitting up	
			Water Tanks for YPRES Water Supply. — Making collapsible Wire entanglements etc	
			Defence Works: — R.E. on new X line, clearing back beam filling & laying Sandbags. —	R.E.
		NIGHT	R.E. clearing drain to new X line. — Pioneers on extension of	
			HAYMARKET. — Pioneers on GARDEN STREET clearing drain & cutting for 3	
			new traverses. — Pioneers on extension of new X line — R.E. fitting	
			Water tanks for Water Supply at YPRES.	
do	17/6/16	DAY	Strength of Company: — As before.	
			Stage: — Making Bee Drains, Trench Water Stands, collapsible Wire	
			Entanglements, Beds for ECOLE etc.	R.E.
			Forward party: — On ECOLE, starting & forming air spaces.	

Army Form C. 2118.

WAR DIARY
or
INTELLIGENCE SUMMARY.
(Erase heading not required.)

Instructions regarding War Diaries and Intelligence Summaries are contained in F. S. Regs., Part II. and the Staff Manual respectively. Title pages will be prepared in manuscript.

96th FIELD COMPANY
No.
Date
R. E.

Place	Date	Hour	Summary of Events and Information	Remarks and references to Appendices
H.Q. A.S.C. A.S.C. Shell St. YPRES	12/6/16	NIGHT	Defence Work:- Pioneers on real X line extension - pinning WEST LANE - Pioneers running South parapet of WEST LANE - Pioneers on entrance of HAYMARKET - No 3 as before North of WEST LANE	RE
do	13/6/16		Strength of Company :- As before	
		DAY	Work :- Hqrs: Making Box drains - French trench mortar stands - Beds for ECOLE - collecting RE stores	
			W.M. Entanglement - Sign Boards etc	
			Defence Work :- Fitting of Water Tanks - Pioneers on extension of new RE x line - No 3 draining WEST LANE - No 3 completing M.G.E. at	
	NIGHT		F15 - Pioneers on X? lying frames - No 3 Infantry sleeping cellars at ECOLE forming suitable ventilating doorways	
do	14/6/16		Strength of Company :- As before	
	DAY		Work :- Hqrs: On 'E' Camp - Making Wire Entanglements - Beds for ECOLE etc	
			Tramrod huts, R.M. cellar at ECOLE - starting forming up shed	
	NIGHT		Defence Work :- Drains of drainage of Grand - Place near line 3 of WEST LANE - No ?	RE
			Standing near X line N of WEST LANE building etc - Similar arrangement	
			huts - B Infantry as cellars at ECOLE - pump opened trapdoors for	
			S.A. - No on water tanks in YPRES	

WAR DIARY or INTELLIGENCE SUMMARY

Army Form C. 2118.

Place	Date	Hour	Summary of Events and Information	Remarks and references to Appendices
H.Q. 96. 2.3.&4. Sections YPRES	20/6/16	DAY	Strength of Company: As before. Sap Road sent to No 2 Sap Yuldren before section relieved No 2 section at YPRES. Work: Sapper: On "C" Camp - making sign posts - wire entanglements - Road to ÉCOLE - sign boards - Yser Steps etc. Infantry fatigue: At Bn Infantry preparing ÉCOLE for Billet - 203 inf. putting up Water Tanks. Pioneer on extension of revêtement - also drainage of STRAND 9 ÉCOLE Sap - Runners to & fro also 14 - 14's Scheme also to Zn. No Infantry working - No carrying parties	
do	21/6/16	DAY	Strength of Company: As before. Sappers: On "C" Camp - Road to ÉCOLE - Wire Entanglements Yser Steps etc. Infantry party: No on ÉCOLE cleaning cellars etc. At Bn Infantry on new X line wiring sandbagging etc - Pioneer on drainage of X line relieving French X line - Concrete cleaning STRAND & FLEET St & cleaning - No letting up Water Tanks - No on avenue firestep - Pioneer erecting 4 Steel M.L.	

WAR DIARY
or
INTELLIGENCE SUMMARY.
(Erase heading not required.)

Army Form C. 2118.

96th FIELD COMPANY R.E.

Place	Date	Hour	Summary of Events and Information	Remarks and references to Appendices
ABA 88 A.19.c.c. Sheet 26	21/8/16		Strength of Company:- as before.	
YPRES		DAY	Styles: On "O" Camp - Making Duck Stops. Wire entanglements etc. Forward party:- N°. 3 advanced section team in ÉCOLE.	
		NIGHT	N°. 2 Infantry on new X Line - clearing entrances - Pioneers. Infantry clearing new earthwork - Pioneers & Sappers finish. Pioneers revetting slit X.4. - Pioneers in GRAND X EXP. St. Pz cleaning relaying. - N°. 3 infantry relaying parapet WEST LANE - N°. 3 infantry & sappers billets at ÉCOLE. N° on Water Supply	
do	22/8/16	DAY	Strength of Company:- as before. Styles: On new D.H.Q. - Making Duck Stops. Wire entanglements etc. w/forward party:- N°. 3 infantry & Pioneers on new X line - battening trench revetting. Clinching new earthwork - Pioneers revetting.	
		NIGHT	Slite X.4. - N°. 3 Infantry in ÉCOLE sandbagging latrine. N° on water supply. - R.E.S. & Pioneers retired - Ruts St Pz.	

WAR DIARY
or
INTELLIGENCE SUMMARY.
(Erase heading not required.)

Army Form C. 2118.

Place	Date	Hour	Summary of Events and Information	Remarks and references to Appendices
HEADQUARTERS École des Garçons	24/6/16		Strength of Company: As before.	
YPRES		DAY Work:	Staple: On new D.H.Q. - making Y-wire Stop. Wire Entanglements etc. "Inward parties": R.E. Infantry on ÉCOLE - shutting a new begger.	
		NIGHT	R.E. fitting up Water Yards for YPRES Water Suppl. - R.E. Infantry on ÉCOLE - R.E. Infantry cutting drain for new X Line - Pioneers excavating new X Line towards MENIN ROAD - R.E. laying improving French towards ONSTAPND - R.E. Infantry on given front - Pioneers digging drain for	P.E.
			FLEET St. - Infantry as given party on new X line drains. STRAND - R.E Pioneers Infantry.	
do	25/6/16		Strength of Company: As before.	
		DAY Work:	Staple: On new D.H.Q. making Y-wire Stop. Wire Entanglements etc. "Inward parties": R.E. Infantry on cellars at ÉCOLE	
		NIGHT	R.E. Infantry on ÉCOLE - on new X Line North of WEST LANE, digging drains & trench.	P.E.
			2/6th REGT. J.H. 7/6th ANDREW H.T. a/Sergt WRAY T.J. & Spr PURSELL W killed (night) by H.E. shell in RUE CARTON.	

WAR DIARY
or
INTELLIGENCE SUMMARY.

(Erase heading not required.)

Army Form C. 2118.

Place	Date	Hour	Summary of Events and Information	Remarks and references to Appendices
H.2. a. 8.8 A. 28. c. Sheet 28 YPRES	27/6/16	DAY	Strength of Company: 11 Officers 210 Rank & File. 2/Lt Stewart Miller joined H.Qrs. Others on D.H.Q. – making Trench Stops & Wire entanglements etc. Forward Parts. – R.E. Infantry on new X line at ÉCOLE	R.E.
		NIGHT	R.E. Infantry on new X Line between WEST LANE & HAY MARKET – R.E. Infantry Working Parties at ECOLE – R.E. on water carts.	
do	28/6/16	DAY	Strength of Company: As before. 2/Lt. K.C.M HANDS joined Company. Works: Same. On new D.H.Q. – making Trench Stops & Wire entanglements etc. Forward parts. R.E. on cellars at ECOLE.	R.E.
		NIGHT	R.E. working on new X line. – R.E. Infantry on ECOLE – R.E on Water tanks YPRES.	
do	29/6/16	DAY	Strength of Company: As before. Works: Same. On new D.H.Q. – making Trench Stops & Wire entanglements etc. Forward parts. R.E. Infantry on ECOLE	R.E.
		NIGHT	Pioneers on new X line, south of WEST LANE – R.E. on new X Line POTIZE end. – R.E. Infantry on ECOLE – R.E. on Water tanks YPRES – Pioneers on HAYMARKET. – Officers on GRAND –	R.E.

WAR DIARY
or
INTELLIGENCE SUMMARY.
(Erase heading not required.)

Army Form C. 2118.

Place	Date	Hour	Summary of Events and Information	Remarks and references to Appendices
H.8.a.16.8 A.28.C. Sheet 28 YPRES.	29/6/16		Strength of Company: As before. 2/Lt A.M. WILLATS & F.S.E EMBERTON joined Company. 18 Infantry Carpenters from 59th Brigade joined Company.	P.F.Sy
		DAY	Work: On new D.H.Q. – Making Yser Stops, Wire Entanglements etc. Covered party: R.B. Infantry on ÉCOLE.	
		NIGHT	R.B. Infantry on ÉCOLE. – R.B. Infantry on Water Tanks. YPRES.	
do.	30/6/16	DAY	Strength of Company: As before. Work: On new D.H.Q. – Making Yser Stops, Wire Entanglements etc. Covered party: R.B. Infantry on ÉCOLE.	P.F.S
		NIGHT	R.B. Pioneers, Infantry on new X line – drain dug, trench deepened, widened, trench boards laid. – R.B. Infantry on ÉCOLE. – R.B. on fitting up Water Tanks. YPRES.	

20th Divisional Engineers

96th FIELD COMPANY R. E.

JULY 1916

July. Vol 10

SECRET

Army Form C. 2118.

WAR DIARY
or
INTELLIGENCE SUMMARY.
(Erase heading not required.)

96th FIELD COMPANY R.E.

Instructions regarding War Diaries and Intelligence Summaries are contained in F. S. Regs., Part II. and the Staff Manual respectively. Title pages will be prepared in manuscript.

Hd. Qrs. 20th Divn.
Forwarded M Prevost
Col. C.R.E. 20th Divn.

Place	Date	Hour	Summary of Events and Information	Remarks and references to Appendices
H.2.6.6.8 A.26.c.8.8 Sheet 28 YPRES	1/7/16		Strength of Company:- 7 Officers. 310 Other Ranks. 78 Horses Mules attached:- 17 Carpenters from 59th Brigade. 13 Infantry loading party from 59th. 60th & 61st Brigades	R.E.
		DAY Works:-	Artyge:- On new D.H.Q. - making Gun Stops. Wire Entanglements etc.	
		NIGHT	Forward party:- On new X line - 2nd Infantry on ECOLE - N.B.13.b.1.9 on Water Supply YPRES. - R.E. on STRAND & HAYMARKET.	
do	2/7/16		Strength of Company: as before	
		DAY Works:-	Artyge:- On new D.H.Q. - making Gun Stops. Wire Entanglements, Smoke hole etc	R.E.
		NIGHT	Forward party R.E. Parties R.E. Infantry on new X Line - Progress on site in X.3. - R.Es Infantry on ECOLE deepening on Pillar. - R.E. on Water Supply, YPRES	
do	3/7/16		Strength of Company: as before	
		DAY Works..	Artyge:- Making Gun Stops - Traverses - Ramps for making Wire Entanglements - Wire Entanglements - Party for Water work at YPRES. - on new D.H.Q.	R.E.

WAR DIARY
or
INTELLIGENCE SUMMARY.
(Erase heading not required.)

Army Form C. 2118.

Place	Date	Hour	Summary of Events and Information	Remarks and references to Appendices
	3/1/16 (Cont'd)	DAY	Onward party: R.E. & Infantry on ECOLE	
		NIGHT	R.E. & Infantry on new X line — R.E. on Broun Trench between new X line — HAYMARKET — R.E. & Infantry on ECOLE — Q.S. putting up Tambo a/c. Water Supply, YPRES.	R.E.
do	4/1/16		Strength of Company; as before. (No action went into forward Ballots)	
		DAY	Work: Repro:— On new D.H.Q. — Male — Wine Entanglements. White Steps. M.G.E. — Ammunition Boxes. Bayard Entrances etc.	R.E.
			Onward party: R.E. & Infantry on ECOLE.	
		NIGHT	R.E. Pioneers & Infantry on new X line — R.E. on Broun Trench between new X line — HAYMARKET — R.E. & Infantry on ECOLE — putting up Water Tambo.	
do	5/1/16		Strength of Company: As before (Work in line taken over by new Company with 5th Bde. 2nd Can.)	
		DAY	Work: Repro:— All about — Ammunition Boxes — M.G.E. — Box Girders Gas Steps. Bayard Frames Vermorel Sprayer Boxes Wine Entanglements.	R.E.
			Onward party: R.E. & Infantry on ECOLE	
		NIGHT	R.E. on JOHN St — R.E. & Infantry on Dugs goes in B.Q. — R.E. Party repg parados A3, A5, A.B. 6. — Q.S. rfg ST JEAN — INFILTIE Railway —	

WAR DIARY
or
INTELLIGENCE SUMMARY.
(Erase heading not required.)

Army Form C. 2118.

95th FIELD COMPANY

Place	Date	Hour	Summary of Events and Information	Remarks and references to Appendices
	5/7/16 (contd) 6/7/16		Bivouacs on CAVAN trench - N°1 Infantry on ÉCOLE - N°2 Salmon Water Tanks for YPRES Water Supply	R2
do		DAY	Strength of Company: As before. N°1: - Major: - Making Wire Entanglements - Wine Steps - Vermorel Sprayer Boxes - Res drains - Dugout frames etc Forward party: - N°2 & Infantry on ÉCOLE - N°1 on Jetty St. N°2: - Infantry on Yards for Water Supply - N°1 & N°2 on ÉCOLE - N°2 on Fleet St. - N°2 & N°1 with Ryer Crews in front line - N°1 duty on John St. - N°2 on St JEAN - WEILTJE tram track - N°1 on Ryer Crews	
		NIGHT	- Bg. - Bivouacs on CAVAN trench.	R2
do	7/7/16	DAY	Strength of Company: As before. Major: - Making Wire Steps, Wire Entanglements, Dugout frames, Vermorel Sprayer Boxes, Notice Boards, M.G.B. Dugouts, Ammo Boxes etc Forward party: -	R2

T2134. Wt. W708-776. 500000. 4/15. Sir J. C. & S.

WAR DIARY
or
INTELLIGENCE SUMMARY.
(Erase heading not required.)

Army Form C. 2118.

96th FIELD COMPANY R.E.

Place	Date	Hour	Summary of Events and Information	Remarks and references to Appendices
H7a A26c Sheet 28 YPRES	8/1/16	DAY	Strength of Company:- As before. Work:- Sappers: Making Wire Entanglements - Fire Steps - Notice Boards - Covers for Water Barrels - M.G.E. - Verandah Sponge Boxes - Dugouts etc. Forward Party:- R.E. on École. R.E. & Infantry on Water I.14.4 YPRES 3. - R.E. & Infy on École - R.E. & Infy & JEAN - WISWESCHE alg. - R.E. on JOHN St. - R.E. Pioneers & Infantry on CAVAN trench.	R.E.2
do	9/1/16	DAY	Strength of Company:- As before. Work:- Sappers:- Making Wire Entanglements - Fire Steps - Covers for Water Barrels - Frames for making wire entanglements - Dugout Frames etc.	R.E.2
		NIGHT	Forward party:- R.E. & Infantry on Dugouts in CANAL BANK - R.E. & Infy on École - R.E. & Infy on Water supply for C/II Brigade - R.E. cleaning FLEET St. - R.E. Pioneers & Infantry on CAVAN trench - R.E. & Infantry on GARDEN St.	
do	10/1/16	DAY	Strength of Company:- As before. Work:- Sappers:- Making Wire Entanglements - Fire Steps - Dugout Frames etc. Forward party:- R.E. Infantry on GARDEN St. - R.E. Infy on École - R.E. cleaning FLEET St. - R.E. Pioneers & Infantry on CAVAN trench - R.E. & Infy on Dugouts on CANAL BANK - R.E. & Infy on Water Supply.	R.E.2

WAR DIARY
or
INTELLIGENCE SUMMARY.
(Erase heading not required.)

Army Form C. 2118.

Place	Date	Hour	Summary of Events and Information	Remarks and references to Appendices
H.T. a 5.9 A & C Sheet 28 YPRES	13/7/16		Strength of Company. as before	
			Work:- Regn: Making Wire entanglements - Wire Stop. Dugout frames. Sign Boards etc	
			Working parts: R.E Infantry on Dugouts in CANAL BANK. - R.B. Pioneers Infantry on CAVAN Trench - R.E. Infantry on ECOLE - O.B. Infantry on Water Supply for Left Brigade - R.B. Infantry on GARDEN St	R.E.
do	14/7/16		Strength of Company: - As before. 9 3 men joined Company from ADVEN.	
			Work:- Regn:- Making Wire entanglements. Wire Stop. Dugout frames Sign Boards etc. Working parts:- R.E a Infantry on Dugouts in CANAL BANK. - R.E + Infantry on ECOLE. - R.E a Infantry on GARDEN St - R.E + Pioneers Infantry on CAVAN trench - R.E Infantry on Water Supply for Left Brigade.	R.E.
do	15/7/16		Strength of Company: - as before.	
			Work:- Regn:- Making Dugout frames Wireentanglements Sign Boards Wire Stops etc Working parts:- R.E Infantry on Dugouts in CANAL BANK - R.E Pioneers Infantry on Front Line. - R.E Pioneers Infantry on CAVAN trench - R.E Infantry on	R.E.

WAR DIARY
or
INTELLIGENCE SUMMARY.
(Erase heading not required.)

Army Form C. 2118.

Place	Date	Hour	Summary of Events and Information	Remarks and references to Appendices
H.T.A.S.9. A.2.S.C. Sheet 28	14/7/15		Strength of Company: As before. No 1 & 3 Sections went to BURGOMASTER FARM towards LE DEFERES.	
YPRES			Work: Strip. - Making Dugout frames. Wire entanglements, Sign Boards etc. framework. No 2 Section on travel time.	3½
do	15/7/15		Strength of Company: As before. No 4 Section rejoined HQ from YPRES. Section clearing up dugouts.	R½
WINNIZEELE	16/7/15		Strength of Company: As before. Company entrained at 7.3 Section marched to WINNIZEELE.	
WINNIZEELE	17/7/15		Strength of Company: As before. Cleaning out billets etc. No 1 & 3 less working on LE DEFERES.	R.E.
do	18/7/15		Strength of Company: As before. No 1 & 3 Sections rejoined Company. Arms Rifle Exercises, overhauling Pontoon equipment, Tool carts, Rivolvers etc.	R.E. R.E.

WAR DIARY
or
INTELLIGENCE SUMMARY.
(Erase heading not required.)

Army Form C. 2118.

Place	Date	Hour	Summary of Events and Information	Remarks and references to Appendices
WINNEZEELE BERTHEN	19/3/16		Strength of Company. As before. Company marched to BERTHEN & billetted for the night.	App 2
LE DON	20/3/16		Strength of Company. As before. Company marched to LE DON & took over billets from 1st Coy. No 4 Section went to convent billets for work in line	App 2
do	21/3/16		Strength of Company. As before. Company also has See Henry out & repairing camps. No 1 Section repairing bombay. No 2 Section joined Company	App 2
do	22/3/16		Strength of Company. As before. Loading up wagons etc	App 2
do	23/3/16		Strength of Company. As before. Company marched to M.I.R.d.2.5. (Sheet 28)	App 2
M.I.R.d.2.5. Sheet 28	24/3/16		Strength of Company. As before. Company testing.	App 2
do BOUQUEMAISON	25/3/16		Strength of Company. As before. Coy left M.I.R.d.2.5 at 2am for HOUPOUTRE to entrain for FREVENT. Arrived at FREVENT at 1pm & marched to billets at BOUQUEMAISON	App 2

WAR DIARY or INTELLIGENCE SUMMARY.

Army Form C. 2118.

Place	Date	Hour	Summary of Events and Information	Remarks and references to Appendices
BOURJUEMAISON / AUTHIE	30/7/16		Strength of Company: As before. Company marched to Billets at AUTHIE.	P/2
AUTHIE / ROSSIGNOL FARM	27/7/16		Strength of Company: As before. Company marched to B.H.Q. at ROSSIGNOL FARM (Sh.57c, Sheet 57D NE) Cleaning up Billets.	P/2
ROSSIGNOL FARM / J.3.c. (Sh 57D NE)	28/7/16		Strength of Company: As before. Leo & Neill's men taken of strength. Mr EMBERTON left Company to join 6th Battalion G.H.Q. Troops. 2nd & 4th Sections went up to forward Billets. Half each of Nos 2 & 4 Sections working in Shops, cleaning out, repairing & preparing Billets.	P/2
do	29/7/16		Strength of Company: As before and 1 additional Officer Lt R.M.G. HUDDART joined Company. 44 Infantry (14 Carpenters & 30 fatigue parties) from 59th Bde joined Company. Carpenter in Workshops Coy in Forward Billets making & repair of tools. 3rd Section went to forward Billets — in dugouts — clearing stores etc.	P/2

MAJOR, R.E.
COMDG. 96th Fd. COY. R.E.

20th Divisional Engineers.

96th FIELD COMPANY R. E.

AUGUST 1 9 1 6

SECRET

Army Form C. 2118.

Vol II

96th FIELD COMPANY R.E.

WAR DIARY
or
INTELLIGENCE SUMMARY
(Erase heading not required.)

Instructions regarding War Diaries and Intelligence Summaries are contained in F.S. Regs., Part II. and the Staff Manual respectively. Title pages will be prepared in manuscript.

Place	Date	Hour	Summary of Events and Information	Remarks and references to Appendices
ROSSIGNOL FARM J.3.c Sheet 57D	30/7/16		Strength of Company: As before. Work: Nights – En Tranchee. Writing France etc. Repairs to Billets. General party – No 3 Section – Ambulance Dugout HEBUTERNE – Repair Dugout for Adv Secn – No 1 party – No 2 Section Trench Boards in VENA trench – No 2 coby Water. No 3 Section repairs to Trench Tramway – No 4 Section on strong points near front line – No 5 Section on new Bde HQ Dugout.	R.E.
do	31/7/16	DAY Work:	Strength of Company: As before. Sections: As before. Concentration: On Tramline, after explosive behind – on new Dugout for Adv Section, Water Main ½ reg to ETAPLES – coby dump at HEBUTERNE – on R.A.M.C Dugout – a new Dugout for Bde HQ. On strong point II – on TREE post – on NAIRN CT defined cleared & carpet trenched	R.E.
		NIGHT		
do	1/8/16	DAY Work:	Strength of Company: As before, 2 Br men joined Company from Base. Nights: Making Wiring Screen – Wire entanglements – frames for Wire entanglements – Russian Saps etc.	R.E.

T2134. Wt. W708—776. 500000. 4/15. Sir J. C. & S.

Army Form C. 2118.

WAR DIARY
or
INTELLIGENCE SUMMARY.
(Erase heading not required.)

Instructions regarding War Diaries and Intelligence Summaries are contained in F. S. Regs, Part II. and the Staff Manual respectively. Title pages will be prepared in manuscript.

Place	Date	Hour	Summary of Events and Information	Remarks and references to Appendices
ROSSIGNOL FARM J.3.c. Sheet 57D	1/8/16 (cont)	DAY	"Forward party" :- Dugout for R.A.M.C. — On Rue 3½ — on Dugouts for Section in HEBUTERNE — deburring & relaying Tramway — On WRANGLE, JEAN BART, NAIRN ST & VILLARS — clearing Dugout in WRANGLE —	R.E.
		NIGHT	Work on WRANGLE, a hot Post. TREE Post. 3 Post in old trench.	
			Strength of Company: as before	
do	2/8/16	DAY	Work :- Arges :- Making Mining frames — Wire entanglements & frames — Bivouac poles etc.	R.E.
			"Forward party" :- Dugout for R.A.M.C — Dugouts for Section in HEBUTERNE — on Rue 3½ — On cmd in JONES — Old Front Line trench deepened.	
			Relieved — repg & laying TRAMWAY — & VERCINGETORIX — & M.T.M. Dugout in WRANGLES :- reps trench Bozines JEAN BART TRAJAN ST.	
			Strength of Company :- as before	
do	3/8/16	DAY	Work :- Arges :- Making Mining frames — Wire entanglements, frames etc.	R.E.
			"Forward party" :- Dugout for R.A.M.C — Dugouts for Section in HEBUTERNE — On Rue 3½ — deepening & widening old Front Line — WRANGLE deepening & widening trench. — VERCINGETORIX & rang Stand Okes	

WAR DIARY
or
INTELLIGENCE SUMMARY.
(Erase heading not required.)

Army Form C. 2118.

96th FIELD COMPANY R.E.

Place	Date	Hour	Summary of Events and Information	Remarks and references to Appendices
do	4/6/16		refg trench boards - refg trenchboards JEAN BART & WRANGLE - refg Tramway - on Augusta in WRANGLE.	
			Strength of Company :- 7 Officers 202 Other Ranks, 77 Horses & Mules	
			Work :- Hqrs :- Making Mining frames - Wire Entanglements & frames etc	
			Forward party :- Dugouts for ROUNE & Section in HEBUTERNE - Bn Bde HQ - on REVEL, making & laying frames for overhead frames - deepening Trench 26 ?	
			on Augusta - deepening & widening Old Tram Line - deepening & widening Banbury	
			Prot. - refg Tramway - refg Trench Boards JEAN BART, VILLARS & TROSSACHS -	
			on Augusta in WRANGLE - VERCINGETORIX, on overhead frames.	
do	5/6/16		Strength of Company :- as before	
			Work :- Hqrs :- Making Mining frames. - Wire Entanglements & frames etc	
			Forward party :- Dugouts for ROUNE & Section in HEBUTERNE - On Bde HQ -	P.S
			connecting Augusta Trench 26 - on Augusta left sector front line - widening & deepening	
			old front line - burying signals cable - parapet sheets in JONES - on tank	
			emplacement VERCINGETORIX - refg Tramway - refg trench boards TROSSACHS	
			JEAN BART, VERCINGETORIX - on Augusta in WRANGLE	

WAR DIARY
or
INTELLIGENCE SUMMARY.

(Erase heading not required.)

Army Form C. 2118.

Place	Date	Hour	Summary of Events and Information	Remarks and references to Appendices
do	6/8/16		Strength of Company: As before.	
			Work: Stypa: Making Mining frames. Wire Entanglements frames for same, etc.	
			Forward party: Dugout for RAINE - Dugouts for section in HEBUTERNE - outside	
			H.Q. - Trench 26 connecting up Dugouts - Left sector front line on stairway for R.E.	
			Dugout - REVEL, extending traverse & making arched traverse - deepening &	
			widening "Old" front line - JONES, excavating for shelter - in Dugout 7 T.M.	
			Dugout in WRANGLE.	
do	7/8/16		Strength of Company: As before, and 6 men joined from ROUEN.	
			Work: Stypa: Making Mining frames, Wire Entanglements frames for same etc.,	
			Forward party: Dugout for RAINE - on Role H.Q. - on Role O.P. - Dugouts	
			for Section in HEBUTERNE - REVEL, extending traverse & widening French -	
			Trench 26 connecting up Dugouts - Left Sector front line starrways to Dugouts R.E.	
			JENA, deepening trench - Treasury repair - A M.G. hospitals MARIE LOUISE -	
			Tank emplacement VERCINGETORIX - JONES, excavating - HERCING & IDAYE, deepening	
			trench for frames - Dugout in WRANGLE - new French Avenue OXFORD ST.	
			NAIRNE, JEAN BART & VILLARS - deepening & widening Old front Line	

WAR DIARY
or
INTELLIGENCE SUMMARY.
(Erase heading not required.)

Army Form C. 2118.

Place	Date	Hour	Summary of Events and Information	Remarks and references to Appendices
do	8/8/16		Strength of Company :- As before.	
			Work :- Night :- Wiring Braves Dugouts Lyn Boards Wire Entanglements etc. Covering party & Dugouts for Section in HEBUTERNE. - On dugouts in Trench 95 = outside AHQ. - Dugout in WRANGLE - shelter in JONES - Loophole plate in PK 2. MARIE LOUISE - deepening JEAN BART - outanko at VERCINGETORIX - wiring French Grande in JEAN BART. VILLARS, TROSSACHS, DUGUESCLIN. - wiring TRAMWAY - widening JENA - deepening widening flat trench Line.	
do	9/8/16		Strength of Company :- As before.	
			Work :- Night :- As on 8th. 9 sundry small jobs. Covering party :- On Bde AHQ - On Bde OP - Loophole in MARIE LOUISE - Making Bays in DUGUESCLIN - Dugout in WRANGLE - shelters in JONES - Dugout in JENA - widening JENA - clearing & deepening CCL front PK 2, widening JEAN BART - widening JENA - making Bombing Straight in AULT - accomodation for Sections in Line. HEBUTERNE - Dugouts in Trench 95 - Dugouts in Left Sector of front Line. -	

WAR DIARY
or
INTELLIGENCE SUMMARY.
(Erase heading not required.)

Army Form C. 2118.

Place	Date	Hour	Summary of Events and Information	Remarks and references to Appendices
do	10/8/16		Strength of Company :- As before. Numbers of their Section went to Pouvant Billet. Work :- Stages :- Making Dugouts. Running frames. Wire Entanglements. Sign boards etc. Forward party :- Deepening PASTEUR - on bombing straight in TRAULT - making loopholes trenches in DUGUESCLIN - deepening widening VILLARS - on Dugouts for Bde H.Q. - on Brigade O.P. - Dugouts in front Line K.17.a.7.7 - Dugouts in Trench 76 - Dugouts for sections in HEBUTERNE - Dugouts in WRANGLE - Water tank emplacement. VERCINGETORIX -	
do	11/8/16		Strength of Company :- As before. Stages :- As on 10th - a sundry small jobs. Forward party :- Bombing straight in TRAULT - Yanks emplacement VERCINGETORIX - Loophole in M.G.E - a new Tramway - a Bde H.Q. - Bde O.P. - Dugout in front Line at K.17.a. K.7. - dug out in Trench 76 - Dugouts in WRANGLE - Dugouts for section in HEBUTERNE -	

WAR DIARY
or
INTELLIGENCE SUMMARY.
(Erase heading not required.)

Army Form C. 2118.

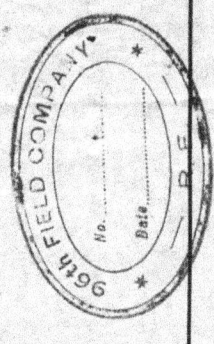

Place	Date	Hour	Summary of Events and Information	Remarks and references to Appendices
do	17/8/16		Strength of Company:- As before.	
			As men of No1 Section went to Billets in SAILLY-AU-BOIS.	
			Work:- Styps:- Making Wire Entanglements, Dugouts, Sign Boards etc.	
			Forward party:- Dugouts for Rue ATQ 7 Bde D.P. - Dugout in front line	
			at K.17. a. 4.7. - Dugout in Trench 96 - Dugout in WRANGLE - RE	
			Dugouts for Section in HEBUTERNE - on Shelter in JONES - Bombing	
			Shaft in RAULT - deepening LABOUR AVENUE - deepening KNOX	
			ST - on Firestep in DUGUESCLIN - M.G.E. Loophole in MARIE	
			LOUISE - Tank emplacement VERCINGETORIX - on new Tramway	
			No 3 Section relieved No 1. See Enclosed billets.	
do	18/8/16		Strength of Company:- As before.	
			Stypes:- On on 18th a similar amount of job.	
			Forward party:- Dugouts for Rue HQ 7 Bde D.P. - Dugout in front line at	
			K.17. a. 4.7. - Dugout Trench 96 - Dugouts for Section in HEBUTERNE - Dugout RE	
			in WRANGLE - Shelter in JONES - deepening CARENCY - deepening	
			FOURNIER & CABER - levelling track by Tramway.	

WAR DIARY
or
INTELLIGENCE SUMMARY.
(Erase heading not required.)

Army Form C. 2118.

Place	Date	Hour	Summary of Events and Information	Remarks and references to Appendices
do	14/8/16		Strength of Company: as before less 2nd Lieut Powell M.C. sent to Base, under age. Wala: Strafers: making Dugouts. Wire entanglements. Shan Boards etc. Forward parties: Dugouts for Bde HQ. – Bde O.P. – Dugout in WRANGLE – Dugouts for Section in HERVTERNE – M.G. E's at GUINDET and OLIVER de CLISSON – revetting DU GUESCLIN – Tramway – framing Notice Boards etc	
do	15/8/16		Strength of Company: as before Wala: As on 14 – a country small jobs etc Forward parties: Dugouts for Bde HQ. – Bde O.P. – Dugout in WRANGLE – Dugout in Trench 96. – Dugouts for sections in the DUTERNE – on Strong Shelter in JONES – on M.G. E's at OLIVER de CLISSON, M.G. E's at PASTEUR laying trench boards – laying trench boards JENA – laying trench boards JEAN BART – revetting and lagging in DUGUESCLIN – on new Tramway – frame notice Boards etc.	

Army Form C. 2118.

WAR DIARY
or
INTELLIGENCE SUMMARY.
(Erase heading not required.)

Instructions regarding War Diaries and Intelligence Summaries are contained in F. S. Regs., Part II. and the Staff Manual respectively. Title pages will be prepared in manuscript.

Place	Date	Hour	Summary of Events and Information	Remarks and references to Appendices
do	16/8/16		Strength of Company :- As before. Remainder of Company in forward Billets. Work :- Packing up wagons, cleaning up Billets, returned to H.Q. etc.	R2
do I.17.d.87.8.	17/8/16		Strength of Company :- As before. Company marched to BOIS de WARNIMONT. I.17.d. Sheet 57D.	R2
	18/8/16		Strength of Company :- As before. Company marched to BEAUVAL	R2
	19/8/16		Strength of Company :- As before. Mounted men with Transport left BEAUVAL & stayed night at VILLAGE de BOCAGE	R2
	20/8/16		Strength of Company :- As before. Remainder entrained at CANDAS at 8.30 a.m for MERICOURT & marched from MERICOURT to MEAULTE. Transport also arrived at MEAULTE.	R2
	21/8/16		Strength of Company :- As before. Company marched to F.S.A.4.b. Sheet "ALBERT"	R2
	22/8/16		Strength of Company :- As before. Dismounted marched to Albert S.D. Transport remained at F.5.d.4.b.	R5

WAR DIARY
or
INTELLIGENCE SUMMARY.

Army Form C. 2118.

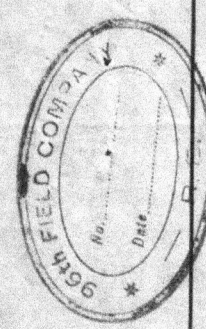

Place	Date	Hour	Summary of Events and Information	Remarks and references to Appendices
A.14.a.5.3 F.21.d.4.6 Sheet - ALBERT	23/8/16		Strength of Company :- as before. Work :- Working parties engaged for work under O.C.'s 3rd Sections on new trenches near Rly Station GUILLEMONT & extension of TRONE VALLEY Work rendered impossible owing to heavy enemy Shell fire.	R/-
do	24/8/16		Strength of Company :- as before Work :- 250 yds trench INVICTA deepened widened - EASTON trench between MELLINERAY & INVICTA deepened. - Digging 300 yds new trench near Ambury	R/-
do	25/8/16		Strength of Company :- as before "less 1 man taken off strength" Work :- Making Gun Boards. Deepening widening INVICTA - deepening FAGAN trench - Latrines at BRIGHTON ALLEY to SAPPER trench. - widening & deepening TEALE trench & WHITE HORSE trench.	R/-
do	26/8/16		Strength of Company :- as before Work :- Making Gun Boards. One new trench from EDWARD B to junction of KNOT & SAPPER trench - extension of INVICTA trench. -	R/-

Army Form C. 2118.

WAR DIARY
or
INTELLIGENCE SUMMARY.
(Erase heading not required.)

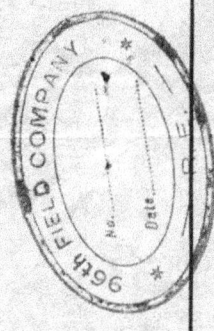

Place	Date	Hour	Summary of Events and Information	Remarks and references to Appendices
do	27/8/16		**Strength of Company:-** As before. Cpl Gibson wounded. Spr Thompson wounded section moved with Transport to L.9.c.9.3.	
			Work:- Making & fixing Sign Boards. On new trench from Einstein elbow of SAPPER. Trench in Southerly direction through GUILLEMONT ROAD - Extension of INVICTA trench - new trench between KNOT & SAPPER.- On new trench from SHERWOOD to LAMB.	R/Z
A.14.a.5.8? L.9.c.9.3	28/8/16		**Strength of Company:-** As before except Spr Bodwin killed.	
			Work:- Making & fixing Sign Boards. Widening & deepening TABLE trench & WHITE HORSE trench - deepening & widening INVICTA - deepening trench between KNOT & SAPPER - Completing new trench from SAPPER to GUILLEMONT RD.- Widening & deepening trench WHITE HORSE to SHERWOOD.	R/Z
do	29/8/16		**Strength of Company:-** As before	
			Work:- Making & fixing Sign Boards. Deepening FAGAN & WHITE HORSE trenches. On new trench from 1Q.194 ALLEY to SUNKEN ROAD. Carrying material to advanced dumps.	R/Z

P. Stevens
MAJOR, R.E.
COMDG. 96TH Fd. COY. R.E.

20th Divisional Engineers.

96th FIELD COMPANY R. E.

SEPTEMBER 1 9 1 6

96th Field Co. R.E.

SECRET

Vol 1/2

Army Form C. 2118.

WAR DIARY
or
INTELLIGENCE SUMMARY.
(Erase heading not required.)

Place	Date	Hour	Summary of Events and Information	Remarks and references to Appendices
A.14. a.5.3. q.a.q.3. Nr. ALBERT	30/8/16		Strength of Company: 7 Officers 212 Other Ranks. Weather: Making 2nd new Bridge. As usual no work done owing to bad weather.	A22
do	31/8/16		Strength of Company: As before. Work: On new C.T. from junction of TEALE & IRISH ALLEY to point in LAMB Trench S of GUILLEMONT RD - Clearing Advanced Trench leading off SAPPER trench - draining IRISH ALLEY & deepening Reserve trench E of TRONES WOOD. (Coldstream Guards (Pioneers) on two latter.)	A22
do	1/9/16		Strength of Company: As before. 2000 less 5 men taken off strength. Lieut HUDDART wounded. also a/L/Cpl Brown a.	A22
do	2/9/16		Work: Deepening & widening INVICTA & FAGAN & draining IRISH ALLEY. Strength of Company: As before	
do	3/9/16		Strength of Company: As before Attack on GUILLEMONT - 1 no. Sec took up position in ARROW HEAD TRENCH by 1 am morning of 3rd. 1 no. Sec in SHERWOOD Trench by 12 am morning of 3rd. 1 no. Sec in LIVERPOOL Trench by 2.30 am morning of 3rd. 1 O.C. in ARROW HEAD Trench.	

Army Form C. 2118.

WAR DIARY
or
INTELLIGENCE SUMMARY.
(Erase heading not required.)

Instructions regarding War Diaries and Intelligence Summaries are contained in F. S. Regs., Part II. and the Staff Manual respectively. Title pages will be prepared in manuscript.

Place	Date	Hour	Summary of Events and Information	Remarks and references to Appendices
A.	3/9/16	(cont)	Nos. 1&2 advanced with attacking troops & made strong posts detailed on 2.9.24. Sunken Rd. Posts completed & used as garrisons by Sec. No 3 Sec. advanced with attacking troops & made strong posts in GUILLEMONT on Pope Boundary of attack. Both not occupied by 2nd 7 R.F. forward post unoccupied. No 3 Sec. advanced on 2nd Amn objective being obtained & constructed 2 strong posts to S.E. of village occupied same at night. Nos. 1 Sec. advanced on 3rd Amn objective being gained & constructed strong posts at Cemetery on WEDGE WOOD-GINCHY Rd occupied same at night with Infantry. O.C. visited posts & front line about 3:30 p.m.	App 1
,,	4/9/16		Nos. 1 Sec. returned under Sec. Sergt. to CARNOY. Nos 2,3 & 4 Sec. were shown tasks to dig new trench on line 2nd Amn objective & in evening were again taken forward to consolidate on line of cemetery front. O.C. visited both Front Lines about 7 a.m. Return taken up to Sec. on 2nd evening about 4 p.m.	App 1
,,	5/9/16		Nos 2,3 & 4 Sec. left GUILLEMONT about 4 a.m. returning to CARNOY about 6:30 a.m. Losses on 3rd, 4th & 5th :— 2/Lt WILLATS wounded, 4 N.C.O's & men killed, 2 N.C.O's & men missing believed killed, 35 N.C.O's & men wounded.	App 2

T2134. Wt. W708—776. 500000. 4/15. Sir J. C. & B.

WAR DIARY
or
INTELLIGENCE SUMMARY.

(Erase heading not required.)

Army Form C. 2118.

Instructions regarding War Diaries and Intelligence Summaries are contained in F. S. Regs., Part II. and the Staff Manual respectively. Title pages will be prepared in manuscript.

Place	Date	Hour	Summary of Events and Information	Remarks and references to Appendices
	6/9/16		Company less Transport at L.9.c.9.3. moved to K.18.a.2.9. Bois de TAILLES.	App 1
	8/9/16		Whole Company moved to CORBIE.	App 2
	9/9/16		do VAUX.	App 3
	10/9/16		Reinforcement 48 men joined Company. Inspection by GOC 25th Divn. (no transport). Pte HUDDART admitted to hospital.	App 4
	11/9/16		Company moved to K.18.a.2.9. Bois de TAILLES.	App 5
	12/9/16		Pte HUDDART rejoined Company.	App 6
	14/9/16		Company moved to L.3.a.9.7. F.23.c.4.2.	App 7
	15/9/16		ditto	App 8
			2/Lt. LYON joined Company.	
	16/9/16		Company moved to A.15.a.3.5. Part of officers and IA moved to 28.k.7.7. 9 part of Transport to ~~BERNAFAY WOOD.~~ Remainder of Transport returned to F.23.c.4.2. and 2/Lieut moved to L.N.W. of GUINCHMONT Spur S.24.d.8.2. All returns marked by	App 9
	17/9/16		by D.L.I. and listed list of trench from T.24.b.8.6 to T.30.c.3. B... and ... that night.	App 10

WAR DIARY
or
INTELLIGENCE SUMMARY.
(Erase heading not required.)

Army Form C. 2118.

Place	Date	Hour	Summary of Events and Information	Remarks and references to Appendices
	17.9.16		4th section erected by 253 D.C.s dug out just beyond the tunnel in line from T.2.b.9.1. to T.3.a.9.6. fine weather for night.	H2
	19.9.16		All section erected by 250 D.C.s completed above tunnel to 4 ft steps to act as H.Q. army. 1xyds — but wider with recessed shewn.	H2
	20/9/16		Company H.Qs Transport at F.23.c.4.2. moved to SAND PITS.	H2
	21/9/16		Transport from F.23.c.4.2. moved to SAND PITS.	H2
	22/9/16		Company moved to MORLANCOURT.	H2
	23/9/16		3 men joined Coy from ROUEN. Company supported by B.G.C 59th Div. Bde.	H2
	24/9/16		Sunday. Coy attended service with 11th K.R.R Coy.	H2
	25/9/16		Company moved to L.3.a.9.7. Henry Valley	H2
	26/9/16		2/Lt HANDS attached to Coy Company from this date.	H2
	28/9/16		Company moved to A.15.a.7.7. Talus Bois.	H2

(P.T.S) Capt
M. Gnt 8
O.C. 96 Coy R.E.

W Hardy Lt Coy
O.C.96.sect

20th Divisiobal Engineers

96th FIELD COMPANY R. E.

OCTOBER 1 9 1 6

Vol 13

96th Field Coy

WAR DIARY or INTELLIGENCE SUMMARY

Army Form C. 2118

SECRET

Instructions regarding War Diaries and Intelligence Summaries are contained in F.S. Regs., Part II. and the Staff Manual respectively. Title Pages will be prepared in manuscript.

(Erase heading not required.)

Place	Date	Hour	Summary of Events and Information	Remarks and references to Appendices
	29/9/16		Dismounted moved to Dugouts at GUILLEMONT, a remainder of transport to MARICOURT.	R.S.
	1/10/16		Work: On new Road to GUEDECOURT & Road E of TRONES WOOD.	R.S.
	2/10/16		Work: Clearing Road from GINCHY to T.7,6,6,7. and working on Trench from T.13.6.9.4. to T.8 central. On new Dump at GUILLEMONT.	R.S.
	3/10/16		Work: On new Dump at GUILLEMONT. Night of 2nd/3rd 10 Officer party set out to take out new trench on line from existing trench at N.33.d.6.5. - N.33.b.6.2. but owing to wet night of 3rd advance post then way, trench taped out on morning of 3rd. early by Infantry (2KRRs R.B.) went out to work on new trench but for then way & no work was done.	R.S.
	4/10/16		2 R.E. BELLOC. L. joined Company. Work: On Track to T.8 - Track from T.8 to LES BOEUFS - Road from GINCHY to T.7.6.7.7. - 2.2.6.7.7. - Track from above to GAS at WATLING ST.	R.S.
	5/10/16		2 R.E. BELLOC. L. left Company, joined 84th Coy. Reinforcement 10 men joined Company. 3 P.Bs men wounded. - One (Pepe Kitchener) died afterwards Work: R.S.3 P.Bs evacuated 2/0 yds Assembly trench in continuation of 3rd line started by 84th Coy.	R.S.
	6/10/16		2 R.E. LYON wounded. Salvaging Kirsch board tracks in E direction from WATERLOT FARM.	R.S.

WAR DIARY or INTELLIGENCE SUMMARY

Place	Date	Hour	Summary of Events and Information	Remarks and references to Appendices
	7/10/16		R₃ & R₃ gr new Commn. Trench from N.28.a.0.3. in N.E. direction to new Mann line R₃ & Infy or new Comm. Trench from WINDMILL TRENCH N.33.d.3.3 a N.33.L.8.4.	R⁄
	8/10/16		Spr Wealm wounded	R⁄
	9/10/16		Whole of Company moved to MEAULTE E.22.L.5.9	R⁄
	10/10/16		Company moved to VILLE-sur-ANCRE	R⁄
			Rn WARDE R.H. joined Company from 8th M Coy as 2nd in Command	R⁄
	11/10/16		9/W BRIDGMAN G.S. joined Company	R⁄
	10/10/16 to 17/10/16		Company training. Bayonet drill Rifle exercise Shooting & Rushing & general instruction	R⁄
	13/10/16		Company paraded with 59th Infy Brigade for inspection by XIV the Corps Commander	R⁄
	19/10/16 to 20/10/16		O.C. Company acting C.R.E. 20th Divn.	R⁄
	18/10/16		Company moved to CITADEL	R⁄
	19/10/16		Company less Transport (remained at CITADEL) moved to huts at the CARTER'S A.8.a.8.3	R⁄
	20/10/16		Company working on erecting shelts & deep-winding underg dugout GINCHY.	R⁄
	21/10/16		ditto	R⁄
	22/10/16		ditto	R⁄

Army Form C. 2118.

WAR DIARY
or
INTELLIGENCE SUMMARY
(Erase heading not required.)

Instructions regarding War Diaries and Intelligence Summaries are contained in F. S. Regs., Part II. and the Staff Manual respectively. Title Pages will be prepared in manuscript.

Place	Date	Hour	Summary of Events and Information	Remarks and references to Appendices
	23/10/16		Company working on erecting Huts & superintending new deep dugout @ GIVENCHY.	RE
	24/10/16		ditto	RE
	25/10/16		ditto	RE
	26/10/16		2/Lt BRIDGMAN, with 5 N.C.O's (instructors) and 51 Recruits left Company to go into back area for training. Remainder of Coy at A.6 & 8.8. moved to huts in Camp at A.8.c.1.4.	RE
	27/10/16		Company working on erecting Huts & superintending new deep dugout @ GIVENCHY.	RE
	28/10/16		ditto	RE
			ditto	RE
			2/Lt FORMBY left to join party in back area.	RE

P T Story
MAJOR R.E.
COMDG. 96th Fd. COY: R.E.

20th Divisional Engineers.

96th FIELD COMPANY R. E.

NOVEMBER 1 9 1 6

SECRET WAR DIARY or INTELLIGENCE SUMMARY.

(Erase heading not required.)

Army Form C. 2118.

(56th FIELD COMPANY R.E.)

Vol 14

Place	Date	Hour	Summary of Events and Information	Remarks and references to Appendices
A.S.C.I.4. F.21.L.3.0. sheet ALBERT combined	29/10/16.		Strength of Company :- 6 Officers 213 Other Ranks. 2 Officers, 5 N.C.O Instructors, 31 Recruits in back area for training. Company working on erecting huts & superintending new deep dugouts GINCHY.	A.2
do	30/10/16.		ditto	A.2
do	31/10/16		ditto	A.2
do	1/11/16.		ditto	A.2
do	2/11/16		ditto	A.2
do	3/11/16		ditto	A.2
do	4/11/16		Company working on executed huts. Dugouts at GINCHY handed over No. 25b Tunnelling Co.	A.2
do	5/11/16		ditto	
do	6/11/16		ditto O.C joined party at rear (training)	
do	7/11/16.		ditto	
do	8/11/16		ditto 2/Lt WILLIAMS joined party in back area.	
do	9/11/16		ditto	
do	10/11/16.		O.C Coy went on leave. Packing & loading wagons.	
do VILLE	11/11/16.		Company at A.S.C.14.9. Fr.L.6.3.0. moved to VILLE.	M.M

Army Form C. 2118.

WAR DIARY
or
INTELLIGENCE SUMMARY.
(Erase heading not required.)

Instructions regarding War Diaries and Intelligence Summaries are contained in F. S. Regs., Part II. and the Staff Manual respectively. Title pages will be prepared in manuscript.

96th FIELD COMPANY R.E.

Place	Date	Hour	Summary of Events and Information	Remarks and references to Appendices
VILLE	12/11/16		Training - Drill, Rifle Exercises etc. Company drill.	
do	13/11/16		ditto	
do	14/11/16		ditto	
do	15/11/16		Detachment in Breda area rejoined Company. Whole Company moved to TREUX	
TREUX	16/11/16		Working on Stables at TREUX, VILLE & MERICOURT.	
do	17/11/16		ditto	
do	18/11/16		ditto	
do	19/11/16		ditto	
do			Fighting Gallows at VILLE	
do	20/11/16		Working on Stables at TREUX, VILLE & MERICOURT.	Making Bayonets
do	21/11/16		ditto	
do	22/11/16		ditto → Run for School at TREUX	
do	23/11/16		ditto	
do	24/11/16		ditto	(over)
do	25/11/16		O.C. rejoined Company from leave & ditto to act as 2nd in Comd on 24.	

T2134. Wt. W708—776. 500000. 4/15. Sir J. C. & S.

WAR DIARY
or
INTELLIGENCE SUMMARY.

Army Form C. 2118.

Place	Date	Hour	Summary of Events and Information	Remarks and references to Appendices
TREUX	26/11/16		Packing Loading Wagons	
TREUX & VECQUEMONT	27/11/16		No 2. Sec. proceeded to VECQUEMONT as advance party. Remainder of Company less No 4 Section marched to VECQUEMONT.	
VECQUEMONT	28/11/16		Working on XIV Corps R.A. School, 17th, 20th, 28th Divnl Schools of Instruction	
do	29/11/16		ditto	

M.Woods Capt RE
o/c 96th Field Coy. RE

20th Divisional Engineers

96th FIELD COMPANY R. E.

DECEMBER 1916

SECRET

Army Form C. 2118.

WAR DIARY
or
INTELLIGENCE SUMMARY.

(Erase heading not required.)

Instructions regarding War Diaries and Intelligence Summaries are contained in F.S. Regs., Part II. and the Staff Manual respectively. Title pages will be prepared in manuscript.

96th FIELD COMPANY

Vol 15

Place	Date	Hour	Summary of Events and Information	Remarks and references to Appendices
TREUX				
VECQUEMONT	29/9/16		VECQUEMONT: Working on XIV Corps R.A. School, and 17th, 20th, 22nd of June School Re. of instruction.	R.E.
do	30/9/16		TREUX – (New Sec.) Working on Stables at TREUX, VILLE and MERICOURT	R.E.
do	1/10/16		ditto ditto	R.E.
do	2/10/16		ditto ditto	R.E.
do	3/10/16		ditto ditto	R.E.
do			ditto ditto	R.E.
do	4/10/16		O.C. rejoined Company after acting as C.R.E. Divn.	R.E.
do	5/10/16		Work as before.	R.E.
do	6/10/16		ditto	R.E.
do	7/10/16		ditto	R.E.
do	8/10/16		ditto	R.E.
do	9/10/16		Packing, loading up wagons	R.E.
do	10/10/16		Company at VECQUEMONT marched to TREUX.	R.E.
TREUX	11/10/16		Whole Company marched to BERNAFAY WOOD.	R.E.

SECRET

WAR DIARY
or
INTELLIGENCE SUMMARY
(Erase heading not required.)

Army Form C. 2118.

Instructions regarding War Diaries and Intelligence Summaries are contained in F. S. Regs., Part II. and the Staff Manual respectively. Title pages will be prepared in manuscript.

96th FIELD COMPANY R.E.

Place	Date	Hour	Summary of Events and Information	Remarks and references to Appendices
BEANAPAY WOOD and S 29 d	12/12/16		Laying Corduroy Road. Trench Boards etc & repairing Dugouts for Lectures. Repairs to Drying Shed & Officers Stable. Making Ration Store	PE
do	13/12/16		ditto	PE
do	14/12/16		On CRB's stable BRIQUETTERIE. On Pipe Line from BRIQUETTERIE to new Stone Lines. Laying Corduroy Road in Camp. & repg Officers Stables. Party working in CRB's workshops	PE
do	15/12/16		Laying CORDUROY Road in Camp. — Party in R.A.C's Workshops — on GUILLEMONT new Camp — on Grenade Stores at GUILLEMONT. — Working on Mule Track.	
do	16/12/16		Wiring OZONE Trench. — Working on Mule Track. — Working on GUILLEMONT new Camp. — on Grenade Stores GUILLEMONT. — Laying Corduroy Road in Camp.	
do	17/12/16		Wiring Intermediate Line — Working on Mule Track. — on new Camp at GUILLEMONT. — on Grenade Store GUILLEMONT. — Laying Corduroy Road in Camp	
do	18/12/16		On new Camp at GUILLEMONT. — on Grenade Stores at GUILLEMONT. — Laying Corduroy Road in Camp. — Wiring Intermediate Line — Working on Mule Track.	

SECRET

Army Form C. 2118.

WAR DIARY
or
INTELLIGENCE SUMMARY.

(Erase heading not required.)

Instructions regarding War Diaries and Intelligence
Summaries are contained in F. S. Regs., Part II.
and the Staff Manual respectively. Title pages
will be prepared in manuscript.

[Stamp: 95th FIELD COMPANY R.E.]

Place	Date	Hour	Summary of Events and Information	Remarks and references to Appendices
BEAUFAY WOOD and SCOTT	19/10/16		Wiring Intermediate Line – Working on Mule Track – on new Camp all GUILLEMONT – on Grenade Store all GUILLEMONT – Laying Corduroy Road in Camp	Nil
do	20/10/16		2/Lt. J.F. GANDY joined Company. Wiring Intermediate Line making out drainage – on new Camp all GUILLEMONT – on Grenade Store all GUILLEMONT.	Nil
do	21/10/16		DAY. Working on new Intermediate Line & digging drainage trench. NIGHT Digging new Intermediate Line during same.	Nil
do	22/10/16		DAY. Working out new Intermediate Line completed & drains dug. NIGHT Completing digging of new Intermediate Line & wiring.	Nil
CORBIE.	23/10/16		Company moved to CORBIE. – Transport by Road arriving 4 pm and Men arrived by Lorries arriving 6 pm.	Nil
do	24/10/16		No. 2 Section left for DAOURS for work on Corps Artillery Schools. Working on Stables at CORBIE on MERICOURT Road and fitting up Machinery etc at Laundry, CORBIE.	Nil

SECRET

Army Form C. 2118.

WAR DIARY
or
INTELLIGENCE SUMMARY.

(Erase heading not required.)

Instructions regarding War Diaries and Intelligence Summaries are contained in F.S. Regs., Part II. and the Staff Manual respectively. Title pages will be prepared in manuscript.

96th FIELD COMPANY R.E.

Place	Date	Hour	Summary of Events and Information	Remarks and references to Appendices
CORBIE	25/10/16		Working on fitting up Machinery etc at Laundry an Stables on MERICOURT Road.	Mw
do	26/10/16		ditto	Mw
do	27/10/16		N.C.O's cinema dinner concert at Laundry. Capt E.B. HUGH-JONES joined Company. Onty left Coy for work on 36 C.C.S. Working on fitting up Machinery & Boilers at Laundry & working on stables on MERICOURT Road.	Mw
do	28/10/16		Capt E.B. HUGH JONES transferred to 83rd Field Coy R.E. fitting up Machinery etc at Laundry — On stables on MERICOURT Rd — Sawing up logs at LECLERE Sawmills — Welling Trees at CORBIE — Supervising work on Prisoners Camp at HEILLY. Sunday small jobs.	Mw
do	29/10/16		ditto	Mw
do	30/10/16		ditto	Mw

MWade Capt R.E.
MAJOR, R.E.
COMDG. 96th Fd. COY. R.E.

War Diary
of the
96th Field Coy., R.E.

January 1917.

Vol 16

SECRET

WAR DIARY
or
INTELLIGENCE SUMMARY.
(Erase heading not required.)

Army Form C. 2118.

Instructions regarding War Diaries and Intelligence Summaries are contained in F. S. Regs., Part II. and the Staff Manual respectively. Title pages will be prepared in manuscript.

Place	Date	Hour	Summary of Events and Information	Remarks and references to Appendices
CORBIE	2/1/17		Packing, loading wagons & cleaning up Billets	MW
CORBIE } CITADEL }	1/1/17		Company moved to CITADEL area.	MW
CITADEL } COMBLES }	2/1/17		Company left CITADEL, Nos. 1.3.4. proceeded to COMBLES (CATACOMBS), 2 & 2 Coy with Transport to WEDGE WOOD. (R.1.d.8.)	MW
WEDGE WOOD COMBLES				
WEDGE WOOD	3/1/17		Cleaning up & improving Billets at CATACOMBS & WEDGE WOOD. Nos 2 & 4 Platoons R.E. on war from Transport. Working at SAILLY Strong Point — setting CUSHY Strong Point — constructing Dugout for new Batta Dump at V.14.a.4.3.	MW
do	4/1/17		Working on SAILLY Strong Point — on C.T. to front line — on CUSHY Strong Point — cleaning & strengthening cellars at CUSHY & CHATEAU — on CHATEAU Strong Point — on R.A.M.C. Aid Post at FREGICOURT & HAIE WOOD.	MW
do	5/1/17		Working on SAILLY Strong Point — on C.T. to front Line — on CUSHY Strong Point — on cellars at CHATEAU & CUSHY — on CHATEAU Strong Point — on COMBLES Strong Point — on R.A.M.C. Aid Post at FREGICOURT.	MW
do	6/1/17		Working on SAILLY Strong Point — on C.T. to Front Line — on CHATEAU Strong Point — on CUSHY & COMBLES Strong Point — M.G. Dugout on CHATEAU — strengthening CUSHY Cellar — on FREGICOURT Aid Post — on HAIE WOOD Aid Post — on RIDT Exchange at FREGICOURT.	RMW

SECRET

Army Form C. 2118.

WAR DIARY
or
INTELLIGENCE SUMMARY.

(Erase heading not required.)

Instructions regarding War Diaries and Intelligence Summaries are contained in F. S. Regs., Part II. and the Staff Manual respectively. Title pages will be prepared in manuscript.

Place	Date	Hour	Summary of Events and Information	Remarks and references to Appendices
COMBLES				
WEDGE WOOD	8/1/17		Working on SAILLY Strong Point — on C.T. to Front Line — on CUSHY Strong Point PUSHY Cellar Dugout — on CHATEAU WELL Dugout — on CHATEAU Strong Point — on COMBLES Strong Point — FREGICOURT Aid Post — FREGICOURT Boot Exchange	MW
do	9/1/17		No 2 Section relieved No 3 Section in forward area. On Strong Points at SAILLY, CUSHY & COMBLES — C.T. to Front Line — CUSHY CELLAR Dugout — CHATEAU Strong Point — HAIEWOOD Aid Dugout — FREGICOURT HAIEWOOD Aid Posts.	MW
do	10/1/17		On Strong Points at SAILLY, CUSHY, COMBLES & CHATEAU — revetting Support Line — C.T. to Front Line — HAIEWOOD Aid Dugout — FREGICOURT Aid Post — FREGICOURT Boot Exchange	MW
do	11/1/17		On Strong Points at SAILLY, CUSHY, COMBLES & CHATEAU — C.T. to Front Line — Support Line — Dugout duck board track to CUSHY — HAIEWOOD Aid Dugout — FREGICOURT Aid Post — FREGICOURT Boot Exchange.	MW
do	12/1/17		On Strong Points at SAILLY, CUSHY & CHATEAU — C.T. to Support Line — CHATEAU — CUSHY Dugouts — HAIEWOOD Dugout — FREGICOURT Aid Post — FREGICOURT Boot Exchange	MW
do	13/1/17		On Strong Points at SAILLY, CUSHY, CHATEAU — HAIEWOOD Dugout — FREGICOURT Aid Post — FREGICOURT Boot Exchange.	MW

SECRET

WAR DIARY
or
INTELLIGENCE SUMMARY.
(Erase heading not required.)

Army Form C. 2118.

Instructions regarding War Diaries and Intelligence Summaries are contained in F. S. Regs., Part II. and the Staff Manual respectively. Title pages will be prepared in manuscript.

Place	Date	Hour	Summary of Events and Information	Remarks and references to Appendices
COMBLES WEDGE WOOD	14/1/17		On Strong Points at SAILLY, CUSNY, CHATEAU - CUSNY Arch board track - FREGICOURT Aid Post - FREGICOURT Post exchange -	Nw
do	15/1/17		Winning Reserve Line - On FREGICOURT Aid Post.	Nw
do	16/1/17		Winning Reserve Line - on CUSNY Strong Point - FREGICOURT Aid Post - FREGICOURT Post exchange -	Nw
do	17/1/17		Winning Reserve Line - On CUSNY Strong Point - FREGICOURT Reserve Post - FREGICOURT Aid Post - FREGICOURT Post exchange. No 3 Sec. relieved No 4 Sec. in forward area.	Nw
do	18/1/17		On CUSNY - Yvon Lane trench board track - On Strong Points at SAILLY. CUSNY 9 CHATEAU - Winning Reserve Line - FREGICOURT Reserve Post, Aid Post Post exchange.	Nw
do	19/1/17		On SAILLY Strong Point - On Aid Post Reserve Post & Post exchange at FREGICOURT - Winning Reserve Line - CUSNY - Yvon Lane trench board track.	Nw
do	20/1/17		Widening Winning Reserve Line - on SAILLY O.P - CUSNY - Yvon Lane trench board track - On Aid Post, Reserve Post & Post exchange at FREGICOURT.	Nw
do	21/1/17		CUSNY - Yvon Lane trench board track - Aid Post, Reserve Post & Post exchange at FREGICOURT - Drainage of Support Line	Nw

Army Form C. 2118.

SECRET

WAR DIARY
or
INTELLIGENCE SUMMARY.
(Erase heading not required.)

Instructions regarding War Diaries and Intelligence Summaries are contained in F. S. Regs., Part II. and the Staff Manual respectively. Title pages will be prepared in manuscript.

96th FIELD COMPANY R.E.

Place	Date	Hour	Summary of Events and Information	Remarks and references to Appendices
COMBLES				
WEDGE WOOD S	22/1/17		Drainage of Support Line - Strutting cellar SAILLY Strong Point - On Aid Post, Reserve Post & Bosh Rechange at FREGICOURT	Nom
do	23/1/17		Resetting, cleaning & widening Support Line - On Aid Post, Reserve Post & Bosh Rechange at FREGICOURT - On Anti-gas Blankets at CHATEAU Battn HQ - Strutting SAILLY	Nom
do	24/1/17		Support trench cellar - On BULLET Cross Roads Strong Point.	Nom
do	25/1/17		Working on Support Line - On Aid Post, Reserve Post & Bosh Rechange at FREGICOURT. Anti-gas Blankets at CHATEAU Battn HQ - Strutting SAILLY support trench cellar.	Nom
do	26/1/17		On Support Line - BULLET Cross Roads Strong Point - widening wing of Reserve Line - On Bosh Rechange at FREGICOURT - On SAILLY strong point cellar.	Nom
do	26/1/17		On Support Line - thickening wing of Reserve Line - on SAILLY Strong Point - Anti gas Blankets for left Battn & Right Battn HQ. - at FREGICOURT Aid Post & Bosh Rechange - SAILLY O.P.	Nom
do	27/1/17		Company moved to FRANVILLERS. Dismounted by Lorry, Transport by Road.	Nom
FRANVILLERS	28/1/17		Rifle & Rifle Reserves. Cleaning up Billets. Kit Inspections etc	Nom
do	29/1/17		Drill & Rifle Reserves, Lewis & Lashings.	Nom
do	30/1/17		Route March.	Nom

Onwards Capt RE
o/DC 96 Fd Coy RE

SECRET

Army Form C. 2118.

Instructions regarding War Diaries and Intelligence Summaries are contained in F. S. Regs., Part II. and the Staff Manual respectively. Title pages will be prepared in manuscript.

WAR DIARY
or
INTELLIGENCE SUMMARY.
(Erase heading not required.)

95th FIELD COMPANY R.E.

Vol 17

Place	Date	Hour	Summary of Events and Information	Remarks and references to Appendices
FRANVILLERS	31/1/17		Physical Drill & Rifle Exercise. Demolition. Fitting up Baths at HEILLY	P.E.
do	1/2/17		ditto. Laying on Trenches. Fitting up Baths at HEILLY.	P.E.
			Making frames & felling trees. Building Incinerators at HEILLY.	
do	2/2/17		Physical Drill & Rifle Exercise. Demolition. Fitting up Baths at HEILLY. Working on frames at A.V.C. stables at HEILLY. Building Incinerators at HEILLY. Making frames & felling trees.	P.E.
FRANVILLERS	3/2/17		Making frames & felling trees. Packing up Stores & loading wagons.	P.E.
MEAULTE	4/2/17		Company marched to billets at MEAULTE.	P.E.
MEAULTE	5/2/17		Repairing & fitting up new Billets. Overhauling & repairing Transport.	P.E.
do	6/2/17		ditto	P.E.
do	7/2/17		Packing up Stores & loading wagons.	P.E.
MEAULTE 8.30a	8/2/17		Company marched to Billets at 8:30a (between TRONES WOOD & GUILLEMONT).	P.E.
8.30a	9/2/17		Subsequent to Billets. - Laying trench board track on Bull Dump Avenue.	P.E.
			Current trench board track on GINCHY Loop with X.P.M.	P.E.
do	10/2/17		Laying run & Emplacements T.9.d.11 & forward accommodation for Sea Form.	P.E.
do	11/2/17		ditto	P.E.

T2134. Wt. W708—776. 500000. 4/15. Sir J. C. & S.

WAR DIARY or INTELLIGENCE SUMMARY

Army Form C. 2118

(Erase heading not required.)

Instructions regarding War Diaries and Intelligence Summaries are contained in F.S. Regs., Part II. and the Staff Manual respectively. Title Pages will be prepared in manuscript.

25th FIELD COMPANY R.E.

Place	Date	Hour	Summary of Events and Information	Remarks and references to Appendices
S.t S.30.a. 16.a.	11/2/17		No 3 Section moved to forward Billets at T.16.a. Making splinter proof accommodation for a Section in advanced area. O.C. went on course for Company Commanders.	R.E.
do	13/2/17		No 4 Section moved to forward Billets at T.16.a. Making accommodation for a Section in advanced area.	R.E.
do	14/2/17		2/Lt R.J. CORK joined Company. also 3 other ranks.	R.E.
do	15/2/17		Making forward Billets for a Section in advanced area – also for Officers.	R.E.
do	16/2/17		Making accommodation for Officers & Section in forward area – attempt made to take up line for C.T. to forward post. – M.G.E behind BENNETT evacuation for dugout & deepening Comm. Trench. Sp. R.W. FORMBY killed night of 16/17th Feby. Sp. TAYLOR.W. wounded (at duty)	R.E.
do	17/2/17		Making accommodation for Officers & Section in forward area.	R.E.
do	18/2/17		Making accommodation for Officers & Section in forward area. – Work on FLANK AVENUE Beaver Dug. – Work on 2 new M.G.E. – on Dugouts for R.A. at MORVAL ORCHARD – On new CT. to "B"jul – Making Stevens dugout. No 4 Section moved to new Billets at T.9.d.11.	R.E.
S.30.a. 16.a. 9.d.	19/2/17		On forward Billets for Section – Trench Boards laid from Pulled to Main road – On FLANK AVENUE Beaver Dug. – on M.G.E behind BENNETT. No 3 Section moved to new Billets at T.9.d.11.	R.E.

Army Form C. 2118

WAR DIARY
or
INTELLIGENCE SUMMARY

(Erase heading not required.)

Instructions regarding War Diaries and Intelligence Summaries are contained in F.S. Regs., Part II. and the Staff Manual respectively. Title Pages will be prepared in manuscript.

96th FIELD COMPANY R.E.

Place	Date	Hour	Summary of Events and Information	Remarks and references to Appendices
S.30.a & T.1.d	20/5/17		On Trench Board Track from R.E. Billets to BULL DUMP – On forward accommodation for Officers Section – On M.G. Emplacement behind BENNETT – On FLANK AVENUE Rear Post.	
do	21/5/17		On FLANK AVENUE Rear Post – On forward accommodation for Officers Section – PRUSSIAN Loups Trench Boards to BULL DUMP – refg Duckboard Track – Track – On nos 1 & 2 M.G. Emplacements.	
do	22/5/17		On FLANK AVENUE Rear Post – On nos 1 M.G. Emplacement – on advanced R.E. Billets – refg Duckwalks in forward area.	
do	23/5/17		On forward accommodation for Officers Station – on FLANK AVENUE Rear Post – refg Duck Walks in forward area – on nos 1 & 2. M.G. Emplacements.	
do	24/5/17		On nos 1 & 2 M.G. Emplacements – refg Duck Walks in forward area – On FLANK AVENUE Rear Post Sgt SANDY wounded (at duty). Spr. Sloan wounded.	
do	25/5/17		On nos 1 & 2 M.G. Emplacements – refg Duckwalk – on FLANK AVENUE Rear Post – on advanced R.E. Billets	
do	26/5/17		On nos 1 & 2 M.G. Emplacements – on advanced R.E. Billets – on FLANK AVENUE Rear Post – refg Duckwalk.	

Continued

MAJOR R.E.
COMDG. 96th Fd. Co. R.E.

WAR DIARY or INTELLIGENCE SUMMARY

Army Form C. 2118

Vol. 18

Place	Date	Hour	Summary of Events and Information	Remarks and references to Appendices
S.30.a T.q.d.5	27/7/17		Working on FLANK AVENUE Bearer Post - 2 ty Brickwalks - On nos. 1 no 3 M.G Emplacements - working on advanced R E Billets	R.E.
do	28/7/17		2ty Brickwalks - Working on nos 1, 2, 73 M.G. Emplacements - On R.E advanced Billets - on FLANK AVENUE Bearer Post.	R.E
do	1/8/17		On advanced R E Billets - on FLANK AVENUE Bearer Post - on nos 1, 2, 73 M.G Emplacements - 2 ty Brickwalks - Wiring in front of PRUSSIAN TRENCH, also to left of Sunken Rd. & 300 yds to right of Sunken Rd. 2/Lt Mitchell W. Wounded (at duty)	R.E
g 30 a	2/8/17		nos 1 & 2 Sections returned to Steenvoorde from forward Billets.	R.E
do	3/8/17		Working on GUILLEMONT Baths - Making Gun Run. Officers & N.C.Os given Mo.3 Section went to CARNOY. Working on GUILLEMONT Baths - Making Gun Run - Getting Box. Examination by Brigade Gas Officer	R.E
do	4/8/17 (Sunday)		2/Lt GANDY, J.F. Wounded at Mantie 30/7/17 sent to Hospital. Working on GUILLEMONT Baths - Making Gun Run	R.E
do	5/8/17		Working on GUILLEMONT Baths - Work in Shops - Company training.	R.E
do	6/8/17		Working on GUILLEMONT Baths - Work in Shops - Company Training.	R.E
do	7/8/17		Attachment of no.3 Section rejoined Company. Working on GUILLEMONT Baths - Work in Shops - Company training. Part of No. 1 & no 4 Sections with 2 officers went to forward Billets.	R.E
S.30.a.2 T.q.d.5	8/8/17		Taking over work in forward area from 83rd Bde M.G - Work in Shops - Training of Backward Salients	R.E

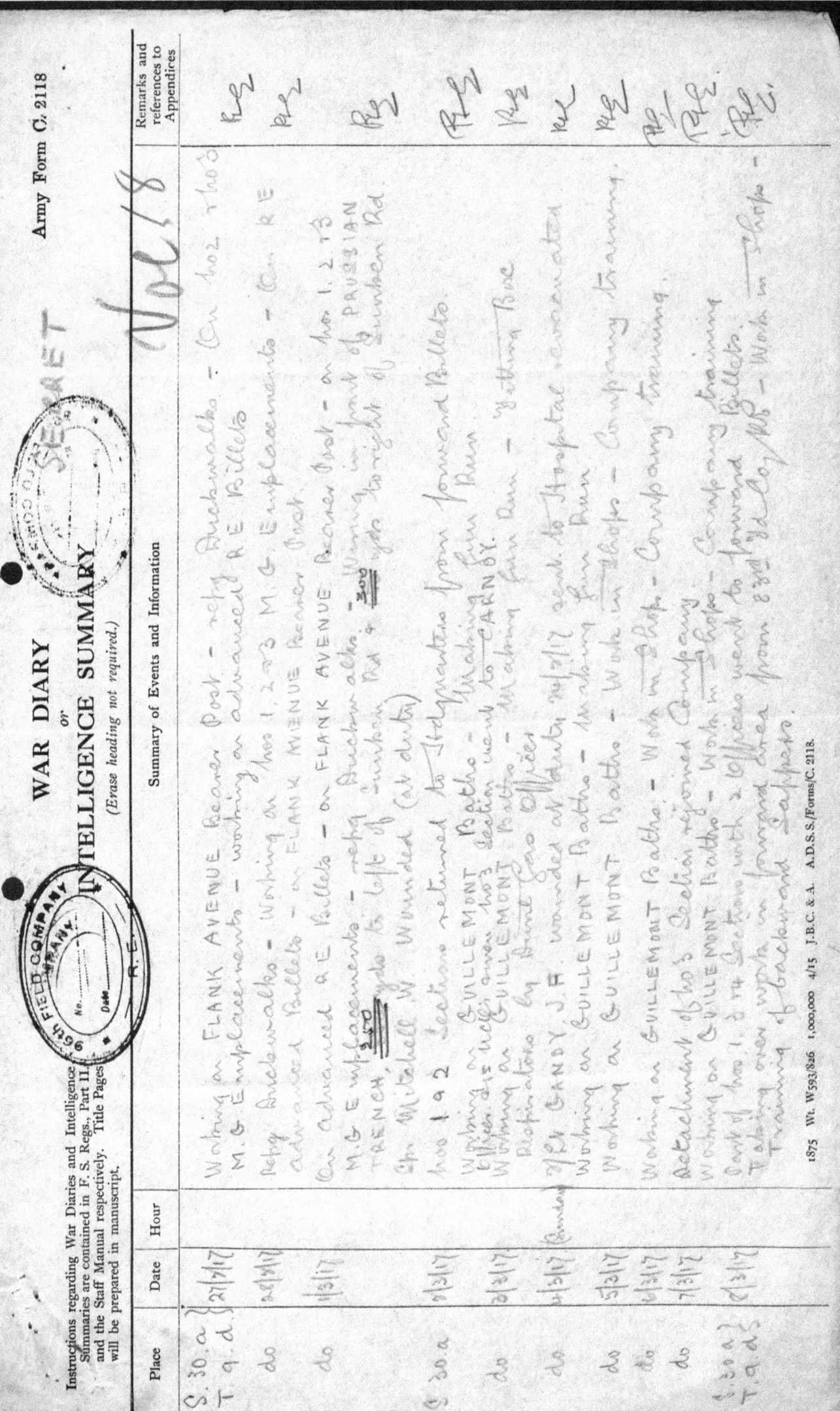

SECRET

Army Form C. 2118

WAR DIARY
or
INTELLIGENCE SUMMARY

(Erase heading not required.)

Instructions regarding War Diaries and Intelligence Summaries are contained in F. S. Regs., Part II. and the Staff Manual respectively. Title Pages will be prepared in manuscript.

Place	Date	Hour	Summary of Events and Information	Remarks and references to Appendices
S.30 a.2 T.q.d.5	9/3/17		Working on Nos 1, 2, & 4 M.G. Emplacements — Work in Shops — Training of Backward Sappers.	ME
do	10/3/17		Working on Signal Dugout near Bull Dump — Work on forward RE Billets — on RAM C Dugout near Bull Dump — retr trench boards BULL Dump Dugs — on Nos 1, 2, 3 & 4 M.G. Emplacements — Work in Shops — Training of Backward Sappers.	ME
do	11/3/17		Work on Signal Dugout near Bull Dump — on forward RE Billets — on RAMC Dugout near Bull Dump — on Nos 1, 2, 3 & 4 M.G. Emplacements — Work in Shops — Training of Backward Sappers	ME
do	12/3/17		2N BANISTER & 10 OR joined Company. Work on Signal Dugout — on RAMC Dugout — on forward RE Billets — on No 4 M.G. Emplacement — digging drain RESERVE LINE.	ME
do	13/3/17		2N BANISTER proceeded to forward Billets. On RAMC Dugout near Bull Dump — Bunks or Sunken Rd LES BOEUFS — on drains for Reserve Line — on No 4 M.G. Emplacement — Work in Shops — Training of Backward Sappers	ME
do	14/3/17		On RAMC Dugout — on forward RE Billets — on Dugouts in Sunken Rd LES BOEUFS — on M.G. Emplacement in "O" X trench — on drains in Reserve Line — Work in Shops — Training of Backward Sappers	ME
do	15/3/17		Widening & deepening Reserve Line — drainage of Reserve Line — on Dugouts LES BOEUFS — RAMC Dugout at Bull Dump — on forward RE Billets — making Police Shy Huck Archery near FLANK AVENUE — Work in Shops — Training of Backward Sappers.	ME

WAR DIARY or INTELLIGENCE SUMMARY.

Army Form C. 2118.

SECRET

(Erase heading not required.)

Instructions regarding War Diaries and Intelligence Summaries are contained in F.S. Regs., Part II. and the Staff Manual respectively. Title pages will be prepared in manuscript.

[Stamp: 36th FIELD COMPANY R.E.]

Place	Date	Hour	Summary of Events and Information	Remarks and references to Appendices
S.30.a T.a.5	16/3/17		On how M.G. Emplacement — on Reserve Line trench, digging, draining — on Brigade Sunken Rd. LESBOEUFS — to R.A.M.C. dugout near BULL dump — a forward R/GS Post — Work in shops — Training of Backward Sappers. No 1 Sec. returned to H.Q. Nos 2,3,4 went to GINCHY/3 & 3 to BULL dump. — 3 Officers at GINCHY. O.E. recruiting new line (to Beaumier Ry-	R.E.
S.30.a GINCHY BULL dump	17/3/17		On Dugouts Sunken Rd. LES BOEUFS — on forward N₂ Billets — R.A.M.C. Aid Post — Work in shops — Training of Backward Sappers. Company relieved by 54 Co in Line. Sapping new DECAUVILLE Line — Sections shifted into 3 cleaning billets on GINCHY.	R.E.
do	18/3/17		On MORVAL – ROCQUIGNY Road — carrying rails & sleepers forward DECAUVILLE	
do	19/3/17		On MORVAL – ROCQUIGNY Road — working on new DECAUVILLE	
do	19/3/17		On new Decauvilly MORVAL to ROCQUIGNY — On new road GINCHY to LES BOEUFS	R.E.
do	20/3/17		do	R.E.
do	21/3/17		do	R.E.
do	22/3/17		do	R.E.
do	23/3/17		Nos 1,2,3,4 Sections moved to billets at T.16 central. Taking up COMBLES – GUILLEMONT – DECAUVILLE Track	R.E.

SECRET

Army Form C. 2118

WAR DIARY
or
INTELLIGENCE SUMMARY

(Erase heading not required.)

Instructions regarding War Diaries and Intelligence Summaries are contained in F. S. Regs., Part II. and the Staff Manual respectively. Title Pages will be prepared in manuscript.

Place	Date	Hour	Summary of Events and Information	Remarks and references to Appendices
S.30.a) T.16 central	24/3/17		On new Deauville Rly. MORVAL to ROCQUIGNY. On new road GINCHY to LES BOEUFS. Taking up COMBLES - GUILLEMONT track.	--
do	25/3/17		On new Deauville Rly MORVAL to ROCQUIGNY. Taking up COMBLES - GUILLEMONT track.	--
do	26/3/17		ditto	--
do	27/3/17		ditto	--
do	28/3/17		ditto	--
S.30.a&b	29/3/17		Nos. 1 & 3. Sections returned to Headquarters. Nos 2 & 4. Sections returned to Headquarters. No 1 Sec. left for N.34.a. central.	--
S.30.a&b N.34.a.	30/3/17		Nos. 2,3 & 4 Sections HQR. moved to N.34.a. central. O.C. left Company to act as C.R.E. 20 Divn. (29/3/17).	--

Murdoch
Capt. RE
O/C 96 Fd Coy. RE.

SECRET

WAR DIARY
or
INTELLIGENCE SUMMARY

(Erase heading not required.)

Army Form C. 2118.

Place	Date	Hour	Summary of Events and Information	Remarks and references to Appendices
0.34.a. Sheet 57.c.S	31/3/17		Erecting Coril. houses etc. - Work on Water Point at DROMORE Jc. - Work on new D.H.Q. ROCQUIGNY. - Reconnoitering Roads & taking samples of water from wells in forward area.	R.E.
do	1/4/17		On new D.H.Q. ROCQUIGNY. - on DROMORE Jc Water Point - Reconnoitering Roads in forward area & taking samples of water from wells	R.E.
do	2/4/17		ditto	R.E.
do	3/4/17		On new D.H.Q. ROCQUIGNY. - on DROMORE Jc Water Point - repairs to both wells ROCQUIGNY.	R.E.
			O.C. rejoined Company after acting as CRE 20 Div.	
do	4/4/17		On new D.H.Q. ROCQUIGNY. - on DROMORE Jc Water Point - completing repairs to both wells, ROCQUIGNY.	R.E.
do	5/4/17		Water Point DROMORE Jc (O.31.6.4.1) completed - repairs to LES MESNIL - ROCQUIGNY Rd	R.E.
do	6/4/17		Repairs to LES MESNIL - ROCQUIGNY a - repairs to LE TRANSLOY - DROMORE Jc - ROCQUIGNY - BUS Road.	R.E.
do	7/4/17		Repairs to ROCQUIGNY - LE MESNIL Road - repairs to LE TRANSLOY - ROCQUIGNY Rd - repairs to ROCQUIGNY - BUS Road	R.E.
do	8/4/17		Working on YPRES (Internationale) Lane, filling in enemy trench - repairs to Adv H.Q. & Billets in BUS - repairs to ROCQUIGNY - BUS Road - clearing trees from BARASTRE - BUS Road.	R.E.

Army Form C. 2118.

WAR DIARY
or
INTELLIGENCE SUMMARY.
(Erase heading not required.)

Instructions regarding War Diaries and Intelligence Summaries are contained in F. S. Regs., Part II. and the Staff Manual respectively. Title pages will be prepared in manuscript.

96th FIELD COMPANY R.E.

Place	Date	Hour	Summary of Events and Information	Remarks and references to Appendices
O.34.a. Sheet 57c	9/4/17		On YTRES line - wiring edging - repairs to billets in BUS - party made ROCQUIGNY to BUS, ROCQUIGNY to BARASTRE, BUS to BERTINCOURT. BUS to BARASTRE - BUS & LECHELLE & VAULVART station.	A2
do	10/4/17		ditto H.Q. section had 27B lea cell Transport moved to YTRES.	A2
O.34.a. YTRES	11/4/17		On YTRES line - constructing posts, draining & wiring dismantling old enemy wire & collecting a dumps - Repairs to ROCQUIGNY - BUS road - retaining roads in BUS, LECHELLE & BARASTRE - repairs to Bde H.Q. & billets in BUS	A2
do	12/4/17		On YTRES line as on 11th inst - Repairs to ROCQUIGNY - BUS road - also road in BUS LECHELLE & BARASTRE & roads ROCQUIGNY - BARASTRE - BUS to BERTINCOURT - BUS to BARASTRE - BUS to LECHELLE & VAULVART Stn.	A2
do	13/4/17		ditto	A2
			Remainder of Company moved to YTRES. 2/Lt WILMOT joined Coy from 84th Fd. Coy R.E.	
YTRES	14/4/17		Coy Billets in RUYAULCOURT - repairs to waterpoint RUYAULCOURT. - laying out Strong Points "A" (P.17.d.9.1.) "B" (P.12.c.1.3) "C" (P.11.a.4.9) scavenging up wire for same - repairs to Coy billets in BERTINCOURT Bde H.Q. YTRES - enabling hand rail round crater at P.17.d.6.5.	A2

A5834 Wt. W4973/1107 750,000 8/16 St.d. Forms

WAR DIARY or INTELLIGENCE SUMMARY

Army Form C. 2118.

(Erase heading not required.)

Instructions regarding War Diaries and Intelligence Summaries are contained in F. S. Regs., Part II. and the Staff Manual respectively. Title pages will be prepared in manuscript.

96th FIELD COMPANY R.E.

Place	Date	Hour	Summary of Events and Information	Remarks and references to Appendices
YPRES P.2b.a.9.4. Sheet 57.C.SW	15/4/17	—	Billet accommodation in RUYAULCOURT & BERTINCOURT — On Bde HQ (YPRES). — repairs to water joint at RUYAULCOURT. — Work on Strong Points "A" "B" & "C" & carrying up pins for same. — Making hand rail round crater at P.17.d.6.5.	RE
do	16/4/17		Excavating Strong Points "A" & "B" making round "B" making frames for splinter proofs — Repg on Strong Point "D" (P.5.b.2.0). — excavating turning at "C" Strong Point. — On Bde HQ in BUS & YPRES. — on billet accommodation in BERTINCOURT, YPRES & on Rde HQ at RUYAULCOURT — making accommodation at BATH YPRES P.18.b.2.6. — fixing road direction posts at N. BERTINCOURT BARASTRE YPRES. — making round crater at P.2.b.1k.3. — filling road crater at P.10.d.5.4.	RE
do	17/4/17		Work on Strong Points "A" "B" "C" & "D" — on Bde HQ BUS & YPRES — billet accommodation in YPRES, RUYAULCOURT & BERTINCOURT — fixing road direction posts in BUS, LECHELLE, YPRES & RUYAULCOURT — On water joint at RUYAULCOURT.	RE
do	18/4/17		Billet accommodation in RUYAULCOURT, YPRES & BERTINCOURT, YPRES & water joint at P.9.b.1k.3. — fixing road direction posts at EQUANCOURT & NEUVILLE. — draining & making direction round crater at P.9.b.1k.3. — being road direction posts to EQUANCOURT & NEUVILLE. — draining & making round frames for Strong Point "A" & "B" — excavating for splinter proof & making splinter proof frames for Strong Point "A" & "B" — cutting down trees & stumps Q.7.c.3.1. — on being material for new June Baths YPRES — excavating for latrines at RUYAULCOURT & obtaining material for same.	RE
do	19/4/17		On Bde HQ RUYAULCOURT — on water joint RUYAULCOURT — erecting road direction posts — draining & repairing Strong Point "A" & "B" — draining Strong Point & Strong Point "D" — at Bath HQ P.6.a.9.5. — Bde HQ BUS YPRES — billet accommodation in BERTINCOURT — dismantling MGE at P.11d central — completion & on new Baths at YPRES, obtaining material for same.	RE

Army Form C. 2118.

WAR DIARY
or
INTELLIGENCE SUMMARY.
(Erase heading not required.)

Instructions regarding War Diaries and Intelligence Summaries are contained in F. S. Regs., Part II. and the Staff Manual respectively. Title pages will be prepared in manuscript.

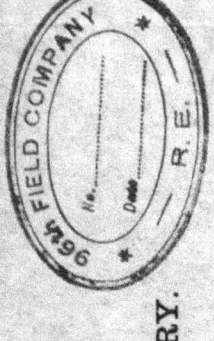

Place	Date	Hour	Summary of Events and Information	Remarks and references to Appendices
YPRES P.26.a.9.4. Sheet 57.c	20/4/17		Forming A batis Q.1.c. 8.6 to Q.1.a. 8.5 and left Battn of left Bde - being reference posts in HAVRINCOURT Wood - new Divnl Baths at YPRES - on Bde HQ RUYAULCOURT - on water point RUYAULCOURT - Bde HQ, Bde QQ, YPRES - billet accomodation Bde, YPRES, BEAT IN COURT, ? RUYAULCOURT, - making diversion round crater RUYAULCOURT.	R.E.
do	21/4/17		On water point RUYAULCOURT - on Bde HQ Artillery Rd - Bde HQ RUYAULCOURT - making diversion round crater RUYAULCOURT - Tram road sys. into RUYAULCOURT - METZ - thickening wire in abatis Q.1.a.9.c. - billeting accomodation Bde, YPRES - Bde HQ YPRES 2 - on Divnl Baths o trench to same - dismantling Electric Light plant at ARROW HEAD.	R.E.
do	22/4/17		On RUYAULCOURT Water point - on Bde HQ RUYAULCOURT - billet accomodation in RUYAULCOURT, YPRES, ? BEATINCOURT - on new Divnl Baths YPRES o trench to same.	R.E.
do	23/4/17		On RUYAULCOURT Water point - on Bde HQ Artillery Rd CQ, RUYAULCOURT - billet accomodation in RUYAULCOURT, BEATINCOURT, Bde, YPRES - on Baths at YPRES - on new Divnl Baths at YPRES o trench to same.	R.E.
do	24/4/17		On RUYAULCOURT Water Point - on Bde HQ Artillery Bde HQ RUYAULCOURT - making road diverting trach HAVRINCOURT Wood Q.I. e.6.6 - on abutmt for mine No same - on billet accomodation Bde - Battn HQ YPRES - new Divnl Baths at YPRES, trach to same making jetta beds.	R.E.
do	25/4/17		Making road diverting trach HAVRINCOURT Wood - making parries for same - draining RUYAULCOURT Road P.12.a.1.3 - on RUYAULCOURT Water pump - on Bde HQ Artillery Rd HQ, RUYAULCOURT - new Divnl Baths YPRES - on Battn HQ YPRES - billeting accomodation YPRES	R.E.
do	26/4/17		On sea fastening on Canal - on Battn HQ Millen accomodation YPRES - on new Divnl Baths YPRES	R.E.

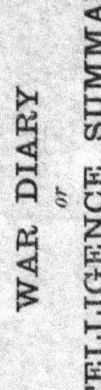

96th FIELD COMPANY R.E.

Army Form C. 2118.

WAR DIARY
or
INTELLIGENCE SUMMARY.
(Erase heading not required.)

Instructions regarding War Diaries and Intelligence Summaries are contained in F. S. Regs., Part II. and the Staff Manual respectively. Title pages will be prepared in manuscript.

Place	Date	Hour	Summary of Events and Information	Remarks and references to Appendices
YTRES. P.L.A. 9.K. Sheet 57/F	27/4/17		No 1 Coy & No 2. Coy. Cantooning on Canal (No 1 See at night, No 2 See day) - On Batth HQ, + Billet accomodation YTRES - Working on BUS - YTRES Road widening + Batho. - on new Quad Batho YTRES. - on Batth Home for RUYAULCOURT.	R/2
do	28/4/17		Wiring RUYAULCOURT Switch. - Nos 2 & 3 Lee Cantooning on Canal (No 2 See at night & No 3. Lee day) - On Batth House RUYAULCOURT. - examining cellar in BERTINCOURT for same. - on Batth HQ RUYAULCOURT - On Batth HQ + Billet accomodation YTRES - on new Bivouc Baths YTRES Station - on YTRES - BUS wagon track. - on YTRES - NEUVILLE track.	R/2

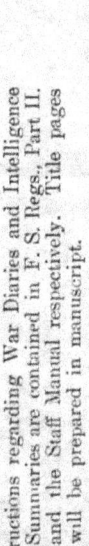

MAJOR, R.E.
COMDG. 96TH F4. COY: R.E.

WAR DIARY or INTELLIGENCE SUMMARY

96 2a Coy R.E.

Place	Date	Hour	Summary of Events and Information	Remarks and references to Appendices
YTRES P.1b a 9.14 Sheet 57c	29/4/17		Strength of Company: 7 Officers 213 O.R.s amen. 74 Horses & Mules. On dry weather track YTRES – NEUVILLE and YTRES – BUS. – on billet accommodation. Making up YTRES – running RUYAULCOURT – NEUVILLE (M.G.E's & chinks posts RUYAULCOURT switch – excavating (M.G.E's 9 day & 14 & men) night). Work in shops.	
do	30/4/17		No 1 & 2 Secs pontooning on Canal (No 1 & 2 day No 4 night) – on YTRES – NEUVILLE track. – on diversion round No 9 of BUS for ROCQUIGNY – BUS – YTRES dry weather track. – on Bath Home at RUYAULCOURT. – on billet accommodation YTRES – Work in Shops.	
do	1/5/17		Erecting hut at Railhead ROCQUIGNY. – camouflaging at Divnl H.Q. – on YTRES – NEUVILLE track. – on diversion round BUS in ROCQUIGNY – BUS – YTRES dry weather track. – on billet accommodation YTRES – on Bath Home RUYAULCOURT.	
do	2/5/17		Camouflaging at Divnl H.Q. – completing hut at Railhead ROCQUIGNY – on hut for Signal School at LECHELLE – working in billets in METZ for Company – felling trees YTRES – LECHELLE Rd. – felling trees BUS – YTRES Rd. – diversion round BUS for dry weather track. – dry weather track YTRES – YTRES Station. – on BUS – ROCQUIGNY dry weather track. –	
do	3/5/17		On Bath Home at RUYAULCOURT. – on Company billets METZ. – on YTRES – BUS dry weather track. – camouflaging at Divnl H.Q.	
METZ YTRES BERTINCOURT	4/5/17		No 1.3.9 & Secs proceeded to billets in METZ. a dismounted att to BERTINCOURT to prepare billets for H.Q. – Working on Billets METZ:	

47306 Maj. Powell 17. – Wounded.

J. Mahy

WAR DIARY
or
INTELLIGENCE SUMMARY.
(Erase heading not required.)

Army Form C. 2118.

Place	Date	Hour	Summary of Events and Information	Remarks and references to Appendices
METZ YTRES	5-5-17		Strength of Company:- 7 Officers 222 men. 7 Officers & others	
BERTINCOURT RUYAULCOURT			On SUPPORT LINE. Taping out and evacuating the drainage and sump. FRONT LINE connecting up posts. No 2 section march to RUYAULCOURT // Work on Billets at RUYAULCOURT	
do—	6-5-17		Reconstructing new support line and clearing trenches from field line for Machine Guns. Reconnoitring trains front drainage in trench line. Taping out Front line. Working on Billets RUYAULCOURT. One day weather broke trace work 9.30 PM to 9.R.3575 (Sheet 57c). One 37052 dap McGuigan P Wounded. No.72243 " " " Wounded at Duty. Front line.	
do—	7-5-17		Strength of Company:- 7 Officers 211 men 7 officers and others. Taping out support line and clearing rifle after. Connecting up front line. Working from Posts to front line with training wire. Work 9.30 PM. Recon. of support line (summary) Work on Billets RUYAULCOURT. Work on Rear 9.30 P.M. to 9.R.2575 (Sheet 57c).	
METZ YTRES	8-5-17		No.2 section moved from RUYAULCOURT to METZ. Connecting up support and front line. Reconnecting posts in front line. Duplicating bridges in Reserve line. Taping out support line on very unstable ground. 9.30 P.M. to 9.R.25.75.8 (Sheet 57c). Work on Billets METZ.	
do—	9-5-17		Reconnecting bridges in trenches. Reconning bridges in Reserve line. Taping out support line. Work on dry weather from East 23 to 9.R. 25.45 (Sheet 57c). Facing boundary aux arrows.	

D.Mack

Army Form C. 2118.

WAR DIARY
or
INTELLIGENCE SUMMARY.
(Erase heading not required.)

Instructions regarding War Diaries and Intelligence Summaries are contained in F. S. Regs., Part II. and the Staff Manual respectively. Title pages will be prepared in manuscript.

Place	Date	Hour	Summary of Events and Information	Remarks and references to Appendices
METZ. YPRES.	10/4/7		Strength of Coy: 7 Officers 211 men. 74 Horses & Mules. Front line with. Moving Tram. G.15.A.8.6. to G.9.d.25.75 (Sheet 57c). Taping out support trench and clearing field of fire. Work in shops. Work on well G.10.a.H.12. (Sheet 57c). Infy Company HQ. B.Hd. G.8.f. B.4.c.H.7. Bell Ammunition Dump. G.15.c.2.8.	May & Juncks G Sheet 57c
do SIEVE WOOD.	11/4/7		On digging and wiring Reserve line B.30.g.7. to B.30.c.6.5. Digging support trench B.14.4.4.7.6 B.30.3.2. Digging Support Trench B.3c.9.7. to B.30.6.5. On well G.10.a.4.2. Infantry Coy HQ making splinterproofs B.4.d.55. - B.4.c.7.7. - B.3.c.4.1. - B.4.c.1.9. Work in shops. No 3 Section moved complete with transport to SIEVE WOOD. 16 H employed on Personnel HQ.	
do	12/4/7		On Infantry HQ Splinterproofs at B.4.c.1.9. - B.3.c.4.1. - B.4.c.7.7. - B.4.d.5.8. Digging support line. Digging front line. Front line wiring. Wiring support line. On Bell Ammunition Dumps B.10.c.8.6. Bell Bomb Dump G.15.c.2.5. On well in TRESCAULT G.10.a.H.62. Work in shops.	
do	13/4/7		On Infy Coy HQ splinterproofs at B.4.c.1.9. - B.3.c.4.1. - B.4.c.7.7. - B.4.d.5.8. Wiring front line. Wiring support line. Digging support line. Digging front line. On Bell Ammunition Dumps B.10.c.86. Bell Bomb Dump G.15.c.2.8. On well in TRESCAULT G.10.a.H.62. Work in shops.	
do	14/4/7		On Infy Coy HQ splinterproofs at B.4.c.1.9. - B.3.c.4.1. - B.4.c.7.7. - B.4.d.5.8. Wiring front line. Wiring support line. Digging support line. Digging front line. On Bell Ammunition Dumps B.10.c.8.6. Bell Bomb Dump G.15.c.2.3. On well in TRESCAULT G.10.a.H.62. Work in shops.	
METZ. YPRES.	15/4/7		No 3 Section returned complete with transport from SIEVE WOOD to METZ. Wiring strong points. Wiring support line. Repairing support line wire where broken by shellfire. On well in TRESCAULT B.10.a.45.65. Infantry Coy HQ B.4.d.5.8. - B.4.c.7.7. - B.3.c.7.1. Wiring front line. Wiring 2nd line. Bridging over blown in culvert. G.10.a.2.2. Bell Bomb Dump. G.15.c.2.8. Bell Ammn. Dump. G.10.c.8.6	

B T Mash

Army Form C. 2118.

WAR DIARY
or
INTELLIGENCE SUMMARY.
(Erase heading not required.)

Instructions regarding War Diaries and Intelligence Summaries are contained in F. S. Regs., Part II. and the Staff Manual respectively. Title pages will be prepared in manuscript.

Place	Date	Hour	Summary of Events and Information	Remarks and references to Appendices
METZ. YPRES	16/9/17		Working on Coy – 74/140 ATO 211 men – 74 horses and mules. Rigging Down Front Mine. Rigging Dugout line. Infantry Coy 118. B40.58 – B40.77 – B50.71. Ball Bomb Dump B15C2.8. Bell Ammunition at Batha METZ. B20C7.7. Well in TRESCAULT B10C4 5 65. Facing Mellin Pump and meter enlargement on right of METZ-TRESCAULT Road. Temp B10C5.5. Handling 2½ yards over enlarging 2½ yards on new line.	Major Afernoon Mod 57c.
do	17/9/17.		Mining Front line. Infantry Coy 110. B40.58 – B40.77 – B50.71. Bell Bomb Dump B15C2.8 Bell Ammunition Temp B10C5.6. Well B10A 45.65. Workers line on right of METZ-TRESCAULT Road. Mining in TRESCAULT Quarry for Bomb Store. Work in Shops.	
do	18/9/17.		Mining front line. Well in TRESCAULT B10C4 5 65. Infy Coy 108. B10A 58 – B10C77 – B50.71. Working on new oval of METZ-TRESCAULT Rd. Making flash murrains around crater at B.17 & 7.0. Quarry for Bomb Store. Rigging comm trench. B11 d 25.9 to B11a 3.0. Mining in TRESCAULT Quarry. Work in shops.	
do	19/9/17		Mining front line Inf Coy (Infantry 108) B40.5.8 – B40.77 – B50.71. Well in TRESCAULT B10C4 5 65. Work on well in TRESCAULT B10A 45.65. Mining in TRESCAULT Quarry for Bomb Store. Bell Ammunition Dump B10C5.6. Fixing ammunition agno hag in WIRE of gaps in wire. Work in shops.	
do	20/9/17		Fixing agnhoards. Work in shops. Standing over ready to relieving Reinwood R.E.	
YPRES	21/9/17		Company (less Transport) moved to YPRES	
LE TRANSLOY	22/9/17		Company moved complete to QUARRY at LE TRANSLOY	
FAVREUIL	23/9/17		Company moved complete to FAVREUIL	
VAULX-VRAUCOURT C29 A.2.4	24/9/17		Company moved complete to VAULX-VRAUCOURT. M.E. 3A4 declines then proceeded to C.29 A.2.4.	

Army Form C. 2118.

WAR DIARY
or
INTELLIGENCE SUMMARY.
(Erase heading not required.)

Instructions regarding War Diaries and Intelligence Summaries are contained in F.S. Regs., Part II. and the Staff Manual respectively. Title pages will be prepared in manuscript.

Place	Date	Hour	Summary of Events and Information	Remarks and references to Appendices
VAULX-VRAUCOURT C.29 a.2.4.	25/7/17		Strength of Coy – 7 Officers 209 men. 73 Horses & Mules. Work on dug outs at C.22a.8.1 – C.22a.5.1 – C.29b.2.4 – C.17a7.0 – C.17a2.0 – C.23b.3.9. Wiring front line. Work in shops. 67712 Spr. Brown R. - Wounded.	Map references Sheet 57c.
do –	26/7/17		Work on dug outs at C.22a.5.1 – C.29a.5.1 – C.29a.2.4 – C.17a7.0 – C.17a2.0 – C.23b.3.9. Wiring front line. Work in shops.	
do –	27/7/17		Work on dug outs at C.22a.8.1 – C.29a.5.1 – C.29a.2.4 – C.17a7.0 – C.17a2.0 – C.23b.3.9. Wiring front line. Work in shops. 50537 Spr. Reed A. Cpl – Wounded at duty.	
FAVREUIL VAULX-VRAUCOURT	28/7/17		Company (less No 1 Section) moved to FAVREUIL.	
do	29/7/17		Work on rifle range, (allows for bayonet fighting baths & advance dressing station.	
	30/5/17		do for 29/7/17	

D.T. MacInnes Capt for O.C. 9.8 Field Coy R.E.

SECRET

9637 Coy RE
WJ 21

Army Form C. 2118.

WAR DIARY
or
INTELLIGENCE SUMMARY.
(Erase heading not required.)

96th FIELD COMPANY R.E.

Place	Date	Hour	Summary of Events and Information	Remarks and references to Appendices
FAVREUIL-VAULX	31/7		Strength of Coy: 7 Officers 2 O/R 3/R & O/R 9 Mins. 74 Nurses & Mules	Map reference Map 57c 9/-
"	1/8		Work on Advanced Dressing Stn Vaulx. Vaulx Baths. FAVREUIL Baths. Work on supper company training	
"	2/8		Work on Advanced Dressing Stn VAULX. VAULX Baths. FAVREUIL Baths. Work in shops company training	
"	3/8		Work on Wiring VAULX line. Taping out position of VAULX line. Work on FAVREUIL Rifle range. Advanced Dressing Stn VAULX. VAULX Baths. Work in shops.	
"	4/8		Work on wire of VAULX line. Spitlocking VAULX line. On Advanced Dressing Stn VAULX, VAULX Baths. On FAVREUIL rifle range. Work in shops.	
"	5/8		Work on Advanced Dressing Stn VAULX. On VAULX Baths. Making gun screens for R.A. & trellis for R.A.M.C. on FAVREUIL Rifle range. & Working on Right & Left details of VAULX line.	
C.20.a.0.0 and VAULX	5/8		Advanced HQ & 3 sections arrived C.20.a.0.0. Transport and 1 section arrived VAULX taking over Billets and work.	

Army Form C. 2118.

WAR DIARY
or
INTELLIGENCE SUMMARY.
(Erase heading not required.)

96th FIELD COMPANY R.E.

Instructions regarding War Diaries and Intelligence Summaries are contained in F. S. Regs., Part II. and the Staff Manual respectively. Title pages will be prepared in manuscript.

Place	Date	Hour	Summary of Events and Information	Remarks and references to Appendices
Bde. O.O. Trust	6/4/17		Strength of Company 7 Officers 206 of other ranks. 73 Horses + Mules	Appointments Mar 3 R.
"	7/4/17		Work on Dugouts. C5a2.4. C5a8.5. C16b1.5. C9d9.4. C10a7.0. Work in Shops	
"	8/4/17		Work on Dugouts C6a2.4. C6a8.5. C16b1.5. C9d9.4. C10a7.0. Work in Shops.	
"	9/4/17		Work on Dugouts C5a2.4. C5a8.5. C16b1.5. C9d9.4. C10a7.0. Work in Shops.	
"	10/4/17		Work on Dugouts C5a2.4. C5a8.5. C16b1.5. C9d9.4. C10a7.0. Work in Shops	
"	11/4/17		Work on Dugouts C5a2.4. C5a8.5. C16b1.5. C9d9.4. C10a7.0. Work in Shops.	
"	12/4/17		Work on Dugouts C5a2.4. C5a8.5. C16b1.5. C9d9.4. C10a7.0. Work in Shops	
"	13/4/17		Work on Dugouts C5a2.4. C5a8.5. C16b1.5. C9d9.4. C10a7.0. Work in Shops	

WAR DIARY or INTELLIGENCE SUMMARY

Army Form C. 2118.

(Erase heading not required.)

Instructions regarding War Diaries and Intelligence Summaries are contained in F.S. Regs., Part II. and the Staff Manual respectively. Title pages will be prepared in manuscript.

Place	Date	Hour	Summary of Events and Information	Remarks and references to Appendices
C20.a.0.0. VAULX	14/7		Strength of Company 7 Officers. 206. 1.S.O.'s & above. 73. Horses & Mules. Work on Dugouts C5a.8.5. C16.b.1.5. C9.a.9.4. C10.a.7.0. Work on Shypos. Reforming Fifteen preparatory to starting Machine Gun Dugouts at C5b.85.55 – U29.b.5.1 – U29.a.9.4.	Appendices. April 17.
NOREUIL VAULX	15/7		Advanced H.Q. & 3 Sections moved to NOREUIL. Work on Dugouts C5a.2.4. C5a.8.5. C16.b.1.5. C9.a.9.4. C10.a.7.0. C5b.95.75. U29.b.5.1. U29.a.9.4. Work on Shypos.	
"	16/7		Work on Dugouts C5a.2.4. C5a.8.5. C16.b.1.5. C9.a.9.4. C10.a.7.0. C5b.85.75. U29.b.5.1. U29.a.9.4. Work in Shypos. Work on trench NOREUIL	
"	17/7		Work on Dugouts. C5a.2.4. C9.a.9.4. C5b.85.55. U29.a.9.4. U29.b.5.1. 150 yds trench dug at U29.b. Work in Shypos. Work on trench NOREUIL	
"	18/7		Work on Dugouts. C5a.2.4. C9.a.9.4. C5b.85.55. U29.a.9.4. U29.b.5.1. Work in Shypos. Work on trench NOREUIL.	[signature]

WAR DIARY or INTELLIGENCE SUMMARY

Army Form C. 2118.

Place	Date	Hour	Summary of Events and Information	Remarks and references to Appendices
NOREUIL & VAULX	19/7		Strength of Company 7 Officers 206 of 6 O.R. Men 71 Horses + Mules. Work in Ringrod C5a2.4. C9a9.4. C5a 95.55 U29a9.4. U29+51. Work in dugouts	Appx references Sheet 57c
"	20/7		Work on Ringrod C5a2.4. C9a9.4. C5b 95.55 U29a9.4. U29+5.1. filling 5 dugouts forto used as mining works. RESERVE LINE Taping out front C5c 8.18.2 to C11.6.2.7.	
I26 32.	21/7		Advanced HQ and 3 Sections opened HQ at. I 2 c 3.2. Work on Ringrod C5a2.4. C9a9.4. C5b 95.55. U29a9.4. U29+5.1.	
"			Strength of Company: 7 Officers 202 N.C.O.s + Men 71 Horses + Mules	

WAR DIARY or INTELLIGENCE SUMMARY

Army Form C. 2118.

Place	Date	Hour	Summary of Events and Information	Remarks and references to Appendices
I, 2, C, 3, 2. Sheet 57/c	22/6/17		Work on 2nd Line.	
do	23/6/17		Working on 3rd Line – on Revolver range at FAVREUIL – on Dugouts S/or Raid on VAULX – NOREUIL Qr – on Baths at VAULX.	
do	24/6/17		On Baths at VAULX – Revolver range at FAVREUIL – factory rebuilding wagons.	
do	25/6/17		Company marched to GOMIECOURT & took over from 460th Field Coy RE.	
GOMIECOURT	26/6/17		Company Drill.	
do	27/6/17		Physical Drill under Gymnasium Instructor L/Cpl Hooker.	
do	28/6/17		Transport moved to ACHEUX en route to GORGES. Remainder – Rifle Exercises.	
do	29/6/17		Remainder marched to ACHIET-LE-GRAND & entrained for CANADAS detraining at latter place marching to GORGES. Transport also arrived at GORGES.	

M Went
O/C 96th Field Coy RE

WAR DIARY
INTELLIGENCE SUMMARY

Army Form C. 2118.

96 3rd Coy R.E.
Vol 22

Place	Date	Hour	Summary of Events and Information	Remarks and references to Appendices
GORGES	30.6.17		Strength of Coy 7 Officers 205 N.C.O.s + men 44 horses + mules. Coy drill, rifle exercises.	R.E.
"	1.7.17		Company marched to ST LEGER-LES-DOMART	R.E.
ST LEGER LES DOMART	2.7.17		"	R.E.
"	3.7.17		Coy drill, physical drill, rifle exercises	R.E.
"	4.7.17		"	R.E.
"	5.7.17		G.O.C. Inspection	R.E.
"	6.7.17		Coy drill, rifle exercises. 2/Lt Gordon Mitchell joined company.	R.E.
"	7.7.17		physical drill	R.E.
"	8.7.17		Sunday. Bathing parade	R.E.

Army Form C. 2118.

WAR DIARY
or
INTELLIGENCE SUMMARY.
(Erase heading not required.)

Instructions regarding War Diaries and Intelligence Summaries are contained in F. S. Regs., Part II. and the Staff Manual respectively. Title pages will be prepared in manuscript.

Place	Date	Hour	Summary of Events and Information	Remarks and references to Appendices
LA CHAUSSÉE	9/7/17		H.Q. and 4 Sections marched to LA CHAUSSÉE.	R.E.
	10/7/17		Parade on bridging	R.E.
	11/7/17		" "	
	12/7/17		" "	R.E.
	13/7/17		H.Q. and 4 Section marched to ST LEGER-LES-DOMART	R.E.
ST LEGER-LES DOMART	14/7/17		Divisional Horse show, Section sent east 1st prize	R.E.
			Coy. drill, reference to physical drill	
	15/7/17		Sunday, trolley parade	R.E.
	16/7/17		Coy. drill, physical drill & rifle exercises	R.E.
	17/7/17		Coy. physical drill. Pontoon & wagon show 1st prize.	R.E.
	18/7/17		C.R.E. inspection.	R.E.

WAR DIARY
or
INTELLIGENCE SUMMARY.

Army Form C. 2118.

Place	Date	Hour	Summary of Events and Information	Remarks and references to Appendices
ST LEGER -LES-	19/7/17		Coy drill, rifle exercises + physical drill.	
DOMART	20/7/17		do -	R.E.1
"	21/7/17		Coy marched to CANDAS, entrained to PROVEN & marched to F.10.a.5.2.	R.E.2
F.10.a.5.2. SHEET 27	22/7/17		Coy training, physical drill.	R.E.2
"	23/7/17		Coy drill + training, physical drill.	
"	24/7/17		do	
"	25/7/17		do	
"	26/7/17		do	
"	27/7/17		do	
"	28/7/17		do	
"	29/7/17		Sunday.	R.E.3
"	30/7/17		Drill -	

P.H. Story
Major R.E.
O.C. 96 Fd Coy R.E.

SECRET

Army Form C. 2118.

WAR DIARY or INTELLIGENCE SUMMARY

August 1917

No. 23

Place	Date	Hour	Summary of Events and Information	Remarks and references to Appendices
Sheet 27 F.16.a.5.2. A.11.c.7.7. Sheet 28	30/7/17		Strength of Coy. 7 Off. 206 O.Rs. Dismounted marched to A.11.c.7.7. (Sheet 28) DE WIPPE CABARET. Arriving 12.20 a.m. rest morning	PF2
A.11.c.7.7.	31/7/17		Company working YPRES - BOESINGHE RD + HUDDLESTON RD. Shift 4pm to 8pm - 38th Division attached + took PILCKEM RIDGE.	A.F.
do	1/8/17		Standing by - very wet day.	PF2
do	2/8/17		Working on Plank road to HUDDLESTON RD - 9am to 3pm	
do	3/8/17		do	A.F.2
do	4/8/17		do	
do	5/8/17		2 Sections on Plank road to HUDDLESTON RD, 2 sections on duckwalk from HUDDLESTON RD	P.F2
B.21.d.5.7	6/8/17		Whole company marched to B.21.d.5.7 (Sheet 28) - near DAWSONS CORNER - constructed new camp.	PF2

SECRET

Army Form C. 2118.

Instructions regarding War Diaries and Intelligence
Summaries are contained in F. S. Regs., Part II.
and the Staff Manual respectively. Title pages
will be prepared in manuscript.

WAR DIARY
or
INTELLIGENCE SUMMARY.
(Erase heading not required.)

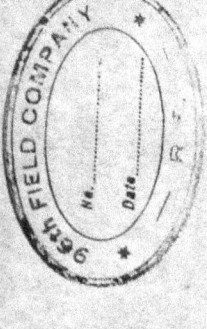

Place	Date	Hour	Summary of Events and Information	Remarks and references to Appendices
Bri d 5Y	7/8/17		Constructing new camp.	K
do	8/8/17		Nos 2 & 3 sections on trench board track HUDDLESTON RD to PILCKEM. Nos 1 & 4 section on DECAUVILLE track, CANAL to HUDDLESTON RD - working in 2 shifts	K
do	9/8/17		do - 40025 Sgt NOLAN wounded - 169245 Sapper FROST wounded & duty 36950 Rfn HARVEY 10KRR killed	K
do	10/8/17		do 49603 Sapper TERRY wounded dry weather	K
do	11/8/17		Working on new Artillery plank track. CACTUS JUNCTION to PILCKEM. + trench board track -	K
do	12/8/17		Tramway wagon track to CACTUS PONTOON bridge - new bridge over YPERLEE completed - working on RAMC Shelters. 75 yds Duckboard track completed - repairing BARD CAUSEWAY - forming dump at GALWITZ FARM. 1 man joined Company.	K

SECRET

Army Form C. 2118.

Instructions regarding War Diaries and Intelligence
Summaries are contained in F. S. Regs., Part II.
and the Staff Manual respectively. Title pages
will be prepared in manuscript.

WAR DIARY
or
INTELLIGENCE SUMMARY.
(Erase heading not required.)

Place	Date	Hour	Summary of Events and Information	Remarks and references to Appendices
Bn. a S.7	13/9/17		PILCKEN RD & HUDDLESTON RD Artillery track made – 150 yds Duckboard track made – MARSOUIN FARM wireless signal station dug out completed – R.A.M.C. Dressing Station & shelters completed – Repair to CACTUS PONTOON track – BARD CAUSEWAY – Sump at GALWITZ FARM completed.	R2
do	14/9/17		Double duckboard track to PILCKEM RD completed – CACTUS PONTOON track marked with white posts – Shore ends of CACTUS PONTOON Bridge made good – R.A.M.C. Dressing station completed.	R2
do	15/9/17		Signboard fixed on track BARD CAUSEWAY – PILCKEM – CACTUS PONTOON – repairing BARD CAUSEWAY. Putney brothers	R2
do	16/9/17		LANGEMARCK captured – Nos 1 & 4 Sections laying tramway to C.B.G.R. – Nos 2 & 3 Sections standing by awaiting orders.	R2
Bn. a S.7. F.10.a.5.2. (Sheet 27)	17/9/17		2 Lt MITCHELL & Spr McILROY wounded while on reconnaissance. Lt MITCHELL died of wounds. Remainder entrained at ELVERDINGHE for PROVEN, going into camp at F.10.a.5.2. (Sheet 27) transport travelled by road.	R2

SECRET

Army Form C. 2118.

Instructions regarding War Diaries and Intelligence Summaries are contained in F. S. Regs., Part II. and the Staff Manual respectively. Title pages will be prepared in manuscript.

WAR DIARY
or
INTELLIGENCE SUMMARY.
(Erase heading not required.)

Place	Date	Hour	Summary of Events and Information	Remarks and references to Appendices
F10.a 5.2.	18/8/17		Company cleaning up & improving camp.	R.E.
do	19/8/17		Sunday. No work.	R.E.
do	20/8/17		Company training	
do	21/8/17		do do	R.E.
do	22/8/17		do do	
do	23/8/17		Cleaning, packing & loading wagons	R.E.
F10 a 5.2. (sheet 27) B10 d 7.3. (sheet 28) B9 d 4.8. (sheet 28)	24/9/17		Dismounted marched to INTERNATIONAL CORNER, entrained for ELVERDINGHE proceeding to camp at B10 d 7.3 (sheet 28) — transport travelling by road to B9 d 4.8	R.E.

SECRET

Army Form C. 2118.

WAR DIARY
or
INTELLIGENCE SUMMARY.
(Erase heading not required.)

Instructions regarding War Diaries and Intelligence Summaries are contained in F. S. Regs., Part II. and the Staff Manual respectively. Title pages will be prepared in manuscript.

Place	Date	Hour	Summary of Events and Information	Remarks and references to Appendices
B10 d.7.5 B9 d.4.6	25/8/17		Working on GERMAN track. VERTE MILL RD ref'd & drained – 70 yds track laid CACTUS PONTOON – repairing PILCKEM RD between C.T.a.C.8.0 + C.T.a.8.7 – 12 yds plank road relaid at C.T.a.8.7 – Working on forming road from HUDDLESTON + RD's to S CHEMIN'S ESTAMINET – forming new road from PILCKEM RD to IRON CROSS RD (370 yds) No 4 Section working in camp	
do	26/8/17		Work on road CACTUS PONTOON to HUDDLESTON RD. Laying 45 yds plank road, 30 yds simple wire pickets + 20 yds turkey track laid – making formation for double road – HUDDLESTON + RD to S CHEMIN'S ESTAMINET, creating drains + ship decking on PILCKEM SWITCH RD 90 yds simple plank way laid forming track & drains. 2/Lt WAITE.F joined Company. No 1 Section working in camp	
do	27/8/17		Work on CACTUS PONTOON to HUDDLESTON RD, 80 yds drained + prepared for turkey tracks, 85 yds simple turkey tracks laid, 30 yds planking laid & ref'g roadway – preparing road formation. S CHEMIN'S ESTAMINET to SWITCH RD – preparing formation PILCKEM SWITCH RD 40 yds planking laid + forming timber drain – HUDDLESTON + ROADS to S CHEMIN'S ESTAMINET, 60 yds formed for road, 3 caves filled, 2 bordrains fixed. 230 yds drain graded & cleaned, 14 yds planking laid. Reinforcements 2 NCO's + men joined Company. No1 Section working in camp.	

SECRET

Army Form C. 2118.

WAR DIARY
or
INTELLIGENCE SUMMARY.
(Erase heading not required.)

Instructions regarding War Diaries and Intelligence Summaries are contained in F. S. Regs., Part II. and the Staff Manual respectively. Title pages will be prepared in manuscript.

Place	Date	Hour	Summary of Events and Information	Remarks and references to Appendices
Bio dy.3 B9 a 4.8.	28/8/17		Work on CACTUS PONTOON RD preparing & laying (113 yds of road, laying 38 yds turkey track, laying 25 yds of fascines making 14 yds motor dummy point — Work on IRON CROSS RD DIVERSION laying 98 yds of plank track, firm bar drain under road, laying 30 yds double under dummy plank. — Work @ GALWITZ DUMP, laying 40 yds plank for loader & dummy wagon — Rep'g road between HUDDLESTON + RD + 5 CHEMINS — drawing between GALWITZ DUMP & 5 CHEMINS. No 3 Section working in camp.	X
do	29/8/17		Work on PILCKEM RD 660 slabs carried, 70 yds decking laid, 150 yds double formation prepared — laying 10 yds lagging & completing drain at junction of ARTILLERY track; cleaning & repairing 500 yds road, draining for same 75% complete — preparing & laying 14 yds turkey walk — CACTUS PONTOON and HUDDLESTON RD, 60 yds planking laid & 45 yds turkey walk laid — rep'g bad places in road — laying top drain & revetting sides of road — rep'g CACTUS PONTOON Bdge — dumps carrying turkey walks & beech slabs.	X

30.VIII.17.   P.E. Stone maj n.z.
O.C. 96th Field Coy R.E.

SECRET

96 Jn Coy RE

WAR DIARY
or
INTELLIGENCE SUMMARY.

Place	Date	Hour	Summary of Events and Information	Remarks and references to Appendices
B10 d 7.3 (Sheet 28)	30/8/17		Working on CACTUS PONTOON – 50 yds Turkey board laid, 117 yds deep in + 40 yds fascined laid, 200 yds drainage done, 100 yds at side of track cleared. HUDDLESTON RD – 5 CHEMINS trav places repaired, making double formation + planking 49 yds – PILCKEM RD. Laying turnrail piece at junction of IRON CROSS RD – 2 drains mis-ed near GALLWITZ FARM. Refg bad places + drainage between 5 CHEMINS ESTAMINET + GALLWITZ 13 yds planking laid, cleaning mud off IRON CROSS RD, filling shell holes + draining same.	RE
do	31/8/17		Work on CACTUS PONTOON to HUDDLESTON + RDS – 110 yds planking laid, 210 yds new drain cut on left of road, 200 yds on right cleared + traced, 2 box drains fixed under HUDDLESTON RD. – 15 yds planking laid end of PILCKEM RD completed lorry turning point, drainage done IRON CROSS RD – 250 yds drainage done on PILCKEM RD, 15 yds Turkey board laid, 20 yds planking, 34 yds aerial reneved – HUDDLESTON + RDS to 5 CHEMINS, 25 yds planking laid, 36 ft revetting, filling in 150 yds drainage. Dismounted marched to ELVERDINGHE + entrained at PROVEN going into Camp at F10 a 5.6 arriving 8.30/pm. Transport went by road.	RE

SECRET

Army Form C. 2118.

WAR DIARY
or
INTELLIGENCE SUMMARY.
(Erase heading not required.)

Place	Date	Hour	Summary of Events and Information	Remarks and references to Appendices
F10 a 5.2. (Sheet 27)	1/9/17		Strength of Company 7 off 207 O.R.	A.D.
			Company cleaning up camp billets & equipment - Inspection of hour respiration by Div. Gas Officer - 3 reinfs joined Coy from No1 Reinf. Bn.	
do	2/9/17		Sunday - Cleaning wagons	A.D.
"	3/9/17		Bathing Parades	A.D.
"	4/9/17		Company training - 4 reinfs joined Coy from No6 Reinf. Bn.	A.D.
"	5/9/17		Company training - making fascines at F15 a 4.2 Sheet 27	A.D.
"	6/9/17		physical drill etc - made 50 fascines at F15 a 4.2	A.D.
"	7/9/17		do - made 70 fascines do	A.D.
"	8/9/17		" - made 80 fascines do	A.D.

SECRET

Army Form C. 2118.

Instructions regarding War Diaries and Intelligence Summaries are contained in F. S. Regs., Part II. and the Staff Manual respectively. Title pages will be prepared in manuscript.

WAR DIARY
or
INTELLIGENCE SUMMARY.
(Erase heading not required.)

Place	Date	Hour	Summary of Events and Information	Remarks and references to Appendices
F10 a.5.2 Sheet 27	9/9/17		Sunday.	RE
do	10/9/17		Company training, physical drill - making 50 fascines at F15 a.4.2. - No 2 Section going forward to prepare billets for Coy at B23 b.64 Sheet 28	RE
do B23 b.64, Sheet 28	11/9/17		Dismounted marched to PROVEN, entrained for ELVERDINGHE, marched thence to B23 b.64 Sheet 28. Transport going by road.	RE
B23 b.6.4	12/9/17		No 1 Section on Duckboard tracks C8 a.8.2 - U23 d.0.5 and C3 a.8.4 - U22 d.6.7. No 2 & 4 Section work on New camps.	RE
do.	13/9/17		No 1 Section Duckboard tracks C8 a.8.2 - U23 d.0.5 and C3 a.8.4 - U22 d.6.7. -- repairing trestle bridge across STEEN BEEK - preparing new billets COMEDY F^m - laying smash track C8 a.8.6 - C8 b.3.4. 50 yds laid - No 4 Section working on IRON CROSS - LANGEMARCK RD. Clearing debris filling shell holes cutting down 4o old panie turnpikes U.5 b.3.1 - U.5 b.6.4. -- No 3 Section camouflaging sites for new Projectile depots ADELPHI. - No 2 Section in camp.	RE

SECRET

Army Form C. 2118.

WAR DIARY
or
INTELLIGENCE SUMMARY.
(Erase heading not required.)

Place	Date	Hour	Summary of Events and Information	Remarks and references to Appendices
B.25 c.6.4	14/9/17		Pan of No 3 Section (9) & Section Officer went forward accommodation at ADELPHI. No 13 & 115 Sapper GRAHAM.J. wounded. No 1 Section working a duckboard track C.9 a.3.4 to D.22 a.6 7.10 yds laid 50 yds repaired, reply trestle bridge near STEENBEEK - preparing duckboard at COMEDY FM. No 3 Section on Regl Hqrs at ADELPHI, erecting Tos Shelter & starting bathing & camouflaging - No 4 Section working on repair IRON CROSS - LANGEMARCK RD. - No 2 Section working in camp.	Pt
do	15/9/17		6 men of No 3 Section went to forward accommodation at COMEDY Farm. No 1 Section repairing duckboard track C.7 a.2.5 - C.8 a.7.9 and C.7 a.2.6 No 2 Section repy duckboard track between HUDDLESTON RD & PILCKEMRD, 38 yds laid, laying 64 yds new track PILCKEM TRACK to PILCKEM + RDS, repy night track to LANGEMARCK 92 yds laid, repy track a. C.13.a., laying single track on left duckboard track at LANGEMARCK - No 3 Section on New Regl Hqrs ADELPHI, erecting creeding steel section work in C.T. - repy Bn Hqrs, at MARK LANE - No 4 Section repg CACTUS PONTOON BRIDGE.	Pt

SECRET

WAR DIARY
or
INTELLIGENCE SUMMARY

(Erase heading not required.)

Army Form C. 2118

Place	Date	Hour	Summary of Events and Information	Remarks and references to Appendices
B23 b 6.4	16/9/17		No 1 Section on duckboard track U28 b 2.0 – U22 d 2.2. laying 105 yds repg bridge across STEENBEEK at U28 a 2.3 – repair do BATT. Hdqrs MARK LANE U22 d 5.8. No 2 Section repair to duckboard track U28 c 9.6 to U22 d 0.5–40 repg left track from MARK LANE U22 d 6.6, on single track around PILCKEM U21d.–100 yds laid – carry g duckboard etc for new track U28 b 2.0 to U22 d 2.2.– No 3 Section on new Bgde Hdqrs + DELPHI, a French Shelter bringing up to dug out, duckboards, digging a camouflaging Ct. for tracks.– No 4 Section working in camp. – Ap 13101 Rfn RICHARDSON T. 10thRR shell shock.	RE
B23 b 3.4	19/9/17		No 1 Section on duckboard track U28 b 2.0 – U22 d 2.2 laying 140 yds repairing bridge across STEENBEEK at U28 a 2.3 – repair do left Bridge 4.9 at U22 d 5.8. – No 2 Section repg night duckboard track 36 yds laid, repg left duckboard track 175 yds laid. Work on PILCKEM DIVERSION 220 yds laid. No 3 Section ditto.– East Corr remetalled for jumping off line. – No 4 Section.– Ne Bgde HQ at ADELPHI.	RE
do	18/9/17		No 1 Section on duckboard track U28 b 2.0 – U22 d 2.2. 1800 yds laid, bridge across STEENBEEK at U28 a 2.3 – repair do Left Bridge HQ U22 d 5.8.– No 2 + 3 Section laying duckboard on PILCKEM DIVERSION. 1040 yds laid, repg left duckboard track + extending 280 yds laid. No 4 Section on New Bgde HQ at ADELPHI which was Completed + occupied by Bgdr.– Jumping off line	RE

SECRET

Army Form C. 2118.

WAR DIARY
or
INTELLIGENCE SUMMARY.
(Erase heading not required.)

Instructions regarding War Diaries and Intelligence Summaries are contained in F. S. Regs. Part II. and the Staff Manual respectively. Title pages will be prepared in manuscript.

Place	Date	Hour	Summary of Events and Information	Remarks and references to Appendices
B23 d.64	19/9/17		Section resting	RE
	20/9/17		Division attacked at 5 a.m. on whole Divl front. 59th Bde a few hrs before on right. The attack was held up by EAGLE TRENCH in centre, but further attack was made at 6 p.m. & further positions were taken - section rested during day in camp & went forward at dusk. 4 parties consisting each of 1 section R.E. 1 platoon D.L.I. (A Coy) & attached Infy went to work on S.P's - owing to situation S.P. V17c 55.15 was the only one constructed in accordance with programme by N°2 Section. The other 3 parties got in touch with Bn. & Coy Commanders & carried out such works of consolidation as they could under circumstances at V23 c.1.6. & V23 a.9.7. & V23 a.75.75. Forward dump at V22 a.67 was shelled set afire, material had to be carried from V28 a.3.6 - 9h/2 Kgt Canadns. O.C. owing to ill health was represented by Capt R.H. WARDE MC RE at Bde HQ.	RE
do	21/9/17		Section resting	RE
do	22/9/17		N° 1,3 & 4 sections erected Nissen huts at BRIDGE JUNCTION & for live transport lines at B20 a.7.4 - N° 2 Section working in camp	RE

D. D. & L., London, E.C. A901 Wt W17/M2017 799 20 5/17 Sch 52 Forms C/2 5814

SECRET

Army Form C. 2118.

WAR DIAGRY
or
INTELLIGENCE SUMMARY.
(Erase heading not required.)

Instructions regarding War Diaries and Intelligence
Summaries are contained in F. S. Regs., Part II.
and the Staff Manual respectively. Title pages
will be prepared in manuscript.

Place	Date	Hour	Summary of Events and Information	Remarks and references to Appendices
B23 b.6.4.	28/9/17		No 3 & 4 Section on Numeral huts at BRIDGE JUNCTION + Burnt transport lines & RE camp side at B20 b.4.1. - No 4 Section in Pigeon HQ. at ADELPHI. No 1 Section working in camp. - No 3 Section went out at night to work on trenchboard track owing to darkness + fog, no work done - EAGLE TRENCH now taken by germs, 5.9" Pigee dirt about RD printers. - 66211 Sap PARTOON. S. wounded at dusty. 16915 Rfn NEWMAN. A. 10115 Rifle. - 27666 Rfn STELFOX wounded. -	Rk 1
do	29/9/17		No 1 + 2 Sections on Numeral huts at BRIDGE JUNCTION + Burnt transport lines - Night No 4 Section repairs to trenchboard track U22 d 15.30 to U22 d 7.6. 30 yds laid - laying of 70 yds new track from U22 d 7.6. - 146779 Sap SMITH. A. G. wounded at dusty.	Rk 2

SECRET

Army Form C. 2118.

WAR DIARY
or
INTELLIGENCE SUMMARY.
(Erase heading not required.)

Instructions regarding War Diaries and Intelligence Summaries are contained in F. S. Regs., Part II. and the Staff Manual respectively. Title pages will be prepared in manuscript.

Place	Date	Hour	Summary of Events and Information	Remarks and references to Appendices
B.23.b.6.4	25/9/17		Nos 1 & 2 Sections erected 4 huts at R.E. Camp BRIDGE JUNCTION - No 3 Section Duckboard track from AU BON GITE to LEFT HAND TRACK EAST of PETREE FARM - No 4 Section on track from U.22.d.7.6 forward, head 40.U.23.a.15.0, laying 290 yds duckboard.	
do	24/9/17		No 4.5.9.10 Sections. ALEXANDER.G. 45909 Sap CHAMBERS.S. 50045 Sap MATHIESON.W. 422697 Cap SMITH.G. evacuated to hospital, suffering from gas.	
do	24/9/17		No 1 & 2 Section on R.E. Camp at BRIDGE JUNCTION erecting 4 huts - no work at night.	
do	24/9/17		No 8.1.2 & 3 Sections on R.E. Camp at BRIDGE JUNCTION, erecting 1 officer hut, 1 Mess hut & 2 other huts & ablution shed. 48703 Sapr. Sergt WANSBROUGH.J. killed, Cap WARDE.R.H. M.C. wounded - 53608 Sgt RYLANCE.J. - 48692 Bgh BOOTHAM. - 50906 L/Cpl BRADBURN.W. - 80724 Spr BROCKWELL.J.W. - 50904 Dvr MURDOCK.W. - 80804 Spr BAYLEY.T. - all wounded. 50739 Spr BOLT.R. wounded at duty - Shell about 4.2. Fell in horse lines by hqrs - 8 horses damaged in all, 2 had to be killed. No 4 Section at night on track from U.22.d.7.6 forward, laying 600 yds duckboard, complete to EAGLE TRENCH. Advance party from 526 In Cy R.E. arrived in camp.	

SECRET

Army Form C. 2118.

WAR DIARY
or
INTELLIGENCE SUMMARY.
(Erase heading not required.)

Place	Date	Hour	Summary of Events and Information	Remarks and references to Appendices
B.13.b.6.4 Sheet 28	28/9/17		Company was relieved by 556 Fd Co - Dismounted marched to ELVERDINGHE & remained for PROVEN area, going into camp at PUTLOVES.	A2
F.10.a.5.2 Sheet 27			F.10.a.5.2 - Transport travelled by road.	

J.B. Story
Major R.E.
O.C. 96 Field Co R.E.

SECRET

WAR DIARY
or
INTELLIGENCE SUMMARY

Army Form C. 2118

96 Ja Coy R.E.

Vol 23

Instructions regarding War Diaries and Intelligence Summaries are contained in F.S. Regs., Part II. and the Staff Manual respectively. Title Pages will be prepared in manuscript.

(Erase heading not required.)

Place	Date	Hour	Summary of Events and Information	Remarks and references to Appendices
F.10 a 5.2 Sheet 27	29/9/17		Company loading pontoons, cleaning up etc	R.E.
do	30/9/17		Sunday.	R.E.
do	1/10/17		Strength of Coy 6 off. 206 O.R. Company marched to HOUPOTRE SIDING, but did not entrain till 8 p.m. & travelled to BAPAUME arriving 9.30 a.m. 2-10-17 & marched to	R.E.
N15 c Sheet 57c	2/10/17		BEAULENCOURT arriving at F Camp 11.20 a.m	R.E.
do	3/10/17		Work on horse standings at N.24 C 9.8	R.E.
do	4/10/17		1 NCO Sergt & 5 Driver joined Coy from Base. Work on horse standings at N.24 C 9.8.	R.E.
do	5/10/17		Lt F.V. SIMPKINSON joined Coy = Work on horse standings at SUC ERIE LE TRANSLOY & Bgde Paths.	R.E.

1875 Wt. W593/826 1,000,000 4/15 J.B.C. & A. A.D.S.S./Forms/C. 2118.

WAR DIARY or INTELLIGENCE SUMMARY

Army Form C. 2118

Place	Date	Hour	Summary of Events and Information	Remarks and references to Appendices
N.18.c.4.6.	6/10/17		Summoned marched do O.21.b.3.5, on the ROCQUIGNY – BARASTRE Rd & embussed & travelled thence to W13.c., transport travelled by road.	TRS
W13.c.	7/10/17		H.Q. & 2 Section moved to W9 b Q.4. 2 Section marched to Q 3.6 d 6.9.	TRS
do			Transport going to V.24.b.5.9. – Taking over from 229 Coy, 40th Division.	
W9 b Q.4 Q3.6 d 6.9	8/10/17		No.1 Section, work on front line left of GIN AVENUE, draining & excavating for frames & improving billets – No 2 Section excavating & improving drainage in front line, relaying & making good trenchboards in RILEY AVENUE & improving billets in GOUZEAUCOURT – No 3 Section, work on sumps at alone at R.2.b.6.0 & work on H.Q. billets – No 4 Section work on ADRIAN huts HEUDECOURT, salving bricks & timber. 2 men no 3 section at Pumping station GONNELIEU & 2 men Pumping station in GOUZEAUCOURT.	TRS
do	9/10/17		No 1 Section work on duckboards & cuddy drains in front line & drains in GLASGOW Tr, FOSTERS AVENUE & GIN AVENUE deepened & cleaned out – No 2 Section found trenchboards & completing drain in RILEY AVENUE; excavating & shaping up ready for reveting in front line, firing baby elephant Pillars in No 5 bay – beamy road for transport in VILLERS PLOUICH – improving billets	TRS

SECRET

Army Form C. 2118

WAR DIARY
or
INTELLIGENCE SUMMARY

(Erase heading not required.)

Instructions regarding War Diaries and Intelligence Summaries are contained in F.S. Regs., Part II. and the Staff Manual respectively. Title Pages will be prepared in manuscript.

Place	Date	Hour	Summary of Events and Information	Remarks and references to Appendices
WQ to Q.4 Q36 & Q.6.9	9/10/17		No 3 Section work on H.Q. billet stables etc. — No 4 Section work on ADRIAN HUT, DEVON RD.	R.E.
do	10/10/17		No 1 Section work on GUN SUPPORT TRENCH - 100 yds trench boards fixed & drains cleaned — GLASGOW TRENCH, 230 yds trench boards fixed & drains cleaned — Baby Elephant shelter erected in front line — No 2 Section work in front line, revetting, new U frames etc. — Unloading wagon at SURREY RD Dump — Work on billets — No 3 Section work on water main GONNELIEU, laying 4" 2" pipe, work on H.Q. billets — No 4 Section, work on DEVON RD — excavation for & erecting ADRIAN HUT - excavating for latrines - erecting 7 drawer shelter.	F.Z.
do	11/10/17		No 1 Section work on GIN AVENUE & SYMES AVENUE, widening & deepening fire bays & firesteps in front line — No 2 Section standing deep dug out at R2D 6.2.4. framing U frames & revetting in front line — Preparing new billets in GOUZEAUCOURT. — No 3 Section work on water supply GONNELIEU. 30 yds of pipe laid, work on H.Q. billet, stables etc. — No 4 Section work on DEVON RD Ramp, erecting adrian hut.	F.Z.
do	12/10/17		No 1 Section, deepening & draining SYMES AVENUE, widening GIN AVENUE, revetting in front line — No 2 Section, revetting & draining in front line, work on dug out at R2D 4.4 & R2D 5.7.2. — No 3 Section work on	R.Z.

SECRET

Army Form C. 2118.

WAR DIARY
or
INTELLIGENCE SUMMARY.
(Erase heading not required.)

Instructions regarding War Diaries and Intelligence Summaries are contained in F. S. Regs., Part II and the Staff Manual respectively. Title pages will be prepared in manuscript.

Place	Date	Hour	Summary of Events and Information	Remarks and references to Appendices
Wg U Q.9 Q36 d.6.9	12/10/17		GONNELIEU Water supply, trench dug 9 x 16 yds of 1" pipe laid, work on H.Q. billet — No 4 Section. Work on DEVON RD Camp; erection of Adrian hut & excavations for latrines; RAILTON Camp; dug out 6 E.S. wagon loads of bricks salved & transported to side of G.O.C. horse SOREL.	H.Z.
do	13/10/17		No 1 Section, work on front line night sector, revetting fireboys & firing trench to widening & cleaning SYMES AVENUE & fired 6A frames, working ships on dugout at R20 b.24½ – No 2 Section & Revetting in front line left sector frames & frames of filling 250 sandbags, work on August at R20 d 5.75 – No 3 Section – work on GONNELIEU water supply, 35 yds trench dug & 42 ft of pipe laid, work on Artillery hut at W15 C. – No 4 Section work on Adrian hut at DEVON RD CAMP, 6 loads of brick salved & removed for G.O.C. horse at SOREL. — 2 loads of tiles salved & transported to R.E.	H.Z.
do	14/10/17		No 1 Section Right Sector, No 9 Bay revetted with V.P.M. rifle rack & strut bar have been fixed, SYMES AVENUE widening & deepening, 2.5 yds U frame, 7 V.P.M. fires. GIN AVENUE, berm cleaned along both sides, deepened & widened 200 yds. – 5 frames fixed in each gallery of August 6 2.4½ – No 2 Section Training in gas drill, preparing pumps for sandbags & laying 450 sandbags, work on August at R20 d.675.	H.Z.

D. D. & L. London, E.C.
W.o.1 W. W 17711/Aug1 750000 3/17 Sch 93 Forms/C2118/4

WAR DIARY or INTELLIGENCE SUMMARY

Army Form C. 2118.

SECRET

Place	Date	Hour	Summary of Events and Information	Remarks and references to Appendices
Wq 6.9.4 Q8.a.6.9	14/10/17		No 3 Section Work on GONNELIEU water supply. Excavation & concrete in BOP. trench pit, also in connection with pumping station - No 4 Section - complete Adrian huts at DEVON ROAD Camp. Excavation for G.O.C. house at SOREL completed, sides revetted & transported. No 1 Section work in Right Sector, Post line - 2 bays revetted & trench drain	PR
do	15/10/17		fired. SYMES AVENUE 24 yds revetted with A frames & RPM - 4 frames fixed in each gallery of dugout at R10.b.2.4.5. - No 2 Section work in left sector. Lowering in tray line, completing bays 63 & 64, entrance to MG shelter. no work on dugout, lack of material. No 3 Section on GONNELIEU water supply 35 yds of trench deepened, levels taken for new sink at GOUZEAUCOURT Baths 5 sited for engine cleaned out - No 4 Section on DEVON ROAD camp, roofing material for kitchen huts, 3 sites cleared, sorting & cutting material for G.O.C.'s house at SOREL. 3 doz of concrete runners laid.	R2
do	16/10/17		No 1 Section in Right Sector steps made in 2 tram bays, trench with 4 frames SYMES AVENUE revetted with A frames & RPM drain cut & graded treadboards fixed 20 yds. 6 frames fixed in each gallery of dugout at R10.b.141. No 2 Section in left Sector. Revetting in bay 61-66. & extension of MG Shelter.	R2

D.D. & L. London. E.C.
(4900.) Wt. W.17119M2012 750/00 5/17 Sch. 82 Forms C2.-9/4

WAR DIARY
or
INTELLIGENCE SUMMARY.

(Erase heading not required.)

Army Form C. 2118.

Place	Date	Hour	Summary of Events and Information	Remarks and references to Appendices
W9 c94 O36 A69	16/10/17		No 3 Section deepening 30 yds of trench for GONNELIEU water supply & latrines made. Engine house cleared & counter shafts erected at GOUZEAUCOURT. No 4 Section work on DEVON ROAD Camp. erected hitter hut & making drainage for latrines, brick laying at G.O.C. house SOREL, preparing timber for same.	FE
do	17/10/17		No 1 Section - widening 8 bays of front line - revetting, deepening & draining 20 yds SYMES AVENUE - deepened & widened 120 yd of GIN AVENUE. - No 2 Section Revetting, preparing for revetting & draining front line - No 3 Section, lowering pipe line at GONNELIEU & GOUZEAUCOURT water supply. - No 4 Section working at DEVON RD Camp & G.O.C. house SOREL Second drainer & bricks for drain windows & bricklaying.	FE
do	18/10/17		No 1 Section working in front line revetting, firebays & fronts deepening - 25 yds deepening & draining in SYMES AVENUE digging sumps - cleaning 250 yds term GIN AVENUE. - No 2 Section draining & revetting front line, fixing angle in pickets & R.M. & erecting shelter for M.G.C. No 3 Section at GOUZEAUCOURT baths, digging trench & laying & threading pipe - No 4 Section at G.O.C. house SOREL, bricklaying & preparing shutters brick - cleaning site for new horse lines at HEUDICOURT	FE

SECRET

Army Form C. 2118.

WAR DIARY
or
INTELLIGENCE SUMMARY.

(Erase heading not required.)

Place	Date	Hour	Summary of Events and Information	Remarks and references to Appendices
Wq 6-94. Q 36 d 69	19/10/17		No 1 Section revetting fire bays in front line, SYMES AVENUE revetting with U frames 4 P.M. & cadding drains & sumps, clearing & deepening drain in GIN AVENUE. No 2 Section draining in front line & revetting with angle irons 4 P.M. No 3 Section working on GONNELIEU & GOUZEAUCOURT water supply, digging trench & fixing pumps. No 4 Section on G.O.C. house & new trench laying in.	RS
do	20/10/17		No 1 Section working in front line revetting 3 bays, SYMES AVENUE both sides revetted, drain cut & graded 18 yd, revetting bad bad of trench in GIN AVENUE. No 2 Section revetting in front line & 150 ft of POPE AVE widened & cleaned up. No 3 Section reforming (Aulieu pump at GONNELIEU & digging trench for pipe at GOUZEAUCOURT. No 4 Section working G.O.C. house & melt, belaying bricks & tiles & working on new home line at HEUDICOURT.	RS
do	21/10/17		No 1 Section working in right Section 2 bays in front line SYMES AVENUE revetting, cadding drain & fixing trench boards, revetting bad bays in GIN AVENUE. No 2 Section in left Section revetting in front line, clearing 100 yds of trench POPE AVENUE & driving mch 150 yds been.	RS

SECRET

Army Form C. 2118

WAR DIARY or INTELLIGENCE SUMMARY

(Erase heading not required.)

Instructions regarding War Diaries and Intelligence Summaries are contained in F.S. Regs., Part II. and the Staff Manual respectively. Title Pages will be prepared in manuscript.

Place	Date	Hour	Summary of Events and Information	Remarks and references to Appendices
W96-Q4 Q36a69	21/10/17		No5 Section on water supply at GONNELIEU - GOUZEAUCOURT. - No 4 Section on G.O.C. horses' mess. Nos 3 & 4 Section relieved Nov 1 & 2 Sections afternoon. 1 work & 1 going into their billets at GOUZEAUCOURT in the evening.	PBZ
do	22/10/17		No 1 Section working on G.O.C. House & mess. - No 2 Section on new horse lines HEUDICOURT, building kitchen hut, erecting stables & pantry floor. - No 3 Section work in Right Section, revetting & draining 4 traverses - doing in large dump at GOUZEAUCOURT Bush. - No 4 Section working deep section tramway & revetair from line trench & revetting by shelter - repairs do water pump & well at GONNELIEU. - R.M.F. HUDDART appd a/Sapt.	PBZ
do	23/10/17		No 1 Section at G.O.C. House at SOREL, building sleeper walls in ante room & running outside walls & chimney. - No 2 Section on new horse lines at HEUDICOURT, erecting stables etc. - No 3 Section revetting & draining 5 traverses in front line & work at GOUZEAUCOURT BATHS. - No 4 Section tramway revetting in front line & completing infantry shelter, repairs do pumping plant at GONNELIEU. 207865 L.Sapt WARNER.C.D. joined Coy from 248 Fd Coy.	PBZ
do	24/10/17		a/Sapt R.M.F. HUDDART transferred do 85 Coy. - Sapt HUGH-JONES.E.B. joining Coy from 83rd. No 1 Section birthdaying at G.O.C. House, preparing roof, preparing woodwork for G.O.C. mess - No 2 Section on new horse lines, fixing stables & finishing floor. - No 3 Section revetting & draining 1 bay & 3 traverses in front line, carry in large dumb at GOUZEAUCOURT BATHS.	PBZ

SECRET

Army Form C. 2118.

WAR DIARY
or
INTELLIGENCE SUMMARY.
(Erase heading not required.)

Instructions regarding War Diaries and Intelligence Summaries are contained in F. S. Regs., Part II. and the Staff Manual respectively. Title pages will be prepared in manuscript.

Place	Date	Hour	Summary of Events and Information	Remarks and references to Appendices
W9 A0.9.4 Q3b d6.9	24/10/17		No 4 Section draining & draining in front line, Infantry Shelters in ARGYLE LANE completed, repairs to pumping plant at GONNELIEU.	RE
do	25/9/17		No 1 Section bricklaying at G.O.C. House, making windows & preparing woodwork for G.O.C. mess. – No 2 Section erecting shelters & billets at new horse lines, HEUDICOURT. – No 3 Section work in front line, mended 4 traverses. Fixing 3 frames in shaft of dug out near SYMES AVENUE, making for ammunition and food dumps at GOUZEAUCOURT BATHS. No 4 Section, trimming & revetting, draining bays, held up often in front line – repairs to shelter in bay 58.	RE
do	26/10/17		No 1 Section on G.O.C. House, gable walls bricked up, roof fixed up, fixed up, high plank built to carry pipes in G.O.C. mess. – No 2 Section on horse lines, erecting stables & Nissen huts. – No 3 Section work in front line revetting & draining 5 traverses 1 bay – 4 frames fixed in deep dug out near SYMES AVENUE, work at GOUZEAUCOURT BATHS – each step 1 Aug 83 near SYMES AVENUE, work at GOUZEAUCOURT BATHS. No 4 Section, front line revetting & trimming bays, new C.T. wanted between NEWPORT TRENCH & front line, 360 jobs erected front niches – repairs to pumping plant at GONNELIEU.	RE

SECRET

Army Form C. 2118.

WAR DIARY
or
INTELLIGENCE SUMMARY.
(Erase heading not required.)

Instructions regarding War Diaries and Intelligence Summaries are contained in F.S. Regs., Part II. and the Staff Manual respectively. Title pages will be prepared in manuscript.

Place	Date	Hour	Summary of Events and Information	Remarks and references to Appendices
W9 c.9.4 Q 36 d 6.9	27/9/17		No 1 Section on G.O.C. House SOREL, roof tiled & chimneys built up, floor laid in one room, building fireplace in G.O.C mess, preparing & erecting woodwork of building. — No 2 Section erecting stables & cookhouse at new horse lines & pump tank. — No 3 Section revetting & draining 2 bays + 5 traverses Dug out at R20 d.4.6, 1 shaft completed, 4 traverses in other shaft, guiding do officers latrine at GOUZEAUCOURT. — No 4 Section work on front line revetting & draining, 2nd dash completed on new C.T. NEWPORT TR do post line, repairs to pumping plant at GONNELIEU. No 1 Section moved to new horse lines at HEUDICOURT	R2
do	28/9/17		No 1 Section work on G.O.C. House SOREL, ridge tiles fixed & roof pointed, pointed board floor laid – building fireplace in G.O.C mess, fixing medium English in do. — No 2 Section working on stables & new horse lines + 1 latrine hut completed. — No 3 Section front line work, draining & revetting 6 traverses & bays – deepening S.Q.M. trip & blocking firebay, dug out at R20 d.4.6 main gallery 280 advft excavated, No 2 shaft completed, guiding do officers bath at GOUZEAUCOURT. — No 4 Section revetting trimming & draining bays do be occupied in front line. — New C.T. NEWPORT TR to front line, 3rd dash completed – repairs to pumping plant at GONNELIEU	R2

D. D. & L., London, E.C.
Army W. W. P14/M1081 750000 4/17 Sch 32 Forms/C2118/4

SECRET

Army Form C. 2118.

WAR DIARY
or
INTELLIGENCE SUMMARY.
(Erase heading not required.)

Place	Date	Hour	Summary of Events and Information	Remarks and references to Appendices
H.Q. T.Q.4 Q36 a69	29/10/17		No 1 Section at G.O.C. house SOREL covering heaters & tarpaulins, ceiling matchboarded in O.C. room, building chimney in G.O.C. mess, just given preparing woodwork & building up stove. — No 2 Section erecting stabling at new horse lines, fixing linings in Nissen huts. — No 3 Section revetting, draining, traverses, bays to front line, making tramway steps in TOM saps, started new support line from RILEY to FOSTER AVE. excavating 200 yds. — excavated 550 cub.ft from dugout R20 d 4.6. refg road screen in GOUZEAUCOURT. — No 4 Section working in front line revetting, draining, building dug. shelters & working on new C.T. from NEWPORT TR to front line, repair to pumping plant in GONNELIEU.	RE

WAR DIARY
or
INTELLIGENCE SUMMARY

SECRET — Army Form C. 2118.

96th FIELD COMPANY R.E.

Place	Date	Hour	Summary of Events and Information	Remarks and references to Appendices
N9 6–9.4 Q36.d.6.9.	30/10/17		No1 Section on G.O.C. House & new SOREL cleaning sites for hoards & model – boarding ceiling, curtain, floor for wardroom house, building fireplace, chimney in mess & laying floor. – No2 Section completing NISSEN hut at new front lines in HEUDICOURT & putting stoves, extending down annex hut – offside new side for billets & levelling & preparing new site. – No3 Section on work forward – never did – re-siding 2 bays & traverses in trestling, clearing berm to 14 bays & traverses, continuing bombing stop in JOM Sap. – Second dash on new support line R20 d.5.3 to R20 a.3.3. dug out 170 yds. – Dug out near SYMES AVE extended 16ft. ∮ gallery also new pipe line in GOUZEAUCOURT. – New Section needling, trimming, chimney in front line – firing M.G.C shelter in NEWPORT T.R. 1 completed dug out ∮ new C.T. return to pumping plant in GONNELIEU.	R
N9 6–9.4 Q36 a 6.9	31/10/17		No1 Section on G.O.C. Annex, hanging door, casing & erecting round door, fireplace & chimney in new boarding floor & fixing fuels in no 1 order workshop. – No2 Section erecting partition in new sheds & whitewashing shops, laying stone blocks, dismantling annex hut & erecting on side of new billets. – No3 Section clearing berm from 5 bays in trestling, new support line, 170 yds. Bombing stop in JOM support gallery, right dug out completed – pipe extension in GOUZEAUCOURT	R

WAR DIARY
or
INTELLIGENCE SUMMARY.
(Erase heading not required.)

Army Form C. 2118.

Instructions regarding War Diaries and Intelligence Summaries are contained in F. S. Regs., Part II. and the Staff Manual respectively. Title pages will be prepared in manuscript.

Place	Date	Hour	Summary of Events and Information	Remarks and references to Appendices
W9 b9,4. Q56 d69	3/10/17		No 4 Section revetting, trimming, draining, occupied bays in front line. New C.T. trimming & excavating, drain NEWPORT TR enemy M.G.C Shelter, handed over pumping plant at GONNELIEU, do 84 & 60. Strength of Coy, 7 Officers 214 O.R.	RH
do	4/10/17		No 1 Section. G.O.C. house SOREL, floor tiled, fixing matchboarding & lining round window, chimney completed in mess, yet fixing in roof, windows made, fixing matchboarding round walls, Officers boarding completed. No 2 Section fixing saddle racks, trench board at horse lines - Roof of Adrian huts at mens billets 85% completed, making 8 frames for walls, shed, drying shed & cookhouse. No 3 Section, revetting in front line doing 2 bays & traverses, constructing bombing stop TOM sap - fixing windlasses, at shaft of dugout & excavating aft of gallery, work on pipe line in GOUZEAUCOURT & strengthening & structure in trench - No 4 Section work in front line, revetting, fixing trenchboards boyed completed - 100 yds of drain deepened & trimmed, mgst poorly revetted 6 bays. New C.T. 50 yds of trenchboards laid & fixed, 6 fire steps & 30 yds of drain excavated, M.G.C Shelter in NEW PORT TR completed.	HM

WAR DIARY
or
INTELLIGENCE SUMMARY

Army Form C. 2118.

96th FIELD COMPANY R.E.

Place	Date	Hour	Summary of Events and Information	Remarks and references to Appendices
Wg 8q.4 Q56 d6.9	4/7/17		No 1 Section G.O.C. house fixing matchboarding & lining, 2 fireplaces bricked up. Camouflage netting fixed on roof. Window frames completed in mess, fixing canvas on walls, mantelpiece tiles laid in hearth, puttying on roof.— No 2 Section working at new bomb line & new billets, removing floor in shed, completing roof of Aaron hut, laying trench boards. No 3 Section in front line, new gun 3 bays & traverses, completing bombing stop in JOM SAP, Gallery 7 Bug Out 85yds in, pipe fixing in GOUZEAUCOURT.— No 4 Section in 18/39 Sector front line, 20 yds of trench revetted, drained trench boards laid, NEW C.T. 100 yds trench boards laid, 2 bays revetted, 4ft shelters erected in NEWPORT TR., erected 2 barricades in GOUZEAUCOURT.	✓
do	5/7/17		Model started. No 1 Section work on G.O.C. house, doors fixed, room matchboarded, canvas fixed, round room, doors & windows fixed in mess, lining walls & room canvas & painting & staining woodwork.— No 2 Section work on new camp, uniform etc. No 3 Section revetting 2 bays-traverses in front line & excavating for bombing stop, GAME SUPPORT line completed to depth of 6ft except for 50 yds. Dug out 11ft 9 gallery excavated, work on pipe line at GOUZEAUCOURT.—	✓

Army Form C. 2118.

WAR DIARY
or
INTELLIGENCE SUMMARY.
(Erase heading not required.)

Instructions regarding War Diaries and Intelligence Summaries are contained in F. S. Regs., Part II. and the Staff Manual respectively. Title pages will be prepared in manuscript.

[Stamp: 95th FIELD COMPANY R.E.]

Place	Date	Hour	Summary of Events and Information	Remarks and references to Appendices
W9 G.4. Q.36 d.6.9	3/11/17		No 4 Section on New C.T. 20 yds of trench revetted + 160yds of trench braced with 20 yds of trench repaired + revetted + necessary for shelters in PENTRE TR. + carrying shelters to site	A.R.
do	4/11/17		No 1 Section complete G.O.R. Hut at SOREL. No 2 Section on New Billet at HEUDICOURT hutting in Aviam hut, erecting cookhouse + drying room. No 3 Section covering in Bomb. dugs in TOM SAP, constructing screen on RILEY AVENUE, 3rd Sect. on GAME SUPPORT, dug a length of 300yds wire repeated of 3 firebays in front line, 1 firebays traverse revetted, continuing bombing stop, dugout at R.21.a.4.6, gallery complete, work on pipeline at GOUZEAUCOURT. No 4 Section, 40yds of trench deepened on New C.T. + 70 yds of trench braced laid, 80yds of falls cleared + shelters erected in PENTRE TR., + barricade erected CAMBRAI RD. + cleaned + shelters erected in PENTRE TR., 20yds of revetment. Section changed over in the evening. No 1 + 2 Sections going forward + 3 + 4 Sections going into new billets at HEUDICOURT.	A.R.
do	5/11/17		No 4 Section move into camp near SOREL to work on road. No 1 + 2 Sections at work on Tram line, carrying + laying 120 trench boards in New C.T. + excavating 120 c ft of chamber in DUGOUT at R.21.a.4.6 + running pump + repairing at GOUZEAUCOURT BATHS	A.R.

WAR DIARY or INTELLIGENCE SUMMARY

Army Form C. 2118.

(Erase heading not required.)

Place	Date	Hour	Summary of Events and Information	Remarks and references to Appendices
W9 b.9.4. Q5b.d6.9 W15.b.4.2 W19.c	5/11/17		No 3 Section improving new billets at HERMIES, finishing a latrine Hut, construction of drying room etc. No 4 Section constructing model W.19.c. outside SOREL + making tank etc in their new camp.	RE
	6/11/17		No 1 & 2 Section work forward, widening & deepening 340 yds of trench in NEW SUPPORT, 250 c.ft. excavated from DUG OUT, laying trench boards in NEW C.T., selecting material & preparing scheme in GOUZEAUCOURT. No 3 Section finishing 2 new billets (a) new hitch & constructing new hitch. No 4 Section working on model, excavating & filling at cooking for file.	RE
do	7/11/17		No 4 Section forward widening & deepening NEW SUPPORT 140 yds, excavated & widened 16 ft of chamber of DUG OUT, new steps on #9. Preparing & screen in GOUZEAUCOURT & taking down the same, refuge working pump & Baths. No 5 Section building 2 new billet & enemy cooking. No 4 Section on trail at SOREL excavating & filling in exceeding profile, construction of truck for truck-over-metal.	RE
do	8/11/17		Nos 1 & 2 Section forward deepening & widening 100 yds of new Sup/pt in GAME SUPPORT, erecting double 12 ft chamber of DUG OUT + new infantry officers shelter in that new. Preparing serene + screens in GOUZEAUCOURT + running pumps & supplying Coolers & Baths.	RE

Army Form C. 2118.

WAR DIARY
or
INTELLIGENCE SUMMARY.
(Erase heading not required.)

96th FIELD COMPANY R.E.

Place	Date	Hour	Summary of Events and Information	Remarks and references to Appendices
N9 b.9.4 Q 3.6 a.6.9 W15 b.1.2 N9.c	8/10/17		No 3 Section work on new billets W15 b.1.2. clearing ground of debris, trenches & erecting cookhouse. No 4 Section on model, excavating & draining, filling in craters on road. No 1 section getting profile erected.	R.E.
	9/10/17		Nos 1 & 2 Section — Work on GAME SUPPORT, deepening & cleaning 50 yds. Laying 100 ft trench board. Dugouts for New Regt Hqrs H.Q. 10ft of Chamber excavated & timbered. 25 ft of trench driven on VILLERS PLOUICH RD 39 ft nearly done except Ledge checked. 4 17ft of screen fixed edge of wall — no hair jumpers 10 by trestle as GOUZEAUCOURT BATHS. No 3 section on new billets. No 4 section on model as SOREL, excavating & filling in revections trestles & shutters. No 1 & 2 section — work on tong line & FUSILIER RES. excavg Sheldon	R.E.
do	10/10/17		GAME SUPPORT fixing screen, sheet trench curves, revtd — 12 ft of Sheldon excavated & driven on Dugout — COPSE RD screens 178 yds mooring & brushwood screen fixed 150 yds hedge thickened & uprights wire fixed yds 2017 fence. — No 3 Section working on new billets — No 4 section on model as SOREL, filling in duty, erecting profile & trestles.	R.E.
do	11/10/17		Nos 1 & 2 Section revetting trace & stops in tong line & erecting Sheldon. 10 ft of Chamber of dugout excavated & timbered, making up tracks over drain (a tramway) PARTRIDGE RD — 20 yds of screen completed on	R.E.

WAR DIARY
or
INTELLIGENCE SUMMARY.

Army Form C. 2118.

Place	Date	Hour	Summary of Events and Information	Remarks and references to Appendices
W9 b 94 Q 36 d 69 W 15 b 12 W 19 c	11/11/17		COPSE RD. 150 feet of thickened 60ft screen prepared & erected; 7 Pioneers in new petrol dump for engines at GOUZEAUCOURT BATHS – No 3 Section improving new billets, bunks etc. – No 4 Section on road clearance, and filling in crown, long flat trestles, reading dead end. No 1 & 2 Section forward work, firing borehole bria in front line near TOM SAP erected in shelters, new eng H.Q. Dug out 4 & 9 revetted & timbered, cleaning up topsoil, covering floor, completing timbering outside signal D.O. at Bt H.Qrs re/pg. plan on & driving pump at GOUZEAUCOURT.	K.E.
	12/11/17		completed screen at COPSE RD. – No 3 Section at new Billets at HEUDICOURT bunking, felling, roof, drying room completed, constructing shelter, frames & hanging sign boards – No 4 Section on road, clearing the Ave, filling in assault trench & trench board track	K.E.
do	13/11/17		No 1 & 2 Sections working on shelters in front line, cleaning & deepening gallery & dug out, chamber completed, framing, revetting & deepening dug outs in ARGYLE LANE & RILEY AVE. – erecting screen for Signal No 3 & 4 Section on road, revetting, filling in, reading out, filling in assault, erecting track a French handrail.	K.E.

Army Form C. 2118.

Instructions regarding War Diaries and Intelligence Summaries are contained in F. S. Regs., Part II. and the Staff Manual respectively. Title pages will be prepared in manuscript.

WAR DIARY
or
INTELLIGENCE SUMMARY.
(Erase heading not required.)

Place	Date	Hour	Summary of Events and Information	Remarks and references to Appendices
W9 b.q.4. Q56 d.6.9 N15 6.1.2 W19.C.	14/10/17		No 1 & 2 Section nothing on the line in front line, performing woodwork for big shelters, continuing excavation ARGYLE LANE & RILEY AVE, dug a 70 yd sewer on COPSE RD. — No 3 & 4 Sections on road, sawing out chiefly filling in, revetting trenches with brush, sawing out full size trenches made near model.	
do	15/10/17		No 1 & 2 Section on New Bgd H Q taking down existing shelters, erecting new dug out – fixing gas door & sandbagging entrances – completing excavation for big shelters in ARGYLE LANE & RILEY AVE, preparing woodwork for the above revetting 2 completed – No 3 Section erecting hidden huts at W9 a 9.3 for 16 q. H.Q. — No 4 Section filling in dead shelters.	
do	16/10/17		No 1 & 2 Section – New Bgde H.Q. as practice, fixing bunks & learners side for shelters, erecting big shelter in RILEY AVE & deepening trench from practice, completing excavation for Brand Shelter in ARGYLE LANE & erecting 2 dugouts, preparing position for new engine in GOUZEAUCOURT. No 3 Section erecting hidden huts at W9 a 7.3, 2 complete. — No 4 Section finishing Off model at SOREL.	

WAR DIARY or INTELLIGENCE SUMMARY

Army Form C. 2118.

96th FIELD COMPANY R.E.

Place	Date	Hour	Summary of Events and Information	Remarks and references to Appendices
W9 6.9.4 Q6 a 6.9 W15 6.12 W14.c	17/11/17		Nos 1 & 2 Section - Wiring back up gate in front line, filling bags, sandbags + pickets in front of Signal Shelter in ARGYLL LANE, deepened trench at & filling earth on top. Repair of telephone RILEY AVENUE, erected shelters near BATT.HQ PARTRIDGE RD - 1 screen 4 yds & 30 yds prepared for erection. COPSE RD. Enemy barrage + windlass over road in GOUZEAUCOURT. - No 3 Section wiring & huts Hqs a 7/5 + making cavalry track from W15 d to W15. No 4 Section also & cavalry track.	Ref
do	18/11/17		No 1 & 2 Section completing 2 hop step gate erecting 3 shelters in PARTRIDGE RD completing Signal D.O. in ARGYLL LANE & RILEY AVE. elephant shelter & lumber completed at New Bn HQ - 62 yds of screen fixed along COPSE RD. Enemy Shrapnel & S.GOUZEAUCOURT BATHS. No 3 & 4 Section completing cavalry track.	Ref
do	19/11/17		Nos 1 & 2 Section resting. Nos 3 & 4 cleaning + packing wagons.	Ref
do	20/11/17		Company moved to VILLERS PLOUICH in accordance with Orders operations organised in conjunction with Divisions on right & left. No 2 Section taking part in attack with reserve Battn. 10 KRR - Nos 3 + 4 Section going forward at night to demolish bridge at G.8.5.4 + M 5.6.5.8. Company in Camp at STATION QUARRY. R.1.3.6.6. No 267481 R.S.M. EDWARDS J.E. + 89478 R.S.M. HILLIER H. commended	Ref

D.D.& L., London, E.C. 4700d Wt. W12481007 750(?) 507 Feb. 23 Forms Co.-Pd.

Army Form C. 2118.

WAR DIARY
or
INTELLIGENCE SUMMARY.
(Erase heading not required.)

96th FIELD COMPANY R.E.

Place	Date	Hour	Summary of Events and Information	Remarks and references to Appendices
R.13.b.6.1.	21/11/17		No 1 Section working on LA VACQUERIE - MASNIERE Rly. No 3 Section attempted to demolish bridge at M.F.C.5.8. No 159962 Sapper MOSS F. killed - No 146766 Sapper SAUNDERS wounded - No 121155 Sapper MARSHALL F. wounded - 211962 Sapper COOPER H. wounded - No 63463 Sapper WHITE C.O. wounded at duty.	
do	22/11/17		No 1 Section working on LA VACQUERIE - MASNIERE Rly. No 2 Section attempted to demolish bridge at M.F.C.5.8. No 50050 Sapper HOFFMAN R. wounded at duty.	
do	23/11/17		No 1 Section erecting wire fence at G.33.c.6.0 - M3.a.8.0 - M3.c.6.0	
do	24/11/17		No 1 & 4 Section wire at G.33.c.6.0 - M3.a.8.0 - M3.c.6.0 completed.	
do	25/11/17		Section improving billets	
do	26/11/17		Section improving accommodation & making new billets at SURREY RAVINE.	

WAR DIARY
INTELLIGENCE SUMMARY

Army Form C. 2118.

Place	Date	Hour	Summary of Events and Information	Remarks and references to Appendices
R13 b 6.1	27/10/17		Making new accommodation at SURREY RAVINE - No 1 Section mining in STATION QUARRY	
do	28/10/17		Parts of Nos 3 & 4 Secs. went up to ocupy dugouts in HINDENBURG Line. Instruction of deep dugouts & report to C.R.E.	
do	29/10/17		ditto	
do			ditto	

E F Penn
Major RE
OC 95th Field Coy RE

95th FIELD COMPANY R.E.

SECRET

Army Form C. 2118.

WAR DIARY
or
INTELLIGENCE SUMMARY.
(Erase heading not required.)

Instructions regarding War Diaries and Intelligence Summaries are contained in F.S. Regs., Part II. and the Staff Manual respectively. Title pages will be prepared in manuscript.

Place	Date	Hour	Summary of Events and Information	Remarks and references to Appendices
VILLERS PLOUICH Sheet 57.C.	30/11/17 to 3/12/17		Enemy attacked on divne & adjoining fronts — Captured GONNELIEU & advanced to GOUZEAUCOURT, but afterwards driven back. Company Transport was got away & moved via METZ to FINS. ALL Pontoon & Trestle equipment could not be rearranged. Large amount of Company Equipment and 20 bicycles were also lost. Company formed parties of Company & attached Infantry & were ordered to man the Trenches RILEY AVENUE & about Line of forward line was held from 10 am 30/11/17 to 4 pm 1/12/17. FUSILIER Reserve line. 4pm to 9 pm on 1/12/17 moved to shelter in VILLERS ROAD at 9 pm for the night & proceeded at 5.30 am on 2/12/17 to hold ROPE AVENUE and moved to FUSILIER Reserve at 6 pm 2/12/17 & remained there until relieved at about 6 pm on 3/12/17. Part of Company were also outfitted for carrying French Mortars & S.A.A. to front line. Part of attached duty were used by R.E. as carrying parties & were afterwards sent back to they battns. Sappers & remainder of infantry stood to but etc at all billets VILLERS PLOUICH & marched to SOREL.	LA VACQUERIE & GONNELIEU & FINS [?]
FINS ? SOREL S	4/12/17		Remainder of Infantry sent back to their battns. Dismounted fortunity Coy moved by Bus to VILLE-SOUS-CORBIE. Transport moved by road to MEAULTE.	M
	5/12/17		Transport moved from MEAULT E. to ORVILLE, minus G.S. wagon, 3 limbers, & water Cart which joined Dismounted fortunity Coy at VILLE.	M
	6/12/17		Transport moved from ORVILLE to AUVEROMETZ. Dismounted marched to AVELUY & entrained for HESDIN. On arrival at HESDIN marched to St DENDEUX.	M

WAR DIARY
or
INTELLIGENCE SUMMARY.
(Erase heading not required.)

Army Form C. 2118.

95th FIELD COMPANY

Instructions regarding War Diaries and Intelligence Summaries are contained in F. S. Regs., Part II. and the Staff Manual respectively. Title pages will be prepared in manuscript.

Place	Date	Hour	Summary of Events and Information	Remarks and references to Appendices
	7/10/17		Transport moved from AUBROMETZ to PLUMAISON.	
	8/10/17		Transport moved from PLUMAISON to ST DENOEUX.	
	9/10/17		Company cleaning up, cleaning wagons, packing & loading.	
	10/10/17			
	11/10/17		Remounted moved by Bus from HUMBERT (after marching from ST DENOEUX) to RACQUINGHEM.	
	12/10/17		Transport moved to THIEMBRONNE.	
			Transport moved to RACQUINGHEM.	
			Drill & Rifle Exercises.	
	13/10/17		ditto O.C. left Company to act as C.R.E. ⟨Div⟩	
	14/10/17		Drill & Rifle Exercises, Training in packing & unpacking Tool Carts. Wiring.	
	15/10/17		ditto	
	16/10/17		Physical drill. Aiming exercises & musketry at ECOVRT range. Nos 1&2 Sec. moved to ZEON GEROUS for work with 61st July Bde.	
	17/10/17		Nos 3 Sec moved to LE CROQUET for work with 60th July Bde.	
	18/10/17		Physical drill. Rifle aiming exercises, wiring practice & training in packing & unpacking Tool Carts.	

Army Form C.-2118.

WAR DIARY
or
INTELLIGENCE SUMMARY.
(Erase heading not required.)

Instructions regarding War Diaries and Intelligence Summaries are contained in F. S. Regs., Part II. and the Staff Manual respectively. Title pages will be prepared in manuscript.

95TH FIELD COMPANY

Place	Date	Hour	Summary of Events and Information	Remarks and references to Appendices
	19/12/17		Drill, Rifle & Bayonet Exercises	
	20/12/17		On sunday jobs for Brigade.	
	21/12/17		ditto	
	22/12/17		ditto	
	23/12/17		ditto	
	24/12/17		ditto	
	25/12/17		Xmas day. Dinner &c.	
	26/12/17		No 4 Section relieved No 3 Sec at near ISAEUS. Musketry at BEAUMONT Range	
	27/12/17		On sunday jobs for Brigade. Drill Rifle Exercises	
	28/12/17		ditto	
	29/12/17		ditto	
	30/12/17		ditto	E.R.A.S.

E W A R Jones
Capt R.E.
o/c 95th Field Coy RE

17

96 2/1 Cay R of C
Vol 27

WAR DIARY or INTELLIGENCE SUMMARY

Army Form C. 2118.

(Erase heading not required.)

Instructions regarding War Diaries and Intelligence Summaries are contained in F. S. Regs., Part II. and the Staff Manual respectively. Title pages will be prepared in manuscript.

Place	Date	Hour	Summary of Events and Information	Remarks and references to Appendices
RAE QUING HEM	1/8/17		On orders to go for Brigade	
	1/1/8		Orders for all sections	
	2/1/8		Nice rifle & bayonet exercise. Two sections suggested course for 6:50 a.m. Bayonet lecture a to Company.	
	3/1/8		Nice rifle exercise, cleaning up and passing out	
	4/1/8		Inspec. knee lecture	
			Important march off from RAEQUINGHEM at 1.50 a.m. for VOORMEZEELE	
	5/1/8		Brief rifle exercise. Dismounted march from RAEQUINGHEM at 3 p.m. march to Equipment station entered for DICKEBUSCH and arrived Bullet on VOORMEZEELE	
VOORMEZEELE	6/1/8		Putting out wiring at all	
	7/1/8		Two the double up on a pilot TERTH AVE. RUSTUM dits Relieving Bay 54 Comp X 30 C 13 3	
	8/1/8		Rest. Perth Avenue	
	9/1/8		Dits	
	10/1/8		Shetty out bay on 2E Bay Kaken 30/31 Amkoor + 10 S.P. attack	

D. D. & I.
A(co1) Wt. W— London, E.C.
20/M2103 250m 00 5/17 Ech 53 Forms Co-of 4

WAR DIARY
or
INTELLIGENCE SUMMARY.

Army Form C. 2118.

Place	Date	Hour	Summary of Events and Information	Remarks and references to Appendices
VOORMEZEELE	11/1/18	—	Hutting erecting 4 shelters. 55 yds duck board track completed to N. of ruined entrance to catacombs of PERTH AVE. Completed lapping out line of new fully in centre of MENIN RD.	
	12/4/18	—	Hutting erecting shelters. 25 yards new duck board track N of PERTH AVE. N.3 strong point work completed. Bivouac work N2 a 3.2 finish, frames + timber completed for 16. Jump[?] K2 a complete.	
	13/4/18	—	Hutting erecting shelters. Rope bridge over ravine completed + carried to PERTH AVE. 75 ft of PERTH AVE. frames + duckboards complete. Filling in around carrying wire to Reserve line. 30 yards new duckboards No.3 S.P. Erecting shelters in Coach House Camp H.30.c. Laying 3 new shelters.	
	14/1/18	—	Hutting erecting shelters, 12 men x 7 m 90.0 gpmt wire. Erecting 6 new huts + laying duck boards in Batt. Camp H30.c. Reverting No. 3 S.P.	
	15/4/18	—	Hutting erecting shelters. 17 yds new duckboards on RESERVE LINE. 10 yards ditto 150 yards repaired home complete on RESERVE LINE.	
	16/4/18	—	Erecting over bay parapet screen. Pumping out gmt not 22.c.4. duckboards 450 yards of splinter I G.0. hut roof complete.	
			Reconnaissance made of front line left Group Centre Bgd.[?]	
	17/4/18	—	Hutting erecting shelters. 36 full arches + 1 half arch erected in PERT A AVE. curb check completed in trench for. Splinter proof erected in HEDGE ROW + new firestep given in LANE [? or LOOP?] St + communication line w of SCOTTISH...[?]	

Cheney [signature] C.O. R.E.[?] [illegible]

WAR DIARY
INTELLIGENCE SUMMARY.
(Erase heading not required.)

Army Form C. 2118.

Place	Date	Hour	Summary of Events and Information	Remarks and references to Appendices
VOORMEZEELE	18/7/16	—	Relief of Battery Staples. 36 Field howrs. Proceed to PERTH AVE. Dugout and one at RITZ Dugout. Lieut Humble gone over to find the Crsf. Now the Reconnaissance of near O.Ps. Handed over. Wagon line at B.Echelon	
	19/7/16	—	Training. Burying wires. Working at O.Ps.	
	20/7/16	—	Heavy gunning of the enemy. Shelling of Dumbarton Wood. Two double reports at intervals, probably Minenwerfer. Reading off. between SP 16.	
	21/7/16	—	Intense gunning of both sides. Enemy fires 9.2" shells in DUMBARTON WOOD from TUNNEL side, bullet gun fire creates a C.R.E. Dump, Workmen Go. Officer rec. Blowing Engine pump at C.R.E. dump. Mail party on out party.	
	22/7/16	—	Hostile shelling started. 10 yds. anthem fire on LSA DUMBARTON WOOD. Purr as at No. 3 S.P. at 9.00 drk. antifrm L.R.	
	23/7/16	—	Heavy enemy shelling. Much ag. war is heavy D. & armoured. B.C. goes abroad for ex. ample et new E.N.C. N.S. Digby Mason in PERTH AVE. Bung. are RITZ Dugout.	

D. D. & L., London, E.C.
(A0001) Wt. W1777/M697 750 m 3/17 Sch 92 Forms/C 2/14

WAR DIARY or INTELLIGENCE SUMMARY

Army Form C. 2118.

(Erase heading not required.)

Place	Date	Hour	Summary of Events and Information	Remarks and references to Appendices
VOORMEZEELE	24/7/18	—	During night were occupied in Trench making works in M.L.R. Everyone was in front shelter in no 4 S.P. Bay to drain, front trenches Islendrus Tale and Tunnel. Bumpers work in Ritz Dugout.	
	25/7/18	—	Shelling. Wiring and improving line DUMBARTON WOOD Dugout. S.P. Ercting bunks at Tacdaw Tunnel. Enlg. G.O.C. map cutting South Trench MLR. Comm Regiment relaying Bumpers Ritz Dugouts Incomplete.	
	26/7/18	—	Working in camp. Cleaning Huts. Remaining day is used MLR with several men of Piers moving S.P. to Comm. cables. Winding filling up graves S.P. to Comm. completed.	
	27/7/18	—	Enemy put heavy in TACDAW TUNNEL Bumper drawing in R.T.B dugouts S.P. in support line employed 25 yds black reveites with A frames new in MLR also driving	
	28/7/18	—	Shelling. Bumpers Ritz dugouts drew cleaned 500 instep upper MLR. Wiring. DUMBARTON WOOD 140 yds completed A frames new in trench. Trench cleaned throw many Ritz and	

WAR DIARY
INTELLIGENCE SUMMARY.

(Erase heading not required.)

Army Form C. 2118.

Place	Date	Hour	Summary of Events and Information	Remarks and references to Appendices
VOORMEZEELE	29/5 to 31/5		Nothing of any importance to report. Enemy's aeroplanes very active. Our own less so.	

E. W. Hugh Jones
Capt. R.E.
O.C. 96th Coy R.E.

96th Field Co. R.E. Army Form C. 2118.

Vol 29

WAR DIARY
or
INTELLIGENCE SUMMARY.
(Erase heading not required.)

Place	Date	Hour	Summary of Events and Information	Remarks and references to Appendices
VOORMEZEELE	3/1/18		Working on INTERMEDIATE LINE & M.K.R & making pouts in NEW SUPPORT LINE in GHELUVELT SECTOR	
	8/2/18		Working	
	9/2/18		Coy HQs moved from Camp at I.31a.1.7 to H.30.a.4.4. Rd 28.	
	10/2/18		Work on INTERMEDIATE LINE & M.K.R. in GHELUVELT SECTOR. Working	
	16/2/18		Working in GLENCORSE WOOD	
	14/2/18	6 p.m.	Transport & HQ left camp at H.30.C. at 12 noon & arrived at STRAZEELE arriving here about 5 p.m.	
	17/2/18 9.30 a.m.		Transport & H.Q STRAZEELE to RACQUINGHEM at 9.30 a.m. Arriving RACQUINGHEM about 2.40 p.m. Remainder of Co. left H.Q. a camp at I.30.m. marches to DICKEBUSCH & entrained at EBBLINGHEM reach to RACQUINGHEM arriving at 9 p.m.	
	18/19/2/18		Cleaning equipment transport inspns. Extra Drill Rifle exercises & musketry training.	
	20/2/18		Entrained R.Only seasons C.S.R. Acquit. M.X.R. off Camp R. Company & transport left RACQUINGHEM at 12.30 p.m. marches to STEEN BECQUE entraining at 6 p.m. for NESLE.	

Army Form C. 2118.

96TH Field Co. R.E.

WAR DIARY
or
INTELLIGENCE SUMMARY.

(Erase heading not required.)

Instructions regarding War Diaries and Intelligence Summaries are contained in F. S. Regs., Part II. and the Staff Manual respectively. Title pages will be prepared in manuscript.

Place	Date	Hour	Summary of Events and Information	Remarks and references to Appendices
NESLE	21/2/18	—	Arrived NESLE at 6.45 AM & marched to CAMPAGNE.	
CAMPAGNE	22/2/18 to 27/2/18		Cleaning and Training — Gas Drill, Section Drill, Rifle Exercises, Open Order. Erection of Weldon Trestle (Theoretical Training).	

E. N. H. L. Jones.
Capt. R.E.
O.C. 96th Field Coy R.E.

27-2-'18

20th Divisional Engineers

96th FIELD COMPANY R.E.

MARCH 1918

96th Field Coy. R.E.

Vol 30

WAR DIARY
or
INTELLIGENCE SUMMARY.
(Erase heading not required.)

Army Form C. 2118.

Place	Date	Hour	Summary of Events and Information	Remarks and references to Appendices
CAMPAGNE	28/2/18		Physical & Company Drill.	
ditto	1/3/18		Section Drill. Rifle exercises. Overhauling & greasing Wilden Treath.	
ditto	2/3/18		ditto	
ditto	3/3/18		Squad Drill. Rifle exercises. Loading wagons.	
ditto	4/3/18		Transport left CAMPAGNE for CHAUNY at 8 A.M. Dismounted left CAMPAGNE by Motor Lorries	
CHAUNY			at 9.30 A.M. Company billeted in 3 Sectors at CHAUNY. N°2 at MANICAMP	
ditto	5/3/18		N°2 at BETHANCOURT. ST QUENTIN 18. - B = C 5 - C 8. in morning.	
ditto	6/3/18		Reconnoitering & setting out an Army Defence Zone, between UGNY le GAY & BESMES	
ditto	7/3/18		ditto	
ditto	8/3/18		ditto & clearing Brushwood	
ditto	9/3/18		ditto	
ditto	10/3/18		ditto & rearranging work to be started by the 191st, 192nd Italian Works Coy ABBECURT & 14th Entrenching Battalion BETHANCOURT	
ditto	"		194th 195th " " " BESMES	
ditto	11/3/18		Warning to move arrived after all parties at work. Dismounted left CHAUNY by Lorries	
OGNOLLES	"		at 2 P.M.— arriving OGNOLLES at 4.30 P.M. Transport moved from CHAUNY at 1.30 P.M. arriving OGNOLLES 9 P.M.	

Army Form C. 2118.

WAR DIARY
or
INTELLIGENCE SUMMARY.
(Erase heading not required.)

Instructions regarding War Diaries and Intelligence Summaries are contained in F. S. Regs., Part II. and the Staff Manual respectively. Title pages will be prepared in manuscript.

Place	Date	Hour	Summary of Events and Information	Remarks and references to Appendices
OGNOLLES	12/3/18		Rifle & Bayonet exercises, Gas drill	R.E.
"	13/3/18		ditto. Reconnoitred lines of defence HAPPENCOURT - BRAY ST CHRISTOPHE - ALBIGNY - VILLERS - ST-CHRISTOPHE - DOUILLY - QUIVIERS with G.O.C. & G.S.O.1. ST QUENTIN 18 A 9 B 3.	R.E.
"	14/3/18		Reconnoitred Switch Line DOUILLY - CROIX MOLIGNEUX with G.S.O.1.	R.E.
"	15/3/18		Rifle & Bayonet exercises. Gas drill. Transport left OGNOLLES 3 P.M. Dismounted Bombers left	R.E.
"	16/3/18		OGNOLLES at 5 P.M. arriving CHAUNY at 4 P.M. Transport arrived 11 P.M. Company billeted as before.	R.E.
CHAUNY			Working on Army Defences from GAUMONT to RESMES	R.E.
"	17/3/18		ditto	R.E.
"	18/3/18		ditto Reconnoitred portion of Line from	R.E.
"	19/3/18		GAUMONT Chateau to UGNY. with C.R.E. & rearranged line	R.E.
"	20/3/18		ditto	R.E.
"	21/3/18		ditto	R.E.
"	21/3/18		German Offensive started. Transport left CHAUNY for St SULPICE. HAM (ST QUENTIN A3) at 2.30 P.M. Dismounted personnel left by motor lorries at 5.30 P.M. arrived St SULPICE at 8.30 P.M. Transport arriving at 10.45 P.M.	R.E.
"	22/3/18		Nos 1 & 2 Sections moved forward to work under 59th Brigade.	R.E.

WAR DIARY
or
INTELLIGENCE SUMMARY.

Army Form C. 2118.

Place	Date	Hour	Summary of Events and Information	Remarks and references to Appendices
			At noon reported at VILLERS ST CHRISTOPHE - then at TOUILLE went to work on line W. of DOUILLY - MATIGNY. Remainder of Section remained in billets	RE
	23/3/18	9.15 AM	Nos 3 & 4 Sections with toolcarts proceeded to demolish bridges over CANAL de la SOMME at BETHENCOURT - ROUY le GRAND (AMIENS 17 L.3) Bridge at Rouy destroyed at 2.30 A.M. 9 Bridge over river at BETHENCOURT at 3.15 AM. over march on CANAL at 9.15 AM. Nos 1 & 2 Sections left Brigade for 59th Coy at 2.30 AM H.Qn & 9 transport moved via ESMERY-HALLON, ERCHEU to OGNOLLES. Nos 2 & 3 Sections returning to 59 Coy taken by Staff Officer 30th Div to prepare bridges for demolition at 6.30 AM. LIBERMONT - RAMECOURT - BUVERCHY - BACQUENCOURT (AMIENS 17 L.4) over CANAL between NESLE & NOYON. Great lack of explosives. Bridges handed over to G.R.E. 30th Div in course of afternoon. Coy concentrated at ERCHEU at 6 PM with transport less Bridging Wagons at OGNOLLES.	RE
	24/3/18	12.30 AM	Dismounted with one limber proceeded to report to 59th Brigade at Rouy le PETIT rested in huts by Railway till 9 AM = then manned line of trenches by Railway at 12 noon. Employed in digging a new line	RE

WAR DIARY
or
INTELLIGENCE SUMMARY.
(Erase heading not required.)

Army Form C. 2118.

Instructions regarding War Diaries and Intelligence Summaries are contained in F. S. Regs., Part II. and the Staff Manual respectively. Title pages will be prepared in manuscript.

Place	Date	Hour	Summary of Events and Information	Remarks and references to Appendices
	24/3/18		from QUIGUERY to MESNIL-ST NICAISE. HQrs & Endicart proceeded to BILLANCOURT. Nos 1.2.9.3. Sections proceeded Coy at BILLANCOURT at 9.PM. No 4 Section remained with Brigade. Transport less toolcarts proceeded to CARREPUITS.	RS
	25/3/18		HQrs 9 Sections proceeded at 5AM to BETHONVILLERS. No 4 Section employed by Brigade in digging trenches to NW of BILLANCOURT rejoined Coy at 1.PM. Nos 1.2.9.3. Sections proceeded to work on new line of Defence AMIENS 1st 9 2nd (3rd 94th) to W of THILLOY-CREMERY. Details Signal School reinforcements etc also employed in work. HQrs No 4 Section at CRUNY till 6.PM then to CARREPUITS. Transport proceeded from CARREPUITS to HANGEST en SANTERRE at 12 noon	RS
	26/3/18		Coy dismounted with 1 limber 91 toolcart concentrated at ROYE at 4 AM proceeded under Brigade orders at 5.30 AM via VILLERS-les-ROYE, ERCHES, ARVILLERS to QUESNEL (AMIENS 14 A.3.) arriving 10.30 AM. Whole Coy concentrated. Left in Lille. Transport less toolcarts 91 limber proceeded to DOMART sur la LUCE. Nos 1.9.3. Sections reported for work under Brigade at 2.PM but rejoined Coy at 9.PM. 76.PM	RS

WAR DIARY
or
INTELLIGENCE SUMMARY.
(Erase heading not required.)

Army Form C. 2118.

Place	Date	Hour	Summary of Events and Information	Remarks and references to Appendices
	27/3/18		Coy employed in digging Defensive line 1½ E of QUESNEL - returned to billets. Transport moved to AILLY SUR NOYE at 11 AM. Bridging Wagons, Battery Wagons & GS Wagons moved to NAMPTY. reported to O.C. Supply Train - hauled at MORISEL	
	28/3/18		Dismounted moved by bus to DOMART - SUR - LA - LYCE. Toolcarts by road at 8AM. returned by Transport from MORISEL dismounted rested "Standing by" in billets. At 2.30 P.M. whole of Transport with Coy ordered to move to BOVES, then on to SAINS en AMIENOIS.	
	29/3/18		Toolcarts & 2 limbers rejoined Coy at dusk employed in digging new Defensive line 1½ E of DOMART at 4.30 AM Coy rested in billets D. DEMUIN. MOREUIL ROAD (AMIENS 17.93)	
	30/3/18		Coy proceeded at 2 PM to BOVES, rested in billets - entrained at 4 PM. in digging new Defensive Line SW of BOIS GENTELLES. (AMIENS 17 F3 F F3) returned to billets 11 PM	
	31/3/18		Coy rested in billets & Transport from SAINS rejoined Coy at 3.30 P.M.	

S.T. Tempair Lt
O.C. 96 Fld Coy lk

WAR DIARY
INTELLIGENCE SUMMARY

Army Form C. 2118.

Place	Date	Hour	Summary of Events and Information	Remarks and references to Appendices
Sheet AMIENS 40009 BOVES	April 1st 1918		All returns authorised clipping line of defence between DOMART-SUR-LA-LUCE and BOVES from 1pm to 8pm. At 8.30pm dismounted personnel went by lorry to FRESNOY-AU-VAL	
FRESNOY AU VAL			arriving at 4.30 A.M. 2nd April. Transport went by road arriving at 9.30 A.M. 2nd April.	
ST AUBIN - MONTENOY	3rd 4th to 8th	2.30pm	Company complete left for ST AUBIN - MONTENOY arrived 8pm. Ref. Sheet 16 DIEPPE 40,000 Cleaning up and training	
BROCOURT	9th		Company joined Div.l R.E. Column & marched to BROCOURT arriving at 4.30pm.	
BOUTTENCOURT	10th		Company marched to BEAUCHAMPS BOUTTENCOURT-SUR-SAMACHES.	
BEAUCHAMPS	11th 12th to 15th 16th 18th 17th		Company marched to BEAUCHAMPS arriving 3.35pm. Cleaning up. Training in pontooning, knotting, lashing, miniature range &c. Major R.E. Stay D.S.O. R.E. evacuated to Base (sick) Selected for Corps Transport left by road at 8.30pm	

Page 2.

WAR DIARY
or
INTELLIGENCE SUMMARY.
(Erase heading not required.)

Army Form C. 2118.

Place	Date	Hour	Summary of Events and Information	Remarks and references to Appendices
EU	18th	6:30 p.m.	For PONT REMY (Sheet 40000, ABBEVILLE) Transport Divisional Personnel and remainder of Transport marched to Eu (Sheet 40000 ABBEVILLE) where they entrained for TINQUES (LENS II 20000) arriving there at 11:30 p.m. At 1 p.m. they marched to GUESTREVILLE. The portion of the transport which had gone by Road also still en route.	
GUESTREVILLE	20th	2 p.m.	Transport arrived.	
	20th to 30th		This was an uninterrupted period of intensive training. Lectures, schemes, shooting on miniature and 200 yds. ranges while OC. Eighteen Reinforcements arrived.	
			1-5-18	
			E.A. Hugh-Jones R.E.	
			E. Capt. 96th Coy R.E.	
			O.C. 96 th Field Coy R.E.	

96 Field Coy.

Army Form C. 2118.

WAR DIARY
or
INTELLIGENCE SUMMARY.
(Erase heading not required.)

Instructions regarding War Diaries and Intelligence Summaries are contained in F. S. Regs., Part II. and the Staff Manual respectively. Title pages will be prepared in manuscript.

Place	Date	Hour	Summary of Events and Information	Remarks and references to Appendices
LENS 11 GUESTREVILLE 9/8	May 1/18		Training Lectures, Schemes, Shooting on miniature "200x" Range, Washing arrgts.	Sheet 36 N.10 c 39
	2nd	9.45am	Company & Transport left GUESTREVILLE & marched to ABLAIN ST NAZAIRE	
	3rd		Sections watering at ABLAIN ST NAZAIRE (in camp)	
	4th	10 AM	Nos 1, 2 & 3 Sections proceeded to forward billets & work on Wittes left flank defences	
	6th		Bridging equipment parked at No Pontoon Park RANCHECOURT.	
	9th		Took over forward work in the left sector from 84th Fld Coy RE	
	10th & 18th		Constructing dugouts, cleaning & repairing trenches, digging & wiring flank defences	
	18th & 28th		Sections relieved on 18th & took over work on right sector, including dugouts, shelters & flank defences. Work carried on till night of 28th	from 8375 ♀ Coy RE
	29th		Sections returned & entered on 4 days training of Bayonet drill, Rifle exercises, Squad drill, Open Order drill, Lewis Gun & Rifle firing	

E.F. Haylitoogh R.E.
Cmd'g 96 Fd Coy R.E.
Lt 96
O.C. 96

WAR DIARY or INTELLIGENCE SUMMARY

Army Form C. 2118.

96 2nd Coy R.E.

Vol 33

(Erase heading not required.)

Instructions regarding War Diaries and Intelligence Summaries are contained in F. S. Regs., Part II. and the Staff Manual respectively. Title pages will be prepared in manuscript.

Place	Date	Hour	Summary of Events and Information	Remarks and references to Appendices
ABLAIN-ST NAZAIRE	31/7/18 to 3/8		"Training" Prepared drill with extended Lewis Guns & rifle firing	ST NAZAIRE RIVER
	4/8		Installed new spray set at ANGRES trollies sent out and Cambs X & S, maintaining Brigade wiring classes	
	5/8		Took Men Bath Station carried out Inspection of Company & Transport by O.C.	
	6/8		9 Section took new tools Section from 34th West Cy RE, commenced work	
	7/8		Constructed deep Dugouts, erecting Baby Elephant shelters, wiring,	
	8/8		Artillery observation Posts, wiring & working on Defences of HILL 65 &	
			Bois de RIAUMONT. Daily inspection of Road Mines, maintenance of Trenches	
	16/8		Took over work in AVION Section from 23rd Mid. Cy RE	
	17/8 to 25/8		Working on deep Dugouts, Baby Elephants shelter, Brigade Artillery H.Q's, wiring & reclaiming ex Trenches to conform to new defences	Sketch
	23/8		6 O.R. took part in successful Trench Raid with South Rifles in N.34 on enemy Dugouts, capturing 6 20lbs Mobile charges of Ammonal, destroying 6 entrances to deep Dugouts & killing many of the enemy	

Army Form C. 2118.

WAR DIARY
or
INTELLIGENCE SUMMARY.
(Erase heading not required.)

Instructions regarding War Diaries and Intelligence Summaries are contained in F. S. Regs., Part II. and the Staff Manual respectively. Title pages will be prepared in manuscript.

Place	Date	Hour	Summary of Events and Information	Remarks and references to Appendices
	25/8		Relieved by 83rd Field Coy R.E. & withdrew to Bark Circus	Bark C.
	26/8		Work on new camp at X.3.d.	ST NAZAIRE
	27/8		30 O.R. in hospital with P.U.O. & 29 excused duty in camp	(river)

E. H. Hugh Jones
MAJOR. R.E.
O.C. 96th FIELD COY. R.E.

Sheet 1.

96 30 Coy R.E.

96 R 34

Sheet ST NAZAIRE RIVER

WAR DIARY
or
INTELLIGENCE SUMMARY.
(Erase heading not required.)

Place	Date	Hour	Summary of Events and Information	Remarks and references to Appendices
ABLAIN-ST NAZAIRE	June 30th		Company Strength 7 Officers and 209 OR	
	July 1st		Continued training Programme	
	2nd		Programme & Firing Rifle evening Physical drill	
			50th Bde Horse Show. Rare Meet 5 events won by this UNIT	
			Inspection of Winners by Corps Commander afterwards	
	3rd		Training Programme continued as above including Mining Classes Company	
	4th		Section took over all work on both sections from each of the Chief Engr	
	5th		Commenced work consisting Hamels Platoon Posts M.G. Emplacements	
	10th		Trench Shelters cement Artillery Observation Posts dug outs & Othello	
	13th		Bridges	
	14th		Forward H.Qrs & Observation Posts. In addition, carried the Instrumentation	
			of the Central Section Lakes 2° 2° on the Left	
			He work consisted of Concrete Platoon Posts Coned OP. Bomb	
			Trench Shelters, the making & fixing of French Door Frames	
			& Screens general Trench Maintenance Ino 1 Coy R.E.	
			Road Metal, & Constructing Dug outs & Shelters and Camps	
			Gas Officer	

14th to 30th July

WAR DIARY
INTELLIGENCE SUMMARY
(Erase heading not required.)

Sheet 2

Army Form C. 2118.

{ 14th to 30th July. }

{ Sheet ST. NAZAIRE RIVER. }

Place	Date	Hour	Summary of Events and Information	Remarks and references to Appendices
	July 18th		No 50053 Sapper AHERN J awarded D.C.M. for gallantry in the field on 22-6-18 during raid on enemy trenches. Company intercalation.	
	20		Four R.E. & O.R. took part in the Raid on enemy trenches carried out 16 (20 Inf Bde) Dundels Casualties no casualties.	
	28		Died at New Defence Dump between M.31.c - M.24.c.	
	22		Back area work consisted of erecting Nissen huts etc at ALBERTA CAMP repairing huts, drainage etc.	
	29		Roads at NIAGARA CAMP sundry repairs at Ventorio Jobs at Divisional H.Q.	

E.H. Hugh Jones
MAJOR, R.E.
O.C. 96th FIELD COY. R.E.

WAR DIARY
or
INTELLIGENCE SUMMARY.

(Erase heading not required.)

Army Form C. 2118.

Sheet ST NAZAIRE RIVER

Place	Date	Hour	Summary of Events and Information	Remarks and references to Appendices
ABLAIN-ST NAZAIRE	July 31st 1918		Company "Strength" 7 Officers 206 Other ranks.	
	August 1st		Working on Centre sub Sector. General platoon posts, new line and posts, erecting shelters, and artillery O.P.	
	2nd		Company H.Qrs. moved to ANGRES M.33.d.1.7.	
	3rd		Section work consisted of erecting M.G. emplacements. Pill-boxes.	
	5th-19th		Artillery O.P. General trench maintenance, erection of filtonating chamber maintenance of Road, Mines, and drainage scheme.	
	20th		Section took over all work from the 83rd Field Coy R.E. in the right sub-Sector comprising the HIRONDELLE defences, 2 sections commenced work at once on Pill-boxes, artillery O.P. drainage, shelter, trench repairs, constructing R.A.P. improvements to A.D.S. deep Dugouts, maintenance of Railway track and R.E. Dumps	
	27th		8 O.R. took part in Trench raid on enemy defences. Coy. mobile Champs and Bangalore torpedoes, they breached the enemy wire and destroyed several dugouts, one sapper was wounded on the return journey.	
	30th		Back area work consisted of improvements to Camps and erecting Road Signs.	

96 Jul Coy RE
9/8 36

Sheet 1

WAR DIARY
or
INTELLIGENCE SUMMARY
Army Form C. 2118.
(Erase heading not required.)

SHEET 83 ST NAZAIRE RIVER

Place	Date	Hour	Summary of Events and Information	Remarks and references to Appendices
ABLAIN ST NAZAIRE	31/8		Company "Strength" 7 Officers and 203 O.Rs	
			at S.10.d.7.7 with 2 Sections	
	1/8		"Aron" H.Q. established.	
			2 Sections working on left sub-sector in ten day relief. The work consisting	
			of Shelton Man Pill boxes, Road Screens, Concrete Pill boxes, M.G Dugouts	
			Horn and Artillery Paridges, Chlorinating Chambers, Battle HQrs	
			Clearing Deep dugouts, Repairs and Maintenance of Trenches	
			Constructing concrete Covers to O.Ps. Maintenance of Railway	
	to		and R.E Dump, alterations and Repairs to A.D.Ss, RAP and	
			Collecting Post for walking wounded. All have wope carried	
			out with a view to Drainage for the oncoming winter.	
			Back area Work done by resting Sections, consisted of the	
			erection of wire Fence on Training Ground at MARQUEFFLES making	
			and Drawing tools, erection of Nissen huts, Cookhouse	
			Incinerators, Notice-boards and General repairs to Camp.	
	27/8		An "Intensive Training" programme Lasting ten days was	
			carried out by all Sections, which comprised Rifle –	

Sheet 2.

WAR DIARY
or
INTELLIGENCE SUMMARY.

Army Form C. 2118.

Place	Date	Hour	Summary of Events and Information	Remarks and references to Appendices
ABLAIN ST.NAZAIRE				SHEET ST NAZAIRE RIVER.
	27/9/18		exercises, running drill, Map reading, Road Mine and Booby Trap demonstrations, extended order drill, Physical exercises and Infantry Schemes.	
	28/29		One Officer and 30 O.Rs reported to Company for attachment for Work and R.E. Training.	
	29/9/18		5 R.E. carrying 2 Bangalore Torpedoes and 3 Mobile Charges took part in a Raid on enemy defences, with 2 Platoons of 11th Battalion K.R.R.C. One R.E. was wounded. Company "Strength" 7 Officers and 207 O.Rs.	

E.B. Hughes Jones
30-9-18
MAJOR, R.E.
O. C. 96th FIELD COY. R.E.

WAR DIARY or INTELLIGENCE SUMMARY

Army Form C. 2118.

96th Army Rd

WR 37

Sheet 1

Place	Date	Hour	Summary of Events and Information	Remarks and references to Appendices
WEST OF AVION	30/9/18		Coy Strength 7 Officers 203 O.R.'s	Sheet A. 44 P.
	Oct 1st & 2nd		No 3 & 4 Sections working on left sub. sector defensive system	
			No 1 & 2 " " " " in ASKAIN ST NAZAIRE	
			" Back area work in ASKAIN ST NAZAIRE	
	3rd		Enemy withdrawal on LENS Front. At 18.15 hours orders received HQ. + No 1 & 2 Sections which were standing by moved forward to LA COULOTTE, accompanied by all Section tool carts + Pontoon wagons carrying "R.E." equipment wire laid &c, arriving there at 20.00 hrs. A detachment of 1 Officer & 28 O.R.'s from 60th Btn & a similar number from 61st & 62nd Btns were reported to the Coy. at 20.05 for work, the total number of attached infy. now being 3 Officers & 112 O.R.'s all of whom, including the Coy were billeted with the 3 Bns of the Brewery.	
	4th		No 3 & 4 Sections rejoined Coy from original rendezvous killets at 06.15 hours. No 3 Sec. remaining in reserve whilst repairs to billets & Tramway, while No 1 Section proceeds to ____	

Sheet 2.

Army Form C. 2118.

WAR DIARY
or
INTELLIGENCE SUMMARY.

(Erase heading not required.)

Place	Date	Hour	Summary of Events and Information	Remarks and references to Appendices
			for making water reconnaissance, and Bows Sample being taken. Lieut Cork made reconnaissance of forward roads. No. 24 Section stood by with the attacked inf.y for work on road from AVION to MERICOURT. Squad from No.2 Section cut a g'way thro destroyed railway bridge which was obstructing the road in AVION.	
	5th	06:15	Coy. & attached inf.y. paraded for work. Sections 1 & 3 as on the 4th. Nos. 2 & 4 worked on road thru MERICOURT & exc. thm 200x of the front line. Squad from No.2 Sec. made ramp for field guns over destroyed bridge site in SALLAUMINES. Representatives of Off.r Field Coy 12th Div. reported to take over work. Our Officers and 10 O.R's. from 96th Field Coy. R.E. went on cycles to BETHONCOURT to arrange billets.	LENS 11
	6th	17:30	The dismounted platoons of attached inf.y. embussed at FOSSE 6 in ANGRES	

Sheet 3.

Army Form C. 2118.

WAR DIARY
or
INTELLIGENCE SUMMARY.
(Erase heading not required.)

Place	Date	Hour	Summary of Events and Information	Remarks and references to Appendices
	7th		Transport & part of Coy H.Q. Left ABZAIN ST NAZAIRE at 09.30 & arrived at BETHONCOURT at 14.00 hrs. Attached infy. went by train to MESNIL BOUCHE, Coy. arrived at BETHONCOURT at 20.00 hrs.	
	8th		Coy billeted in bazens. Cleaning up.	
	9th		Training programme commenced.	
	10th		Drew trying equipment from pontoon park. Training & recreation, including large amount of pontoon drill, selection of suitable reference to attack sclerias, recce to muscles & bridging sclerias.	
	30th		Preparing to entrain for VERU en route to join 3rd Army in the CAMBRAI area. Bn strength 7 Officers + 207 O.R.'s 6 O.R.'s joined the Coy. during the month.	

E.T. Hugh Jones
MAJOR, R.E.
O.C. 96th FIELD COY. R.E.

96 2/Coy R.E. Vol 36

WAR DIARY
or
INTELLIGENCE SUMMARY.

SHEET No 1.

Army Form C. 2118.

Place	Date	Hour	Summary of Events and Information	Remarks and references to Appendices
	31/12		Company including Transport left BETHENCOURT (SHEET hens 11) at 01.15 hours for SAVY STATION and entrained at 08.00 hours for VÉHU (SHEET hens 11) arriving VÉHU 15.00. Dismounted personnel entrained 16.15 for CAMBRAI arriving 18.30 hours, billeted in houses. Mounted personnel left VÉHU 16.30 and proceeded by road to CAMBRAI arriving 22.30.	
	1/1/19		Company "cleaning up" generally	
	2/1/19		Standing by awaiting orders, to move. Cleaning and watering billets.	
	3/1/19		Company left CAMBRAI at 15.30 and marched to CAUROIR arriving 17.50.	
	4/1/19		Continued the journey at 11.30 and arrived ST AUBERT 14.00 hours.	
	5/1/19		Company resting at ST AUBERT	
	6/1/19		Training "Physical drill" lectures and Footcart-Packing.	
	7/1/19		At 14.45 the Company left ST AUBERT, and proceeded to VENDEGIES arriving 17.30.	
	8/1/19		The march was resumed to JENLAIN at 18.00, the Company arriving 17.30	
	9/1/19		Standing by cleaning billets etc.	
	10/1/19		Left JENLAIN 13.30 and proceeded to St WAAST la Vallée arriving 17.30, joined the 61st Infantry Brigade.	

WAR DIARY or INTELLIGENCE SUMMARY

Army Form C. 2118.

SHEET No.2

Place	Date	Hour	Summary of Events and Information	Remarks and references to Appendices
	11/18		Notification received 09:00, that Hostilities cease at 11:00 hours. Company left ST WAAST 13.00 and proceeded to GOEGNIES. Dramatic personnel arrived 18.30, and Transport 30 minutes later, having had to make a detour, owing to mine craters on the line of march. All billeted in the CHATEAU DE ROGERIE.	
	12/18		Section started work on road bridges at D.25 b.3.4. Sheet 51. and No 4	
	13/18		ditto	
	14/18		Section moved to HAVAY with Tplant for work on Road craters	
	15/18		Section working on Roads at between HAVAY and GIVRY	
	16/18			
	17/18			
	18/18		Company allotted an area for work erasing German signs and indications this work was carried on daily.	
	19/18			
	20/18			
	21/18			
	22/18		Company moved to TAISNIERES at 13.30 arriving 16.30 hours and joined 59th Infantry Brigade.	
	23/18		At 09.30 Company marched to WARGNIES-LE-PETIT arriving 14.00 hours	
	24/18		left WARGNIES-LE-PETIT at 09.30 and arrived ST MARTIN at 15.30.	

SHEET VALENCIENNES 1.8

Army Form C. 2118.

SHEET No 3

WAR DIARY
or
INTELLIGENCE SUMMARY.
(Erase heading not required.)

Place	Date	Hour	Summary of Events and Information	Remarks and references to Appendices
SHEET VALENCIENNES 12	25/11/18		Company left ST MARTIN for ST VAAST 09.30 arriving 13.00 and rested one day. Cleaning up, and washing was gone.	
	26/11/18			
	27/11/18		Left ST VAAST at 09.30 and marched to CAMBRAI arriving at 14.00 hours.	
	28/11/18		Company rested one day.	
	29/11/18		The Transport under 60th Infantry Bde Group moved off at 08.25 for BEUGNATRE N.E. of BAPAUME. (Sheet LENS 11)	
	30/11/18		Dismounted personnel entrained 09.00 hours for ARQUEVES. (Sheet LENS 11. F.6) One reinforcement joined the Company during the Month. Company Strength for month ending November 30th 1918 as follows:- Officers 7. Other Ranks 204.	

H.C. Edwards
Capt R.E.
o/c 96th Field Coy RE

WAR DIARY
or
INTELLIGENCE SUMMARY.

Army Form C. 2118.

96th Fd Coy R.E.

Instructions regarding War Diaries and Intelligence Summaries are contained in F. S. Regs., Part II. and the Staff Manual respectively. Title pages will be prepared in manuscript.

(Erase heading not required.)

Place	Date	Hour	Summary of Events and Information	Remarks and references to Appendices
	30/11/18		Transport left BEUGNATRE for BLENVILLERS-AU-BOIS (SHEET LENS 1) Remainder personnel detrained at ARQUEVES and marched to FAMECHON arriving at 20.00 hours.	
	1/12/18		Transport moved to FAMECHON arriving 12.00 hours.	
	2/12/18		Company working on own billets by FAMECHON. No 3 Section moved to HUMBERCAMPS (Shell Lens 11) for work on R.E.A. Camp, &c.	
	3/12/18		Remainder of Company improving Billeting Accommodation.	
	4/12/18		No 2. Section moved to TOUTENCOURT for similar work with 59½ Inf. Bde.	
	5/12/18		No 1. Section moved to TOUTENCOURT for similar work.	
	6/12/18			
	7/12/18		Sections working on	
	8/12/18		No 4 Section moved to HUMBERCAMP and joined No.3 Section	
	to		Company making Billeting Accommodation at LA CAUCHIE, HUMBERCAMP, LA HERLIERE	
	23/12/18		GAUDIEMPRÉ, HÉRISSART, RAINCHEVAL & LA BAZEQUE, also erecting new Huts,	
			making new R.A.M.C. Camp at TOUTENCOURT and new Camp at HURTEBUSE FARM, FAMECHON.	
	24/12/18		Sections reallied to FAMECHON for the Xmas Rest & Dinner	
	to 27/12/18			
	28/12/18		Resumed work on the different camps as above.	
	to 30/12/18			

E.W. Hugh Jones
Major R.E.
O.C. 96 Fd Field Co R.E.

96 Fd Coy Army Form C. 2118.

Vol 40

WAR DIARY
or
INTELLIGENCE SUMMARY.

(Erase heading not required.)

Place	Date	Hour	Summary of Events and Information	Remarks and references to Appendices
HURTEBISE FARM	30/12/18	—	Company "Strength" 7 Officers and 197 OR	Sheet Lens 11.
	1/9		Sections employed improving Billeting accommodation at HUMBERCAMP, RINCHEVAL, TOUTENCOURT, HERISSART, GAUDIEMPRÉ, VAUCHELLES, LA CAUCHIE, LA BAZEQUE, LA BRET and HURTEBISE FARM	
			One section withdrawn from TOUTENCOURT HQ and detachment sent to VAUCHELLES to take over work from 83rd Field Company RE	
			2 ORs reinforcements joined Company during the month	
			2 Officers 49 other ranks and 16 animals proceeded from UNIT on demobilization during the month of January.	
			2 OR's awarded the Meritorious Service Medal	
	30/9		Company Strength 4 Officers 144 other ranks	

E.A. Hugh Jones
CAPT. R.E.
O.C. 96th FIELD COY R.E.

96th Coy R.E.

WAR DIARY
or
INTELLIGENCE SUMMARY.

Army Form C. 2118.

Sheet June 11.

Place	Date	Hour	Summary of Events and Information	Remarks and references to Appendices
HURTEBISE FM	31/1		Company "Strength" 5 Officers and 164 Other Ranks	
	1/2		Denomined Personnel employed improving Peeling Decauville at	
			HUMBERCAMP, GAUDIEMPRÉ, SAUCHELLES LA BAZEQUE, HUTTEBISE FARM	
			MONDICOURT and DOULLENS	
	24/2		24 O.Rs and 9 Animals proceed from Unit on	
			Demobilization during February as follows:	
	26/2		5 O.R. proceed on draft to 1st Br Drainery as follows:	
	27/2		one O.R. to 228th Field Coy R.E. two O.R. to 222nd Field Coy R.E.	
			and two O.R. to 231st Field Coy R.E.	
			One O.R. accured the "Military Medal"	
	28/2		Company "Strength" 4 Officers and 108 O.Rs.	

E.F. Hyde Jones
MAJOR, R.E.
O.C. 96th FIELD COY R.E.

WAR DIARY or INTELLIGENCE SUMMARY

Army Form C. 2118.

WL 42

Place	Date	Hour	Summary of Events and Information	Remarks and references to Appendices
HURTEBISE FARM	31/19 2/19 3/19		Company Strength 4 Officers and 108 other Ranks. Dismounted Personnel employed improving Billeting accommodation and erecting loading Platform at MONDICOURT, repairs to HENU CHATEAU, and repairs to wells at GRENAS.	
			2 Officers and 17 other Ranks proceeded to XVII Corps Concentration Camp for dispersal during March.	{LENS SHEET 11}
	15		28 Animals were despatched from this UNIT during the month of March for dispersal.	
			9 other Ranks proceeded on draft to the 30th Division distributed as follows:- 6 OR to 200th Field Coy.R.E, 2OR to the 201st Field Coy.R.E. and 1 OR to 202nd Field Coy.R.E.	
	29/3 30/3		2 O.Rs also proceeded on draft to the 41st LONDON DIVISION. Company Strength 2 Officers and 62 other Ranks	

31. MAR. 1919

J.C. Oswald
O.C. 96th FIELD COY. R.E.

WAR DIARY
INTELLIGENCE SUMMARY
(Erase heading not required.)

SHEET LENS 11.

Place	Date	Hour	Summary of Events and Information	Remarks and references to Appendices
HURTEBISE FARM	1/4/19 to 28/4/19		"Effective Strength" of the Unit :- 2 Officers and 62 other Ranks. Dismounted personnel employed, improving & building accumulators, repairing walls at GRENAS, POMMERA, LA GAUCHIE, and HUMBERCAMP. Repairs were also effected to HENU CHATEAU, and the stables at GRENAS CHATEAU. 2 Other Ranks proceeded to XVII Corps Concentration Camp during the month for Dispersal. 8 animals were despatched from this Unit during the Month for Dispersal, and 4.2 horses taken on Strength the latter number being the total animals on charge. 1 Other Rank re-enlisted in British Belgium Army and proceeded to ENGLAND on furlough. A draft of 4 Other Ranks comprising 2 volunteers and 2 retainable personnel proceeded to the 41st LONDON DIVISION. "Effective Strength" of the UNIT :- 2 Officers and 50 Other Ranks.	

LIEUT. R.E.
O.C. 96th FIELD COY. R.E.

Army Form C. 2118.

WAR DIARY
or
INTELLIGENCE SUMMARY.
(Erase heading not required.)

96th Coy R.E.
W.D. 44

Remarks and references to Appendices: **MAP:- LENS 11.**

Place	Date	Hour	Summary of Events and Information	Remarks
HURTEBISE FARM	3/9		Effective Strength of the Unit :- 2 Officers and 50 other Ranks. Dismounted personnel continues on unfinished hutts & repairing Railroad	
FAMECHON			OZEINS, PONNIERS, LA CAUCHIE, HUMBERCOURT. Repairs in progress. Alterations to loading platform at MONDICOURT & the disposal of the G.S. Field Ambulance were fixed & orders for transp. to divisions. 92nd proceeded to XVII Corps Concentrated Camp Grounds for dispersal between huts &c. 1 L.O. Section left the Unit on the instant for Army Annual Collecting Camp, Candas, for dispersal, having only 3 L.O. horses in charge. Corpl at Sapr proceeded for service with 4th Dvn Army of Occupation on the 9/11/18.	
	29/11		Effective Strength of the Unit :- 2 Officers & 26 Other Ranks	

H.C. Edwards
Capt. R.E.
O.C. 96th FIELD COY R.E.

www.ingramcontent.com/pod-product-compliance
Lightning Source LLC
Chambersburg PA
CBHW080900230426
43663CB00013B/2586